The politics of women's rights

THE POLITICS OF
WOMEN'S RIGHTS

April Carter

LONGMAN
London and New York

Longman Group UK Limited,
Longman House, Burnt Mill, Harlow,
Essex CM20 2JE, England
and Associated Companies throughout the world.

Published in the United States of America
by Longman Inc., New York

First published 1988

British Library Cataloguing in Publication Data
Carter, April
    The politics of women's rights. —
    (Politics today).
    1. Women's rights — Great Britain —
    History — 20th century
    I. Title II. Series
    323.3′4′0941   HQ1593

ISBN 0-582-02400-5 CSD
ISBN 0-582-29519-X PPR

Library of Congress Cataloging in Publication Data
Carter, April.
    The politics of women's rights.

    (Politics today)
    Bibliography: p.
    Includes index.
    1. Women's rights — Great Britain. 2. Women —
Great Britain — History.   I. Title.   II. Series.
HQ1236.5.G7C37 1988   305.4′2′0941   87–2870
ISBN 0-582-02400-5 (CSD)
ISBN 0-582-29519-X (PPR)

Set in 10/11pt Plantin Comp/Edit 6400
Produced by Longman Singapore Publishers (Pte) Ltd.
Printed in Singapore

CONTENTS

CONTENTS

FOREWORD

Books have a life of their own. Admiring greatly her previous work, always thought-provoking and always on a different and a difficult subject, I asked April Carter to write on the politics of women's rights in a series on "The Politics of . . .", this and that, which I have edited with Patrick Seyd. I hoped for a fresh look at this important subject, obviously important in practice to about half humanity and still the subject of neglect by most of the other half, but a subject that in terms of theoretical and polemical books has recently become, in publishing terms, anything but neglected, and even somewhat, if not tired, certainly predictable. But our series had a standard form, mainly aimed at students of politics: to show how a problem has emerged in the context of contemporary history, to describe the main institutions and pressure groups related to it, and then to argue what should be done in terms of public policy. But this can be a mechanical formula: good books have a life of their own.

April Carter finally wrote something rather different that should reach a wider audience, so the book appears outside the series; indeed she has written, I think, something more important, widely needed and unusual than I had expected. Certainly she gives us historical context and her views on rights and equality are clear and explicit. But mainly she has set out criteria by which we can judge how much progress has in fact been made in the post-war period towards the emancipation of women and equality of the sexes; and having set out such criteria, as a good political and social philosopher, she has actually attempted to answer these questions, as a good social historian would.

The result of actually examining the evidence is a measured judgement of worthwhile progress made, but still a very long way to go, not simply to bring advanced theory into practice but to bring common working and occupational practices into anything like commonsense judgements of fairness. Dr Carter does identify and examine the main specifically feminist theories and doctrines and also specific institutional and attitudional obstacles to achieving equality of the sexes but others have done this before, with varying success; or often success in argument is hard to measure because, while grievances are relatively obvious, goals are more hard to define and much feminist writing has, like much other radical writing, become too internalised. What is unique and valuable in this book is that it sets out measures of progress so that assessments can then be made of actual progress in key fields of employment, wages, health care etc. And this is done with a calm dispassion that should command trust and respect, I believe, both from those who may think she goes too far and those who may think the contrary. If you want to know amid all the theorising what the practical issues are and what has happened, you will find it here.

Bernard Crick
   Professor of Politics Emeritus
      Birkbeck College, London

AUTHOR'S PREFACE

The purpose of this book is to give an overall picture of the changing position of women in Britain over the last forty years, and to examine the political, legal and social processes responsible for these changes. It is a book for the general reader interested in women's rights but not already familiar with the growing literature on women and on feminism. I owe a considerable debt to the research and writings of those who have uncovered details of women's inequality, analysed political and legal attempts to promote women's rights, recounted feminist activity and developed feminist thinking. The Equal Opportunities Commission and National Council of Civil Liberties have provided invaluable information.

A number of people have read portions of earlier drafts and helped me to see what to keep, and what to rewrite or discard. My thanks to Eileen Brock, Madeleine Butchart, Margaret Canovan, Christine Greenhalgh, Alan Lawrance and Anne Stott. I owe an especial debt to Lisa Foley, who spent time in digging out facts and figures for earlier chapters and gave me her direct and perceptive criticism on the book. Finally, I am grateful to Bernard Crick who suggested this topic to me, for his patience in waiting for me to finish and for his encouragement and constructive criticism.

This book is dedicated to Penny, Kate, Jenny and Hana, who represent the future.

April Carter

LIST OF ABBREVIATIONS

ACAS	Advisory, Conciliation and Arbitration Service
ACTT	Association of Cinematograph, Television and Allied Technicians
ASTMS	Association of Scientific, Technical and Managerial Staffs
CBI	Confederation of British Industry
CPAG	Child Poverty Action Group
CSO	Central Statistical Office
DE	Department of Employment
DHSS	Department of Health and Social Security
EEC	European Economic Community
EOC	Equal Opportunities Commission
GLC	Greater London Council
LSE	London School of Economics
NALGO	National and Local Government Officers' Association
NCCL	National Council for Civil Liberties
NEC	National Executive Committee
NHS	National Health Service
NUT	National Union of Teachers
PEP	Political and Economic Planning
RUC	Royal Ulster Constabulary
SDP	Social Democratic Party
SOGAT	Society of Graphical and Allied Trades (SOGAT '82)
TASS	Technical, Administrative and Supervisory Section of the Amalgamated Union of Engineering Workers
TGWU	Transport and General Workers' Union
TUC	Trades Union Congress
USDAW	Union of Shop, Distributive and Allied Workers
WISE	Women in Science and Engineering

INTRODUCTION

When looking at the history of women's rights in this country it is easy to be misled by the popular assumption of uninterrupted social progress. The position of women has been complicated by the effects of economic change, by varying social attitudes to sexuality and by alterations in the ideal of femininity. There have also been enormous disparities in women's lot, depending on their social class. In all ages women have tended to be economically and legally subordinate to men, but the degree and nature of that subordination has taken many different forms and, in many periods, has allowed greater freedom to a minority of women.

Under feudalism the position of women was very varied. Serfs were treated as the property of their lord and the women might also be treated as sexual property. Women born into the aristocracy were often married off as young girls to further dynastic alliances and were unable to refuse. But women of birth could also inherit and manage their own estates, or could acquire learning and political influence through the church, whilst craftswomen were members of the medieval guilds alongside men or in some cases formed their own guilds. Therefore, as feudalism gave way to a more individualistic form of society, women lost privileges and opportunities and were more systematically excluded on grounds of sex from university education, from the professions, from the craft guilds and from politics. Upper-class women between the sixteenth and eighteenth centuries could, however, acquire learning and enjoy a degree of social freedom. It was the Victorian era that encouraged the narrowest ideal of femininity, equating it with ignorance, pretty accomplishments and lack of sexuality, demanding from women gentility and domesticity. But at the very time this image of womanliness was being promoted a feminist movement was also being born.

Poor women, whether married or not, usually had to work. The

Victorian period embraced a number of contradictory trends in the employment of working women. Industrialisation completed the destruction of most women's skilled crafts and encouraged employers to exploit women as a pool of cheap and unskilled labour, thus building into the development of trade-unionism male hostility to female competition for jobs. Nevertheless the expansion of industry ensured that women remained important in the labour force in the manufacturing sector. Early legislation to control the excesses of unrestrained private enterprise gave special protection to women and children from degrading and injurious labour in the mines, and from inhumanly long hours of work in the factories. Despite some immediate advantages, this protection treated women as fit subjects for paternalism and helped to strengthen the distinction between men's and women's work. The Government was much less inclined to intervene to prevent women dressmakers going blind from overwork, or to protect domestic servants, since these occupations did not offend against the ideals of feminine modesty and domesticity as did work in the mines.

The mid-Victorian period marked the virtual exclusion of working women from the public realm of political agitation and trade-union organisation. Women had played a relatively important role in the political movements of the late eighteenth century and up to the first Reform Bill of 1832. They were also active in the Chartists' struggle, although Chartism only briefly included a demand for the vote for women. From the middle of the century the more limited nature of political agitation tended to exclude women, and working women may have partly absorbed the middle-class ideal of feminine domesticity. There was a parallel decline in female trade-unionism. Women had earlier organised their own Friendly Societies and had taken part in labour strikes, demonstrations and riots in the early decades of the nineteenth century. Between the 1830s and 1870s there was, despite a continuing strand of union organisation in the textile industry, a comparative lull in women's trade-union activity, although towards the end of the century women joined in the new wave of industrial militancy and working-class women gave important support to the feminist campaign for the vote.

Despite the setbacks of the mid-Victorian era for women in all social classes, there was fairly continuous progress in the assertion of certain fundamental rights for women dating from the 1850s, so that on balance women were much more emancipated by the end of Victoria's reign than they had been at the beginning. The demand for the rights of women was a natural extension of the ideas of liberty, equality and fraternity symbolised and promoted by the French Revolution. Mary Wollstonecraft (1967) made this link explicit in her *Vindication of the Rights of Woman*, written in 1792, two years after she had defended Tom Paine against Burke in her *Vindication of the Rights of Man*. If women's rights had been achieved as part of a successful popular movement for radical democracy, they might have been conceived and implemented in an egalitarian political context. But the reforms won by women after 1832 – like those achieved by working men – were granted piecemeal under pressure, for benevolent or pragmatic reasons, and did not directly challenge prevailing social inequalities or social attitudes. As a result, the reforms tended in practice to benefit middle-class women more than their poorer sisters, who could not resort to the courts or enjoy higher education or a professional career. Many arguments for reform avoided claiming the equality of women, and some women who fought hard to remedy particular injustices accepted the natural inferiority of women, or women's primarily domestic role, and refused to support the demand for votes for women. The prolonged resistance to granting women the vote was due, apart from specific political obstacles at various times, to its symbolic significance as a formal recognition of full political and social equality and a denial of the Victorian womanly ideal.

The gains that Victorian women did win laid the basis for the comparative freedom of twentieth-century women, and started to remedy three key areas of inequality: the rights of married women, education of girls and careers for women. Victorian reformers raised two other issues of central importance for women – practice of birth-control and the right to vote – but met determined resistance to change. Real progress had to wait till the early decades of the twentieth century.

Married women were, despite their desirable social status, in a much worse position legally than the despised single woman at the beginning of the Victorian era. Married women had no rights at all against their husbands, no property rights and no rights over their children, since the wife ceased on marriage to exist as a separate legal personality. The first step towards recognising that the wife was entitled to be treated as a person in her own right was the passing of the Matrimonial Causes Act of 1857. This Act in its final form made divorce available through the courts (previously it had been under the jurisdiction of ecclesiastical courts and had required a special Act of Parliament), and gave a separated or divorced wife some protection from her husband. It also allowed her to keep earnings or property acquired after she left her husband, and enabled her to enter into contracts and to go to court.

The Act embodied a sexual double standard – not to be abandoned until 1923 – which enabled men to divorce their wives for adultery, whilst wives could only sue for divorce if adultery were aggravated by cruelty, desertion or certain sexual offences. The position of married women was gradually strengthened over the next three decades by legislation and court decisions, which denied the husband the power to insist on his conjugal rights or to forcibly restrain his wife, made it possible for wives to claim maintenance before going to the workhouse and gave a mother some rights to guardianship of her children – though she did not gain equal rights to custody. The first Bill to give married women ownership of their own property was brought before Parliament in 1857, but partly because of the Divorce Bill being debated that year it was defeated. A series of Married Women's Property Acts in 1870, 1882 and 1893 did eventually give wives entitlement to keep their own earnings and to hold, acquire and dispose of property, whether gained before or after marriage, and to act on their own behalf in legal matters.

In education the daughters of the wealthier classes suffered greater sexual discrimination than working-class girls. The latter were less likely – until the advent of compulsory education in 1870 – to go to school than their brothers, but if they did they went to the same village or church school. Middle-class girls went to special schools for girls, or were taught by a governess, and acquired feminine accomplishments but little solid knowledge. The pioneers of serious academic education for girls were acutely aware of the importance of education in promoting women's independence, in enabling single women to have some alternative to the humiliating post of governess, and indeed to enable governesses to raise their status by improving their own educational qualifications. Queen's College and Bedford College were founded in London in the late 1840s and here sympathetic members of the university lectured to women, many of whom in turn became teachers and lecturers. Graduates of these colleges took the lead in establishing secondary education for girls, opening up public examinations to them and promoting university training for women. The principle that girls should have access to higher education was accepted by the Commission of Enquiry on Schools, which reported in 1868, and there was significant progress in creating such opportunities both in schools and at university level in the next decade.

Education made new careers available to women. Large numbers of single women became teachers and soon dominated that profession. By the end of the century women had entered journalism, a few went on from university to become mathematicians, scientists and even, in the 1890s, engineers. Their most dramatic success was in medicine: Florence Nightingale transformed the unskilled and disreputable job of nursing into a skilled and dedicated vocation; and the well-publicised efforts of a few women broke down the barriers to women becoming doctors – by 1895 there were 264 women registered as doctors in Britain. The principle of careers open to women had been established by the end of the Victorian period (although they were debarred from both the higher levels of the Civil Service and the law until after the Sex Disqualification Removal Act of 1919), but both social prejudice and restrictive professional practices tended to exclude all but the most talented and determined women. The progress made in the nineteenth century in creating work opportunities for women established certain spheres – teaching, nursing and various forms of clerical work – as especially suitable for them. Whilst this meant that single women had achieved much more independence and greater scope for their talents than before, it also created a new form of occupational discrimination, in which women's work enjoyed lower status and still lower pay, so that the pattern of middle-class women's jobs reinforced the discrimination practised in industry.

Issues of a more personal and emotive kind were raised when Charles Bradlaugh's Malthusian League tried to publish information about methods of contraception. Incessant childbearing was a burden upon the health, energy and personal freedom of all married women – Queen Victoria herself complained bitterly about the pains of pregnancy and labour – but it bore especially hard on the poor, who often tried to induce miscarriage and sometimes resorted to infanticide. Abortion had been made a crime under the law in 1803. But because advocacy of contraception attacked sexual prudery, idealisation of the large family and religious doctrines it was met with denunciation by the churches and the medical profession, social outrage and legal prosecution. The trial of Charles Bradlaugh and Annie Besant under the Obscene Publications Act in 1877 for publishing literature on birth-control provided enormous publicity for their cause. They won their case on appeal, but the Obscene Publications Act was used to harass others distributing literature on contraception until the 1890s. Public opinion did apparently begin to move towards the evident advantages of family limitation, but setting up birth-control clinics and publicity about contraception methods continued to excite scandal and hostility well into the twentieth century.

The most famous demand in the movement for women's rights had been the demand for the vote, which was first raised publicly by the women's suffrage campaign in the 1860s, when John Stuart Mill presented a petition on this issue to Parliament. Despite some support in Parliament, and continued pressure from organisations committed to campaign for the vote throughout the nineteenth century, there were no concessions to women at the parliamentary level. Women did acquire some political rights in local government in the 1870s and 1880s: they became members of school boards, parish councillors and Poor Law guardians, and after 1888 women ratepayers could vote in municipal and county elections though they could not be elected to these councils until 1907. In the years before the First World War the campaign for the vote became more intense, involving thousands of women in mass protests and the increasingly militant demonstrations, prison sentences and hunger strikes of the suffragettes. When the vote was conceded in 1918 it was presented as a reward for women's contribution to the war effort and was limited to women over 30 who were also householders or wives of householders. Paradoxically women over 21 were immediately afterwards given the right to enter Parliament, and by 1923 there were eight women MPs. The Sex Disqualification Removal Act of 1919 gave women the right to serve on a jury and to serve as magistrates. The activity of women who entered politics and continuing pressure from feminist organisations was reflected in a substantial body of legislation passed in the 1920s increasing the rights of married women, divorced and separated wives, unmarried mothers and widows as well as single women seeking a career. When in 1928 women finally acquired the right to vote on equal terms with men in parliamentary and local elections, the movement for female emancipation appeared to have achieved its central aims.

Fifty years later, when the survivors of the campaign for votes for women met to celebrate that victory, members of the Women's Liberation Movement demonstrated to protest about the continuing inequalities and disadvantages suffered by women in 1978. The position of women in British society since 1945, the gains for women's rights in this period and the obstacles to full equality, and the problems inherent in the definition of women's rights today, are the subject-matter of this book.

In the first four chapters we examine changes in women's status, women's attitudes, women's legal rights and women's economic experience during the forty years since the end of the Second World War. The focus of each chapter is somewhat different. Chapter 1 looks particularly at the social history of women in the 1940s and 1950s, while Chapter 2 sets out the specific economic, legal and political inequalities suffered by women in the period 1950–70, before efforts to redress these inequalities resulted in legislative reform during the 1970s. Chapter 3 concentrates on the growing militancy among women in the late 1960s and 1970s, the scope of new legislation on women's rights, the impact of new attitudes towards sexuality upon women, and the new feminist perspectives on such issues as violence against women, pornography and women's mental and physical health. Chapter 4 considers the impact of legislation and women's gains and losses in the economic and political climate of the 1980s. The purpose of this first part of the book is to provide a brief but comprehensive survey of the developments affecting women, their responses to them and of the efforts to promote equality or to liberate women.

The second part of the book (Chapters 5–7) is more analytical. We examine in greater depth the political processes involved in achieving laws to improve women's position and the difficulties women face in getting their concerns taken seriously in the political arena; and then explore how effective key legislation has been, and the problems of using the law. The final chapter summarises some key themes in recent feminist theory and briefly relates them to the existing social realities and future possibilities. The dominant emphasis is therefore on women's opportunities in the public domain and political or legal methods of bringing about change, but the discussion does explore at various points the interconnection between women's position in the home and their public role, and the importance of more personal issues both for women individually and for feminism.

Part one
THE POSITION OF WOMEN SINCE 1945

Chapter one
THE IMPACT OF WAR AND OF LONG-TERM SOCIAL TRENDS

INTRODUCTION

Our purpose in the first part of this book is to explore how the rights of women have changed between 1945 and 1985. We use the concept of rights here not only to cover specific legal rights granted to women – important though these are – but also to cover general rights to social, economic and political equality. It is impossible to divorce these rights from the position of women within society and prevailing social attitudes, from the organisation of the economy and the general distribution of power. It is also important to see how women seem to have perceived their own role and rights at various periods since 1945, and to examine the impact of feminist campaigns and ideas.

Our starting-point is the impact of the Second World War on British society and the contradictory pressures exerted on women during and after the war. As a result of the war women did make some gains, but these were fairly negligible. Feminists themselves were divided in their view of the best course to pursue in strengthening women's rights: should women be encouraged to concentrate on their role as wives and mothers but be given stronger economic and legal rights as housewives, or should they seek economic independence and equality in the world of work? In practice in 1950 most married women were likely to choose domesticity, partly because of the ideology of femininity fostered during the late 1940s and early 1950s.

The position of women after 1945 was not, however, shaped solely by the effects of the war and its aftermath, it was also influenced by longer-term social and economic trends. The nature of the family and women's position within it was gradually changing and many women were not in practice content with a purely domestic life. During the 1950s increasing numbers of married women started going out to work, thus setting in train further long-term changes.

THE EFFECTS OF WAR

The two world wars had similar effects on women during the actual period of hostilities. In both wars women were needed to take over the jobs in the economy normally done by men, and in both wars women did heavy, technical and dangerous work which was seen in peacetime as 'man's work'. During the war the Government stressed women's responsibility to assist the national war effort, and towards the end of the First World War, women's auxiliary corps attached to the army, navy and air force were created. But women were recruited for some form of war work earlier and more systematically in the Second World War than in the First.

Indeed, Britain made more extensive use of women than any other country between 1939 and 1945, even the USSR, although unlike the Soviet authorities the British Government did not allocate any women to combat duties. Conscription of single women was initiated in December 1941, when women were given a choice between the auxiliary services, civil defence and certain jobs in industry, and by 1943 virtually all single women under 40 were engaged in some kind of war work. In addition 80 per cent of married women under 40 were mobilised and many mothers of young children did full- or part-time work in industry. Conscription of women was, however, extremely controversial when it was introduced and at first the War Cabinet resisted the idea. Conscription was adopted because the need for women's contribution to the war effort overrode reluctance to expose women to danger or hardship and the desire to keep wives and mothers at home (Bullock 1967: 138–9, 253–5).

The women's auxiliary services tended to act in a traditionally feminine and supportive role to provide clerical and domestic assistance to the armed forces. But some women played an important part as wireless and radar operators, as fighter controllers and as air-ferry pilots. The Special Operations Executive did recruit women as well as men to work behind enemy lines with local resistance groups, and a number of women were parachuted into occupied territory. Women also undertook responsible and dangerous work during the blitz, helping to operate anti-aircraft batteries, acting as air-raid patrol wardens and joining in rescue work after a bombing raid, and driving ambulances. The Women's Voluntary Service, created in 1938, worked with the civil defence forces assisting with food, shelter and evacuation of people from bombed districts (Calder 1982: 224–5, 308–10).

Young women who did not join the women's services or go into nursing were drafted into munitions factories and aircraft factories, or into shipyards and railway yards. Some women had been employed in engineering before the war, but the total number in engineering and allied industries rose from just over 400,000 in June 1939 to 1.5 million by December 1943 (Bullock 1967: 63). Women were also needed as in the First World War to boost food production and were sent out to farms as land-girls. Women with children and older women worked in local factories or offices and shops. During the war women learned to do a number of jobs in industry that, as the Ministry of Labour recorded, employers had previously thought beyond their skill or strength (DE 1975: 30).

In order to encourage mothers of young children to work in industry the Government had to make provision for working mothers. Canteen services and local authority restaurants provided some practical help, but the main issue was setting up nurseries for children below school age. Progress in nursery provision was at first slow. The Ministry of Health doubted the need for nurseries; mothers of young children did not always wish to use the nurseries available; and the Ministry of Labour initially favoured a scheme of registered child-minders, arguing that nurseries required female labour which might otherwise be used elsewhere. Nevertheless, pressure to release women for war work, and the campaigning efforts of bodies enthusiastic in principle for state nurseries, did result in 1,450 full-time nurseries for small children under 5 by September 1944, plus other types of care for small children, compared with just over 200 nurseries of different sorts in 1938 (Riley 1979: 83).

The war drew more women into the Civil Service and other professions, and also gave them new opportunities of promotion. The legal barriers which before the war had forced many middle-class women to stop work on marriage were suspended in the Civil Service, the London County Council, the BBC, the teaching profession, the police and other public services.

So from the standpoint of feminists who measured women's progress by their range of job opportunities and ability to continue working after marriage and childbirth, the Second World War did widen women's horizons. But did these gains survive the war, and did women make the kind of dramatic advance they achieved after the First World War, when they were granted the right to vote? The answer to both questions is a qualified 'no', but the Second World War did result in some limited progress for women's rights.

In one respect women's experience after both world wars was the same: when their labour was no longer urgently needed they were put under pressure to leave their jobs and make way for demobilised servicemen. After both wars they were also eased out of jobs regarded as more appropriate to men, and working-class women were segregated into female work in the factory and the office, and in various types of service. So after 1945 most married women withdrew from their jobs, although surveys of women workers during the war indicated that the majority wanted to go on working afterwards. Employers were no longer willing to help women by organising shifts for part-time workers, and the nursery facilities provided during the war were withdrawn, despite protests by child welfare and women's organisations.

If women's economic position worsened after the First World War, their political and legal position was, as we saw in the Introduction, immensely improved in the ten years following 1918. Nothing comparable happened after 1945. The only specific legal gain women made as a result of the Second World War was that the marriage bar was dropped: an end to discrimination against married women teachers was formally enshrined in the 1944 Education Act, and the Civil Service abandoned the marriage bar in 1946, since the wartime influx of married women into temporary jobs showed that marriage did not, as previously asserted, make women less efficient and reliable (Myrdal and Klein 1968: 53). So young professional women could look forward to combining marriage with a career without facing an explicit legal obstacle, and were not forced to choose between matrimony and their profession.

There are two obvious reasons why women gained more after the First World War. The first is that they suffered from much greater and more visible injustices before 1914, and their contribution during the war years lead to a widespread public feeling that the greatest of these – the lack of the vote – should be remedied. The second is that there had been prolonged, widespread and well-publicised feminist agitation in the years before 1914, so women's rights were a live political issue still in 1918, even though there had been a suspension of feminist agitation during the war. In spite of the continuing efforts of a number of women's organisations and of women in the labour movement in the 1930s and 1940s, women's rights were not centrally on the agenda for the post-war Labour Government that came to power in 1945. Most liberal opinion believed that now women had the vote remaining inequalities would automatically be eliminated over time.

The third reason which can be more cautiously advanced to explain why women made so few gains after 1945, despite their role during the war, is that although both wars tended to promote political radicalism, the social and cultural radicalism that followed 1918 can be contrasted with the conservative tone encouraged in Britain in the late 1940s. Certainly this applied to women. Some of the signs of women's emancipation in the 1920s – for example the boyish fashion in clothes and hairstyles, women smoking cigarettes and the sexual permissiveness associated with the jazz age – may have been superficial and only have applied to certain social circles. But women writers like Vera Brittain have testified to the greater personal and social freedom women won after the First World War. Conversely fashion in the late 1940s espoused the long-skirted, tight-waisted feminine New Look, and advertisements and women's magazines promoted an image of demure femininity, repudiating women's more 'masculine' role during the war. When a Labour Government was swept to power in 1945, with a big parliamentary majority for the first time, it did seem to promise major social change. But the changes that did take place occurred in the creation of the Welfare State and the drive towards post-war reconstruction through housing programmes and in measures of nationalisation. The Labour Party was sympathetic to women's equality at the level of general principle, and women had been able to attain some prominence in the Party. But Labour was also strongly influenced by the trade unions, which tended to be almost exclusively concerned with their male membership and hostile to women who threatened jobs or wages for men. The Labour Government was hampered too by its post-war indebtedness, and economic stringency made it more difficult to be generous to women. Thus the Government refused in 1947 to implement the principle of equal pay for women in the public sector (Macdonald 1977: 148). Unequal pay for men and women doing the same job was one of the most glaring forms of discrimination still suffered by women.

Commitment to welfare fostered by the experience of the war and confirmed by the election of a Labour Government did, however, result in a number of indirect gains for women, especially working-class women. For example the 1944 Education Act provided schoolchildren with free school meals, which women socialists had campaigned for in the inter-war years, primarily to improve the health of underfed children, but also to relieve mothers of one domestic chore in the middle of the day.

The Family Allowances Act of 1945 realised one goal of Labour women's organisations, who had campaigned for the state to pay direct to women money for their children which they could spend on the household, and which would release them from total dependence on their husbands in financial matters. The original draft of the legislation

by the Coalition Government had envisaged that the allowance would
be paid to husbands, but Eleanor Rathbone led a successful pressure
group of women's organisations which succeeded in getting the Bill
amended to make the payment to wives (Banks 1981: 168-9). The
allowance did not cover the first child, and after 1945 the amount of
allowance did not keep pace with the rise in the cost of living, so it was a
marginal contribution to the economic independence of housewives.
But it could be seen as a minor advance.

Not all women agreed, however, that the welfare provisions
originating in the war favoured women's real interests. Both the
Beveridge Report and family allowances were criticised at the time.
The Beveridge Report of 1942, usually hailed as the foundation of the
Welfare State, quite explicitly set out to strengthen marriage and to
encourage married women to stay at home: 'The attitude of the
housewife to gainful employment outside the home is not and should
not be that of the single woman. She has other duties.' The Report also
treated the wife as a dependant of her husband, qualifying for benefit
through him; if she chose to go out to work and contribute
independently she would receive lower benefits than a single woman.
Beveridge recommended family allowances mainly in order to
encourage the birth-rate: the allowance would be a 'signal of the
national interest in children'. Some women's groups, for example the
National Council of Women of Great Britain, protested against the
dependent status of married women in the Report; and a contemporary
survey of soldiers' wives suggested that some working-class women
viewed with cynicism the aim of more childbearing and the proposed
level of allowances (Wilson 1977: 140-1, 150-1, 153-4).

FEMINIST PERSPECTIVES AFTER 1945

Despite the doubts some women had about the nature of the Welfare
State that emerged out of the war years, there was in this period a close
alliance between feminists and advocates of welfare, leading to what
Olive Banks has termed 'welfare feminism' (Banks 1981: 153-79). This
alliance had developed in the 1920s, when the most obvious goals of
the women's suffrage movement had been attained, and when a
number of feminists became strongly aware of the deprived and
subordinate position of many working-class women. Eleanor
Rathbone, who was one of the first women MPs – elected as an
Independent in 1929 – and a suffragist since the 1890s, had been one of
the strongest advocates of a family endowment scheme. Her aim was to
recognise the social importance of motherhood, and to secure women a

15

modicum of economic independence within marriage by a state payment direct to mothers. She regarded herself as a 'new feminist' in contrast with the earlier tradition of feminism that had concentrated largely on trying to ensure women the same rights and opportunities as men. She wished women to assert their own distinctive values and contribution to society rather than copying men (Lewis 1983: 137–9). This brand of 'new feminism' was espoused by a number of leading feminists in the post-war period, like Vera Brittain, who welcomed the Welfare State for encompassing the cooperative and caring ethos associated with women and for allowing women to be recognised for their unique role (Wilson 1980: 164).

The original equal rights emphasis of feminism, expressed through campaigns for legal reform and for the vote, was not, however, entirely abandoned in the 1940s. The main issue was the claim for equal pay for women, which by 1944 could muster public support. In fact the House of Commons voted for an amendment to the 1944 Education Bill giving women teachers equal pay, but when Churchill made dropping this amendment an issue of confidence the Commons abandoned their support for it (Calder 1982: 406). Nevertheless, the long struggle for equal pay for women had reached a new stage. The Civil Service women's associations joined with other women's organisations in 1944 to create an Equal Pay Campaign Committee, and the large public-sector unions supported equal pay in principle, though they proposed it should be introduced in stages. A Royal Commission set up in 1944 also endorsed the idea of equal pay in the public services. The Labour Government failed to implement this principle on economic grounds, and the campaign gained momentum in the 1950s. The final outcome was that the Conservative Government agreed in January 1955 to introduce equal pay in the Civil Service phased over seven years, and this decision set a precedent for other public services (Fogarty, Allen, Allen and Walters 1971: 233–6).

There is not a total conflict between the aims of the new feminists and the aims of the original equal rights campaigners. Indeed, Eleanor Rathbone saw her family endowment scheme strengthening the case for equal pay for women, since the standard argument for paying men more was that men had to maintain a family. In principle, once women had full rights of citizenship it seemed reasonable that they should have the right to pursue a career or earn good money on equal terms with men, but should also have the right to devote their energies to motherhood. In practice, however, there is a conflict of emphasis and values between those who try to ensure women equal economic and political power and the opportunity to go out to work even if married with children, and those whose priority is protecting the rights of women who leave paid work and concentrate on nurturing a family.

The new feminism raised important and potentially radical ideas about the real and long-term goals of women's emancipation. But in the social context of the 1940s and early 1950s it did little to advance women's rights; and it was in danger of being mistaken for a conservative belief that women's place was in the home, especially as this brand of feminism tended to stress traditional male and female roles in the family and to idealise the family as the nucleus of social life. Whatever the proclaimed value placed by society on the housewife, official policy and the law tended to suggest her work was valueless. During the war government legislation on compensation for war injuries initially restricted compensation to wage earners and members of the civil defence organisations, so a mother of children would qualify for nothing. A campaign by women's organisations succeeded in amending the legislation so that it covered all adults injured in the war, but the rate of compensation for a woman was only two-thirds that of a man (McDonald 1977: 148). In divorce proceedings a woman who had been a housewife had no legal claim to a share in the family home unless she had made a financial contribution, or had joint legal title to the house. Feminists campaigning for the rights of married women had difficulty in making headway. Labour MP Edith Summerskill unsuccessfully took up the case of a housewife, who claimed the right to her savings on the housekeeping allowance, after a court ruling that under common law the money belonged to her husband. She also failed to get a Bill through Parliament in 1952 to help wives whose husbands defaulted on maintenance (Banks 1981: 221). Even the partial victory for women on the Family Allowance fell far short of Eleanor Rathbone's project for family endowment.

RETURN TO DOMESTICITY

Feminists of any description were an isolated minority in the late 1940s and early 1950s. As a result of the post-war pressure on women to leave their jobs in favour of men, by 1947 only 18 per cent of married women (excluding those separated from their husbands) went out to work. There was also strong social pressure on women to aspire to femininity and domesticity above all else. This pressure was reflected in and strongly reinforced by the women's magazines, which were the most explicit medium purveying what Betty Friedan later termed 'the feminine mystique'. Women's magazines had begun to acquire a mass circulation in the late 1930s, and during the war the Government had used them to get across official information and to involve women as much as possible in the war effort. But after the war there was soon a change of emphasis and reassertion of feminine interests. By the early 1950s, according to Joy Leman's survey of women's magazines, 'features on weddings, childcare, fashion, cosmetics and 'home-making' ... became more prominent' (Leman 1980: 76). Another study found that by 1951 women's magazines extended their range and depth in dealing with subjects of interest to housewives – for example medical advice, child care, marital problems, furnishing and decorating the home – but had also narrowed the focus to the domestic sphere. Many women's magazines in the early 1950s strongly discouraged married women from going out to work, through their advice columns and in their fiction. Evelyn Home of *Woman* advised her readers:

> It is safe to say that most women, once they have a family, are more contented and doing better work in the home than they could find outside it (White 1970: 142).

This emphasis on women's role at home not only stressed the importance of bringing up children but also urged wives to be sympathetic and supportive to their husbands, whilst taking care to maintain men's conviction of their own superiority, and status as head of the family. So the domestic virtues were placed firmly in the context of women's acceptance of an inferior role.

The women's magazines not only encouraged women to stay at home after marriage and to be good homemakers, they also propagated an ideal of femininity which suggested the only goal of any real woman was romance and marriage. Marjorie Ferguson undertook a content analysis of the feature, beauty, problem pages and of the fiction in the three most widely read women's magazines between 1949 and 1974, and found that the overwhelmingly dominant theme was 'getting and keeping your man'. The tone of voice varied from the robust to the romantic. An article in *Woman's Own* in 1949 entitled 'Feed the brute' lamented the fact that girls did not spend more time learning domestic science at school. But fiction in particular struck a more ethereal note. The introduction to a story called 'The frost and the flower' in *Woman's Own* in 1952 indicated its theme:

> This is all that the average girls asks – a little happiness that belongs to herself, a heart to keep and a home to tend (Ferguson 1983).

The magazines carefully excluded realities of sexual and family life that would disturb the picture of domestic bliss. Sex outside marriage was never mentioned, and although difficulties in marriage could be admitted, the possibility of separation and divorce were apparently taboo in the 1950s and early 1960s.

The message of the women's press was not, however, unequivocally in favour of married women staying at home. Some feature articles did discuss the practical problems of working wives, and although advertisements focused less on work than during the war, they did also show women at work, though usually in feminine and supposedly glamorous roles like air hostesses. There was some recognition that highly qualified women with an expensive training would benefit both society and themselves by combining a career with marriage, and magazines aiming at the upper end of the social scale were less exclusively domestic in their range of features. Career women were, however, viewed as an exceptional minority, to be contrasted with 'most women'. Moreover, this minority was put under pressure by the prevailing psychological theory of child development, which stressed the damage mothers could do to their infants and young children by failing to maintain an intimate and continuous relationship between child and mother. Professional women were particularly likely to be familiar with John Bowlby's theory of 'maternal deprivation', and so to feel guilt if they sacrificed their children to their career; though the theory also filtered into the advice columns of women's magazines. Whether Bowlby's theory really followed from his evidence – derived from evacuee children during the war – has since been seriously questioned; widespread acceptance of it during the 1950s suggests it conveniently dovetailed with the social conservatism, and the stress on womanliness rather than women's rights, of that period.

Within the self-selected circle of those who read women's magazines the message appears to have been broadly accepted. A questionnaire to *Woman's Own* readers suggested the conservatively feminine attitude of 'the typical young British woman' in 1955. Marriage was the main goal of 91 per cent of those still unmarried, and although almost all wanted to continue working after marriage, over 80 per cent wanted to stay at home once the first child was born. The women were strict in their personal life-style, over half did not drink and two-thirds did not smoke, and they appeared to be predominantly religious (at least to the extent of declaring faith in God) and to be wholly uninterested in the implications of science and technology or in politics (White 1970: 152–3).

Despite the apparent willingness of the majority of women to accept the feminine and domestic role allocated to them, a number of social trends were beginning to undermine the ideal of the wife who devoted her time and energies entirely to motherhood and the home. There is also clear evidence that many women found being a housewife full-time frustrating and unsatisfying – though the discontents of the 'captive housewife' were articulated and publicised more widely in the 1960s than in the 1950s.

THE CHANGING HOUSEHOLD

Women's lives reflected changing population trends. As a result of better food, sanitation and health care people were living much longer by the 1950s than 100 or even 50 years before. A young woman who had reached the age of 20 by 1951 could on average expect to live another 50 years (CSO 1983: 91). Secondly, the size of the normal family had dropped sharply since the beginning of the century. During the inter-war years a gradual spread of information about contra-ception, increased concern about the welfare of children and higher aspirations to decent living standards, all encouraged a significant drop in the size of the average working-class family. Smaller families may have been in part a result as well as a cause of women's increased independence, but were certainly vital in freeing women from prolonged childbearing. Young women in the 1950s inherited the benefits of longer life, better health and the power to limit the number of children they had. They were also tending to marry younger and have their babies closer together than their mothers had done, so by the age of 30 many women with growing children had time and energy to spare, and another thirty years at least of active life ahead of them.

Women benefited as well from the long-term economic trend towards an increase in a very wide range of consumer goods and household appliances. During the inter-war period there had been an expanding production of relatively cheap and smart clothes made from new fabrics, of canned and processed foods and of labour-saving devices like electric irons, vacuum cleaners and gas and electric fires. The post-war austerity and rationing made life difficult for many housewives, but even then many families had access to the products of the previous consumer revolution. Although the labour-saving devices available did not magic away the toil of housework they did make life easier than it had been for working-class women in the past.

The common-sense assumption that modern household appliances reduce the physical labour involved in housework is challenged by a number of surveys suggesting that the number of hours women spend on housework had not fallen in the 1950s compared with the inter-war years (Arnold 1985: 12–15). One reason appears to be that standards of cleanliness have risen as washing clothes and cleaning floors becomes easier. There has also been a change in the distribution of time spent on various jobs: more time spent on shopping and less on preparing food, for example. But there is some evidence that women who do go out to work manage to do their housework in about half the time taken by women who are full-time housewives. Looking after young children could help explain this discrepancy, so possibly could the amount of help given by other members of the family when a wife goes out to work. But an American study suggests that the key factors are psychological: a full-time housewife is inclined to be more house-proud and to feel the need to demonstrate her contribution to the household more than a wife who also brings in money (Vanek 1980: 82–90). Full-time housewives may also spend more time on things they like doing – going out shopping could well fall into this category for many.

There is evidence that attitudes among both women and men to the role of the husband in the family, and his correct relationship with his wife, were changing during the 1950s. The belief that the man should be the head of the household, and the often-related belief that the man should be the sole breadwinner, were still fairly widely held in the early 1950s. Male authoritarianism was more overt in working-class than middle-class circles, but was still reflected in the form of the marriage service of the Church of England, while wifely submissiveness was still propagated by women's magazines. The ability to provide for a wife and children was also a symbol of masculine pride and competence, and was often linked to the conviction that women ought to stay at home and look after the husband's needs. So long as the husband was the sole wage-earner, allocating his wife a weekly allowance (and often keeping from her the details of what he earned), he was also in fact in a superior economic position. Although many strong-minded women did dominate their homes, and there were varied patterns of distributing and controlling the man's wage-packet, the man who paid entirely for the home was probably more likely also to be the master in it. Ferdynand Zweig in his study of *The Worker in an Affluent Society* suggested a tentative but interesting correlation between women who went out to work after marriage and those who expressed feelings of equality with their husbands (Zweig 1961: 32). He also found a difference in generations, with younger men and women tending to talk about equality in the marriage.

Even though women were beginning to enjoy better relationships in marriage, the divorce rate was much higher in the 1950s than it had been in the 1930s. This increase in divorce can be explained by the fact that the grounds for divorce had been extended in 1937, and legal aid made available in 1949, so it was easier for partners in a miserable marriage to end it. But the annual rate of divorce in the early 1950s – around 30,000 per year – aroused social concern that the institution of marriage was losing its stability and led to the setting up of a Royal Commission (Smart 1984: 32–3). Although divorce exposed the economic vulnerability and lack of rights enjoyed by the wife, nevertheless over half of the applications for divorce were regularly filed by women. This suggests that a significant minority of women were extremely unhappy in their marriages – especially as the social stigma then attached to divorced women, together with the legal complications of divorce, would discourage any woman from undertaking it lightly. It may also suggest that women were demanding more from life than in the past.

WORKING WIVES

The fact that women wanted more for themselves, or their families, is why many of them chose to go out to work after marriage, when the opportunity was available. The potential supply of labour by married women – except for those with very young children who, in the absence of child-care facilities, found it very difficult to get a job – was matched by an increasing demand for it after 1950 as a result of the rearmament programme promoted by the Korean War, and of the general growth of the British economy during the 1950s. So the proportion of wives at work rose steadily: by 1957 almost a third of 12.8 million married women in Britain were going out to work (Klein 1957: 9).

In the poorest families women have always worked because the family needed the money, and this remained true in the 1950s. Two surveys of working-class wives at the beginning of the 1950s (by Seebohm Rowntree in York and Ferdynand Zweig in Lancashire) found that about a third of each group questioned went out to work 'to make ends meet'. But a higher proportion in each case suggested that they were motivated by the wish to earn 'extras' for the home or 'luxuries', which included furniture, the children's educational expenses and holidays (Myrdal and Klein 1968: 84–5). Juliet Mitchell has pointed out that interpretation of this kind of answer should take into account the tendency of women to deprecate their own contribution and that 'extras' may make a vital difference to the standard of living for the family (Mitchell 1981: 129). Indeed, Zweig concluded that working-class men overcame their reluctance to their wives working because of the advantages of the extra money (Zweig 1961: 44–5).

If the economic motive was most important for the majority of women, a significant minority in all these surveys gave as their main reason for getting a job the desire to meet other people, or enjoyment. A Mass Observation Survey in 1957 confirmed that some women returned to work because of personal boredom or loneliness (Klein 1957: 13–14). That women staying at home as housewives often felt that what they did was unimportant to themselves, or to the world as a whole, was also indicated when a radio programme on the subject of lonely housewives, broadcast in 1961, led to the presenter, Elaine Grande, being inundated with letters. One correspondent wrote: 'Being at home all day is terribly boring, frustrating and to my mind very *inferior*' (Gavron 1966: 110–11).

Ferdynand Zweig's 1959 study of married women working at a radio valve factory in Mitcham found that most enjoyed their work, and that 42 out of 67 preferred going out to work to staying at home, saying they got bored and fed up at home, and they enjoyed companionship at work. But 15 of the sample liked housework better – finding it more independent or interesting – and only worked for the money. About half the women met regularly outside work hours to go shopping and to the cinema or dance clubs (Zweig 1961: 118, 172–3).

Zweig's study does suggest the arguments for women staying at home as well as those for their going out to work. Since the jobs most women were able to get were routine and repetitive, with little inherent job satisfaction, it could be argued that work at home is potentially more creative and leaves women freer to regulate their own time. So the problems of loneliness, boredom and frustration might be seen as the result not of women immersing themselves in a traditional feminine role, but of the conditions of modern family life, which tend to shut women up in their homes with small children. Young mothers often lived far from their own parents or close relations and did not know their neighbours. One of the best-known sociological studies of the 1950s was Wilmott and Young's comparison of the close-knit families and neighbourliness of Bethnal Green with the isolation of the same people when moved out to suburban housing estates (Wilmott and Young 1957).

In practice, however, most married women found that the best remedy for loneliness and boredom was to get a job. This also had the advantage of giving them a modicum of financial independence, and it seems often to have boosted their confidence and self-respect, and their status within the home.

Going out to work did not, however, apparently reflect in any way women's commitment to female emancipation in principle, nor did the experience of work (at least in the short term) usually strengthen women's beliefs in equal rights. The Mass Observation Survey of 1957 found that married women who answered the questionnaire did not state a belief in women's equality or right to work, and had started work again solely for practical or personal reasons. Single women interviewed did not in most cases think of a permanent job, but of temporary jobs until they married and had a family; even among the highly educated, only a third definitely wished to continue their career after marriage, and a third intended to give up their profession on marriage. The only references to women's equality were made by a few men; and the survey found that whilst just under a third of the married men interviewed disapproved strongly of married women working, 23 per cent strongly approved and the rest gave conditional approval. In fact the men were less likely to reject the idea unconditionally than their wives thought. This survey suggested that although male disapproval was a significant barrier, women's attitudes reflected social stereotypes of the feminine role more strongly than did those of men (Klein 1957: 13–14).

Despite the apparent acceptance by many women of a narrowly defined and traditional femininity, women were suffering from frustration and feelings of suppressed revolt. The fact that so many women chose to go out to work, even allowing for strong financial pressures and for the apparently purely personal rather than feminist reasons for doing so, suggests that women were in reality choosing a wider role when they could. Moreover, even if the women who chose to return to work did not normally see their action in the context of women's rights, the new pattern of women's work did have broader social implications. The Finer Report on one-parent families commented:

> Women's work used to be undertaken in the interval between school and motherhood and the sting of occupational inequality was mild. Today, motherhood is taking place in the interval between school and work and the sting of inequality has become sharp indeed (DHSS 1974, Vol. 1: 37).

Whilst this comment involves some historical over-simplification, ignoring the extent to which working-class women have always worked, it does indicate how the new social trend gave support to those women who were becoming aware of the extent of women's inequality in the sphere of work and in society in general.

Chapter two

WOMEN AS CITIZENS 1950–1970 – SECOND CLASS

INTRODUCTION

In this chapter we document the most important ways in which women were still treated as inferiors up until 1970. We concentrate particularly on women's disadvantages at work, since the economic resources and social status enjoyed by people are largely determined by their jobs. The position of women naturally reflects the class divisions of our society, so working-class women were by far the worst off; but women in all classes were on average disadvantaged compared with men in the same class. Moreover, women suffered from a number of forms of discrimination by the state and by financial institutions purely on the grounds of being women or wives, irrespective of class. Finally, women were very poorly represented in politics and all positions of power and responsibility in public life; their political inequality mirrored their lack of power in economic and social life.

The forms of inequality and discrimination that we discuss in this chapter are those which are generally accepted as unjust in terms of the dominant liberal beliefs of British society. Liberalism stresses that all individuals should have equal legal and political rights, should enjoy equal opportunities for freedom and self-development and should be granted equal respect. Women have had to struggle to assert their claims to be regarded as full persons endowed with reason and entitled to the full benefits of liberal society. By the middle of the twentieth century women's right to equal treatment had been accepted in principle, but was denied in practice by many of the embedded social attitudes and practices of society. There is an inherent conflict between treating women primarily as independent workers and citizens, and treating them primarily as wives and mothers with no economic or political responsibilities. Debates about women's emancipation have centred on these two alternate roles for women ever since the Victorian period; the coexistence of these liberal and patriarchal views in post-war Britain resulted in women's inequality, and in many anomalies in the treatment of both men and women.

This conflict of beliefs was reflected in attitudes to women's work. Whilst it was assumed that single women would and should earn their living, and it was increasingly assumed that married women with no children, or whose children were at school, would work, at the same time it was often asserted that women were not serious about their jobs. Women's lower pay and generally lower-status jobs reflected the fact that society still thought their central role was in the home and that their pay was relatively unimportant.

As a result the significant minority of women who were responsible for maintaining family dependants often found it hard to earn a decent wage and were forced back on state security. The belief that women will be provided for by loving and hard-working husbands has always meant, when translated into social practice, that single women expected to look after elderly parents, single mothers, separated or divorced wives, widows and women whose husbands are disabled or irresponsible are left at a serious disadvantage. This stereotype also places pressure on men to provide adequately for their wives in all circumstances, even if the marriage breaks up and they gain new family commitments. Therefore women's inequality at work resulted in direct hardship and injustice for many women and unreasonable burdens for some men, as well as devaluing women's work and denying them the range of opportunities and advantages open to men.

The choice of dates for this chapter inevitably involves some over-simplification. The trend towards more married women going out to work, the change in political climate from the cold-war conservatism of the early 1950s to the fashionable radicalism of the late 1960s, and the growth of permissiveness affecting personal sexual relations and cultural attitudes all had an impact on women. So there was by 1970 much more support for ensuring women true equality and a greater belief in women's right to freedom and self-development than there was in 1950. Indeed, there was evidence of increased public interest and concern over women's rights by the mid 1960s. But 1970 was a watershed. By then there was quite widespread awareness among women of the injustices they had suffered and a desire for change. A new feminist literature began to appear and local feminist groups were being formed; women workers went on strike and women trade-unionists pressed the issue of equal pay; and the national press paid attention to women's demands. Long-standing feminist organisations intensified their pressure for equal rights and a number of MPs pressed for legislation. As a result of new public concern, women's protests and pressure-group activity a range of laws specifically designed to give women equality with men were passed during the 1970s. In this chapter we document the inequalities these laws were designed to remedy.

WOMEN AT WORK

Women suffered discrimination in many spheres during the 1950s and 1960s, but their inequality was most marked and most universally experienced in the area of employment. Women usually earned a great deal less than men, the jobs in which women predominated were low-status jobs and badly paid, and there were extremely few women in top jobs in industry or the professions. The complex set of reasons for this inequality in the work-place included traditional beliefs about women's primary role as wives and mothers, the special problems of married women with children or old people to care for, the assumptions about what counts as 'women's work', and the attitudes of women themselves.

Women were badly paid compared with men throughout the period 1950–70, and the gap between men's and women's earnings stayed fairly constant during these two decades. Women earned on average about half the amount of their male colleagues in both manual and non-manual categories of work, but all women workers were on average paid much less than men. In 1960, for example, a woman doing a full-time manual job earned on average roughly £7. 10s. per week, a woman in a white-collar job £10; the corresponding figures for men were slightly under £15 for a blue-collar job and about £19 for white-collar employment (DE 1974: 29).

In order to understand the causes of women's low pay it is necessary to look first at women in full-time work, where their position is most directly comparable to men, and then to examine separately the special problems of the large number of women part-time workers. Why then did the full-time weekly earnings of women by 1968 constitute on average only 53 per cent of the weekly earnings of men? (Westergaard and Resler 1975: 102). Averages do of course conceal the fact that the gap between men and women was greater in some kinds of work than in others, but in any occupation men tended to earn more than women. The reasons for this differential included the fact that men tended to have jobs regarded as more highly skilled and more responsible, the way jobs were graded and that men could often claim longer experience or length of service. In addition, one major reason why men in manual jobs tended to earn more was that they were very much more likely to work well-paid overtime: figures for 1961, 1966 and 1971 show that on average men worked six to seven hours more per week than women. Finally, women in this period still suffered from explicit discrimination in pay for many jobs. But a Department of Employment (DE) paper noted that even where equal pay had officially been introduced by the 1960s, for example among clerical workers in the Civil Service and among teachers, average earnings of women were still lower than those of men. The paper concluded that substantial differences in average earnings of men and women were to be expected, and that only 'a limited part of the difference' could be explained by discrimination (DE 1974: 29). The paper did not, however, analyse the difficult question of what really counts as discrimination.

The real gap between the earnings of men and women cannot, however, be measured solely by differences in earnings. Women also did worse than men when it came to fringe benefits, especially women in manual jobs. The April 1970 New Earnings Survey found that there was not much difference between men and women white-collar workers over sickness benefits (almost all were covered), but there was a greater discrepancy in membership of pension schemes: 78 per cent of the men but only 50 per cent of the women belonged to such schemes. Women manual workers did markedly worse than men on both counts: only 48 per cent of women against 65 per cent of men were covered for sickness, and only 19 per cent of the women enjoyed pension rights compared with 50 per cent of the men (DE 1974: 35).

Women in full-time work were, however, economically privileged compared with those in part-time work. The number of women doing part-time jobs grew in the 1960s, fairly slowly in manufacturing industry where the proportion rose from 13.7 per cent of the female work-force in 1961 to 18.7 per cent in 1971, but the proportion was much higher in other kinds of work. Estimates for the total number of women working part-time depend on how the figures are collected. The Census of Employment based on the work-place showed that at least one in three women employees were part-time by 1971 – nearly 3 million women. The Family Expenditure Survey on the other hand, based on a sample of households, put the proportion of part-time women employees at 45 per cent in 1971; this survey would include women in domestic service and picks up women in seasonal employment (DE 1974: 13; and DE *Gazette* Nov. 1973). Very few men worked part-time, the Census of Employment found that one in twenty did so in 1971.

There are, of course, advantages for married women in part-time work; it makes it easier for them to look after children of school age – though it does not solve the problem of school holidays – and makes it easier to combine the burden of housework with a job. But part-time work has major disadvantages. It is badly paid, hourly rates for part-time workers tend to be lower than for full-time workers, and part-timers have been much less likely to enjoy paid holidays, sick pay or pension rights. Part-time jobs also tend to be dull, repetitive and unskilled. Therefore women working part-time suffered the drawbacks of all women workers in manual or routine jobs, but in more extreme form. In addition part-time workers are very vulnerable to being laid off in times of recession, often with no right to redundancy pay.

Women's low pay has clearly been linked to the type of jobs they have been expected to do, which tend to be unskilled or to require fairly limited qualifications. Women have typically been cleaners, waitresses, shop assistants, typists, clerical workers or telephonists. When women do work on the factory floor they frequently do unskilled manual labour. These tendencies were well illustrated by a study of women in manufacturing industry by the Ministry of Labour in 1968. Women made up 29 per cent of the work-force, but they accounted for only 5 per cent of skilled production workers and 4 per cent of managers and superintendents. On the other hand, 91 per cent of canteen staff were women, 62 per cent of clerical and office staff and 45 per cent of unskilled production workers. Women were not only concentrated in certain types of work but in certain sectors of industry and certain services. Within manufacturing industry women were grouped primarily in textiles, clothing and footwear; food, drink and tobacco; and electrical engineering; while within the service industries women predominated in distributive trades, miscellaneous services like laundries and catering and in the less skilled office work in insurance, banking and finance. So although the number of women at work increased by about 2 million between 1950 and 1970, the choice of jobs normally open to women did not widen significantly. Women were absorbed mainly into clerical and unskilled work.

Even women with good educational qualifications or special training have in general been badly paid and grouped into certain 'feminine' areas in business and the professions. So it is clear that although the low pay and status of women's jobs is due to the unskilled nature of the work, a reverse factor has also been operating: that jobs usually done by women are downgraded in pay and status precisely because they are seen as 'women's work'. So social prejudice is reflected in the work-place. This downgrading of women's skills meant underrating the work of cooks or secretaries, but was particularly obvious at the professional level, where nurses and teachers, despite their skills and responsibilities, were notoriously badly paid. Apart from the caring professions of medicine and education and social work, women also tended to be well represented in librarianship and to a lesser extent in market research and public relations. But women were largely excluded from what were seen as the masculine realms of engineering, physics, chemistry, architecture or accountancy. Since women broke into many of the professions early on in their struggle for emancipation, their progress at this level has been very poor. Analysis of census data shows that whereas in 1911 women made up 6 per cent of the 'higher professions' like doctors and lawyers, in 1951 their share was only 8 per cent.

Women who did enter the professions tended not to get to the top. Despite the fact that 58.8 per cent of schoolteachers were women, they were significantly under-represented among heads of schools, and women academics very seldom became professors. Nor did women do well in getting top jobs in management. The 1966 Sample Census indicated that only 1 per cent of working women became managers in establishments with more than twenty-five employees, and women made up only 13 per cent of managers of large establishments. Moreover, when women did make it into management they tended according to a Political and Economic Planning (PEP) Report on *Women in Top Jobs* to be buyers or market researchers rather than the actual manager of the store or works (Fogarty, Allen, Allen and Walters 1971: 10). The Labour Party Study Group on Discrimination (1972) Green Paper on *Discrimination Against Women* noted that in banking there were only six women managers despite 5,000 women working in banks, the majority of whom were bank clerks under 25. A few individual success stories could be set against this picture of the exclusion of women from spheres of power, prestige and wealth: the first woman ambassador was appointed in 1962 and the first woman High Court judge created in 1965. But the position of women at work, even of those who were privileged, generally reflected their inferior status in society as a whole.

Attitudes to women at work were very strongly influenced by the traditional assumption that a woman's central vocation was to marry and rear children. This belief had multiple ramifications. Firstly it justified inequality in the work-place. The fact that men would normally have to provide for a wife and family was a standard public justification for women receiving lower pay, and the fact that most women would marry and have children was taken to mean that they could not expect, and did not want, a career like a man's. Apart from the general ideological impact of the traditional view of the female role, the assumption that women would leave their jobs to have children directly influenced employers in making appointments and provisions for training. It also influenced their general view on women as employees. The Confederation of British Industries (CBI) argued in their evidence to the House of Lords Select Committee on the 1972 Sex Discrimination Bill that women were less motivated to work hard, were more likely to leave their jobs than men and had higher absenteeism rates than men. Although the memorandum conceded that none of these things tended to be true of older married women, and also conceded that some absenteeism was due to family responsibilities, the general emphasis and tone of the memorandum suggested that women were unreliable employees and tended to justify what the CBI regarded as a rational form of discrimination: 'The employer is presented with a choice between men and women which, made on the basis of past experience and future expectation, will frequently favour the man' (House of Lords 1972–73 Vol. 1: 147).

In fact women who did have babies faced considerable difficulties if they wanted to stay on at work, and because of the lack of child-care facilities it was impossible for most women to do so. The years spent at home put a woman returning to work in her thirties at a disadvantage compared with her male counterpart. Leaving work to look after young children was also an additional barrier to women getting vocational training, as training courses were designed primarily for men and so seldom provided for people over 30. Yet a 1965 survey found that three-fifths of the women who said they would like vocational training were in fact over 30 (DE 1975: 36).

Beliefs about the kind of work suitable for women were almost as firmly rooted as the belief in women's family role. Many jobs women took were of course a direct extension of work in the home: cleaning, washing, cooking and serving meals or making clothes. Others provided services to people – shop assistants or receptionists – or involved providing assistance to a male employer: secretarial work. Professional jobs emphasising health, education and caring also reflected the traditional role of women in looking after the sick, the young and the old. Women's other areas of employment have been defined partly by economic requirements. Women working in factories have since the Industrial Revolution provided a source of cheap unskilled labour, which is one reason why historically male trade-unionists have often been hostile to women's claims, though

31

they have also tended to perpetuate women's place at the bottom of the labour hierarchy. The influx of young women on to the labour market earlier this century coincided with an extension of clerical jobs which were relatively undemanding, while allowing lower-middle-class women to work in a clean and ladylike environment. Between 1911 and 1966 the proportion of women in the total workforce rose from 29.6 per cent to 35.6 per cent and most of this increase has been accounted for by women moving into lower-level office jobs. The total number of office workers in Britain increased by over 150 per cent in the period 1911–61.

Views about women's physical, psychological and mental nature have strongly influenced the pattern of work open to women. Surveys of male employers in the 1960s and 1970s have indicated the strength of their resistance to women encroaching on male preserves. A survey carried out by the Office of Population Censuses and Surveys in 1973 found that 75 per cent of the respondents thought men more likely to be 'fit, strong, able-bodied' than women, 52 per cent thought men more likely than women to have relevant intellectual abilities as shown by tests and there was a general tendency to rate men more highly on all desirable personality traits. The survey also indicated, however, that a small minority thought women were more likely to have desirable characteristics and just under a third tended to rate men and women equally. So in addition to the employer's own attitudes other factors were clearly influential. The other main factor suggested by the survey was the force of tradition. When asked why women were never employed in certain categories of work the answer 'always has been a man's job' was given by over half the sample for all the non-manual jobs listed and for skilled manual jobs; for various other categories of manual work 'physical reasons' were cited most often and 'always been a man's job' came second (DE 1975: 28–9, 17).

In general women have not been considered fit for physically demanding or skilled manual work, for jobs requiring 'masculine' intelligence and interests – mathematics, science or technology – or jobs involving power and authority over other people. These attitudes and beliefs were often translated into explicit advertising of jobs for men only. The DE did a survey in September 1972 of 7,000 advertisements and found that 19 per cent asked specifically for men and 21 per cent specifically for women; 56 per cent implicitly encouraged both men and women. Advertisements directed only to men offered a fairly wide choice, often of skilled work, and included high-status jobs in architecture, accounting, banking and insurance. Women were offered a limited choice of mostly low-status jobs in clerical, secretarial, catering and hotel work. An analysis by the Institute of Personnel Management of appointments advertised in their journal during 1971 – a sample restricted mainly to personnel and management jobs – found that 46.9 per cent of all the advertisements were for men, 8.5 per cent for women and the rest open to both. But a breakdown of the more senior jobs found that 67 per cent specified men only and none asked for women (DE 1975: 8–9).

The discrimination inherent in social attitudes and traditions of work was institutionalised in a number of professions and occupations by restricting entrants to the necessary training. The National Council of Women gave evidence to the Lords Select Committee on the Anti-Discrimination Bill which covered this problem. The Council referred to the well-known quota system of university medical schools which had, until the late 1960s, been 80 per cent men to 20 per cent women, though by 1970 the proportion had risen to 29 per cent women. Discrimination in training tended to be carried over into appointments. The Council noted that qualified women doctors sometimes complained of such discrimination, and gave an example:

> Ten years ago, a woman gynaecologist, with all the necessary academic qualifications, managed to progress to the short list of four consultant posts, but in each case a man secured the job. This gynaecologist was informed by a member of the third appointing committee that the successful candidate had a wife and three children to support, whereas she was single and did not require the extra money (House of Lords 1972–73, Vol. 1: 128).

The Council also commented on hostility shown to women at almost every level of the newspaper industry, claimed that the National Union of Journalists Training Scheme operated a *de facto* quota of 25 per cent places for women and cited evidence that women trained in both journalism and photography found it harder to get jobs after their training than men.

Professional women were, however, better off than women who wanted to break into skilled manual crafts, since they were not totally excluded from training. For example, in the newspaper industry women could and did become journalists, but could not be compositors, even though women had done this job in both world wars. The Donovan Report (Royal Commission on Trade Unions and Employers' Associations 1968: 93) concluded:

> Many of the attitudes which support the present system of craft training and discrimination against women are common to both employers and trade unionists and deeply engrained in the life of the country. Prejudice

against women is manifest at all levels of management as well as on the shop floor.

Between 1967 and 1971 over six times as many boys as girls entered apprenticeships, and three-quarters of the girls were being trained in hairdressing and manicure (DE Memo, House of Lords 1972–73, Vol. 1: 3). Young women were also much less likely to receive day-release training than men: the figures for 1969 were 10.4 per cent women compared with 39.7 per cent men. The industries employing the largest number of women tended to be the ones in which the lowest proportion of women had day-release training: for example only 2.3 per cent in the distributive trades and 3.4 per cent in textiles (Labour Party Study Group on Discrimination 1972: 9).

The failure of women to break out of a fairly narrowly defined female sphere of work can therefore be largely explained by the strength of the explicit barriers and social pressures preventing women doing 'men's' work. But it is clearly necessary to take account of women's own attitudes. At least four factors seem to have affected how women saw their own job prospects. First, women have been consciously (and no doubt unconsciously) influenced by awareness of the hostility, prejudice and formal barriers they were likely to encounter if they tried to enter a traditionally male preserve. This awareness was illustrated by a study of grammar-school girls in London and the South-East, in which nearly a quarter explained unwillingness to take up engineering by pointing to known discrimination against girls (DE 1975: 15). Only a small minority are likely to choose a career in order to fight for women's rights, or to brave hostility and ridicule to fulfil their sense of vocation. Secondly, the practical difficulties of combining a job with looking after children or sick relatives is clearly a major reason why many women have not wanted to take up extra responsibility at work. A survey of 222 married women workers in a Leicester hosiery factory carried out between 1959 and 1962 found that 171 of them did not want to become supervisors, even though the management favoured promoting married women. The main reason given was the conflict between job responsibilities and the home; moreover, only one of the twenty-three married women who were supervisors had children of school age or younger (DE 1975: 19). A 1971 PEP study of women and careers found that the career aspirations of married women graduates fell, but that single women tended to become more ambitious (Fogarty, Rapaport and Rapaport 1971: 207).

The third factor, which is derived from women's own preferences, rather than their realistic assessments of difficulties, is that many women have wanted to do traditional feminine jobs and few have aspired to get to the top. Surveys of girl school-leavers and of women graduates show clearly that most of them chose to look for clerical or shop work or at higher educational levels for teaching, nursing or social work. The surveys do not always clarify the reasons for choice, and individual decisions are of course shaped by social conditioning which indicates what men and women ought to want. But within our society women have often liked caring for people and have tended to be less ambitious than most men. The claim that women do not want managerial jobs has often been put forward by employers, and can be a convenient excuse for limiting women's opportunities; but has been confirmed by women themselves in a number of studies. The 1971 PEP study of women in top jobs found women who preferred to continue doing their creative jobs in the BBC, rather than try for higher management posts (Fogarty, Allen, Allen and Walters 1971). Over 80 per cent of women workers in a food factory said they had not applied for a supervisory post because they did not want the job, and many said they had no interest in doing it. Even those women motivated to obtain responsible jobs have quite often been happy to stay where they were and not to seek further promotion (DE 1975: 15). Finally, women have notoriously lacked self-confidence, and the tendency to underrate their own abilities has clearly inhibited them from competing with men where they feel the odds are against them, and reinforces a tendency to accept traditional feminine roles.

Women's own view of themselves has been shaped by the deep-seated beliefs about women's nature and social role built into the practices of our society. Although women's position has been slowly changing since the middle of the nineteenth century, and women by the 1950s were enjoying much greater independence and esteem, nevertheless the law, the state, the churches and society at large still assumed women's natural inferiority to men and their economic and legal dependence on their husbands. So women's position at work, the sphere which in modern society largely defines men's power, status and individual self-respect, both reflected and reinforced the continuing inequality of women.

TRAINING GIRLS TO BE WOMEN

The position of women at work was in part shaped by their early education, which handicapped them in competition for jobs and tended to direct them towards traditionally female types of work.

Education for girls represented a compromise between giving girls a general academic education like that given to boys, and steering them towards what were regarded as more feminine subjects and preparation for their later role as housewives. The main academic curriculum was ostensibly the same for boys and girls, but in practice boys tended to take science subjects in much greater numbers while girls opted for the arts. Girls were also encouraged to study domestic science, whereas boys did woodwork and metalwork. Widely held views about the aptitudes of girls and their social destiny influenced careers advice which often helped to channel girls into their segregated female jobs.

All these points were made in a memorandum by the Union of Women Teachers to the House of Commons Select Committee on Willie Hamilton's Anti-Discrimination Bill in 1973. They commented that:

> Perhaps the greatest single contributory factor to the position of women as second class citizens in the matter of employment has been the lack of opportunity for girls in schools to participate in the technological developments of recent years (House of Commons 1973c: 93).

One barrier to girls taking science and maths was the widespread belief that boys are naturally good at these subjects and girls bad, which tended to influence teachers' expectations and to undermine girls' confidence. Girls were sometimes positively discouraged from taking science at higher levels, though this was not universally true, especially in all-girl schools. But girls' schools suffered problems in science teaching, since there were few women with scientific degrees available to teach physics or chemistry, and science facilities were often poor.

There is some experimental evidence from Western societies that girls do better on average in verbal exercises and worse in mathematical and spatial exercises, a difference which only becomes pronounced in adolescence. There is no agreement on whether these differences are innate, but it is widely accepted that cultural conditioning and the teaching process itself have accentuated differences. It is also generally agreed that in the present cultural context there is a very considerable overlap between men and women in their aptitudes, a fact demonstrated by experiments. So the very small numbers of women doing physics, chemistry or mathematics at university meant that girls with potential in these subjects were being diverted into areas considered more feminine like languages or biology.

An even greater barrier to women succeeding in professional careers was the fact that many women of high intelligence were being excluded from higher education altogether; this was true as well of working-class men, but girls in all social classes were less likely than their brothers to reach university – about a quarter of university students were women, which was no real improvement on the position before the Second World War. Women were, moreover, less likely to acquire any form of higher education than men.

During the 1950s British education was still dominated by selection on the basis of the eleven-plus examination which streamed pupils into grammar, technical and secondary modern schools, though by the 1960s comprehensives were becoming more common. Under the eleven-plus system girls did proportionally better than boys in getting into grammar school – indeed some county councils deliberately equalised the number of boys going into grammar schools by giving them 'handicap' grades (Mitchell 1964: 73). But the proportion of girls leaving grammar schools at 15, 16 or 17 was higher than the proportion of boys at each age; and proportionally more girls left comprehensives early. As a result fewer girls gained five or more O levels, and fewer achieved A levels. Of all students who were at university in 1962–63 only a quarter were women, though women made up two-thirds of teacher training colleges (Greenhall 1966: 3). The tendency of girls to opt out of higher education reflected the attitudes of parents, who often did not expect girls to go to university and might be unwilling to support them. Girls' own beliefs about appropriate feminine roles, and possibly a greater unwillingness to tolerate school regulations which treated them as children, also encouraged them to leave school early.

Educational theory in the late 1950s and early 1960s tended to accept the implications of eleven-plus streaming and assume only a gifted few were equipped to enjoy higher education, and the great majority must be trained for a suitable (normally working-class) occupation. In the case of girls this attitude overlapped with the general social view that women could be divided into a small minority of clever career women and the great majority of ordinary women whose main role was to rear a family. Two reports which considered whether girls should be trained primarily for that feminine role came down in favour of schools giving emphasis to girls' expectations of marriage and children, and so treating them differently from boys. The Crowther Report on education, published in 1959, distinguished between the 'intellectually abler' girls, destined for higher education, and the less able who could expect to do clerical work or to be shop assistants. The Report considered schools did not have much scope for giving clever girls 'any education specifically related to their special interests as women', but it argued that the needs of most girls were

37

'much more sharply differentiated from those of boys of the same age than is true of the academically abler groups'. Reasons given were the new trend for very early marriage and the greater maturity of adolescent girls. The writers of the Report were concerned that training girls for clerical work, for example by teaching shorthand and typing, lacked educational content, though this consideration does not seem to have influenced their view of the desirability of training girls for courtship and marriage. 'Though the general objectives of secondary education remain unchanged, her direct interest in dress, personal appearance and in problems of human relations should be given a central place in her education.' (Central Advisory Council for Education (England) 1959, Vol. 1: 33–4.) Despite the provision made by schools to teach girls domestic science, whilst boys concentrated on carpentry and ironwork, the Crowther Report thought schools had not adjusted sufficiently to the fact that 'marriage now looms much larger and nearer in the pupils' eyes than it has ever done before'. The Newsom Report, *Half our Future*, published in 1963 came to similar conclusions about the need to give girls a specifically feminine training. 'To girls especially the personal aspect of vocation to marriage is already apparent. The interest is ready-made: there is an opportunity to give it depth of meaning' (Central Advisory Council for Education, 1963: 116).

The Crowther and Newsom Reports embodied the ideas and values of 'the feminine mystique', at a time when these attitudes were already beginning to be eroded. The same year that the Newsom Report came out with its argument that girls must be educated for 'their main social function', home-making and motherhood, because 'women are biologically and psychologically different from men', the Robbins Report on higher education was also published. Robbins urged a major expansion of higher education, with the aim of promoting the British economy, and argued that the talent was available to fill an expanding higher education sector. A Labour Government came to power in 1964 under Harold Wilson, committed to technological progress and breaking down élitism in education. Robbins was swiftly acted upon: twenty new universities were created and thirty polytechnics, and colleges of education, in the past dominated by women, offered three-year degree courses in place of two-year teaching diplomas. Although at first the proportion of women among the new students rose slowly, the numbers of women students did increase absolutely, and the expansion of higher education has significantly widened opportunities open to women. Crowther and Newsom on the other hand were not implemented. The spread of comprehensive schools committed to the principle of equal opportunities did not result in a widening of choice for girls in the subjects they pursued, but the comprehensives certainly did not endorse theories which sought to narrow the curriculum for girls. Labour Ministers of Education were, moreover, unlikely to embrace the views expressed by Newsom.

WOMEN AND THE STATE

Women achieved formal equality as citizens in 1928, when all women became entitled to vote. But the state still perpetuated the long legal tradition of treating married women as appendages of their husbands, and in its social security provisions based policy on the assumption that women would normally be dependent on men.

The question of women's rights as citizens has been raised most directly in recent years by legislation on nationality and immigration. The basic assumption has been that married women acquire the nationality of their husbands and lose their independent rights under British law. When the British Nationality Act of 1948 was passed it made one concession to women as a result of a campaign by women's organisations, and allowed a British woman who married a foreigner to keep her original nationality. But the Act still retained a double standard for men and women, since British men could confer their nationality on their wives (though under the Act this right was not automatic), but British women could never confer their nationality on foreign husbands.

As political pressure to restrict immigration from the Indian subcontinent, the West Indies and from former African colonies increased during the 1960s, the rules were made more stringent and resulted in a reduction in the existing rights of women. Under the 1962 Commonwealth Immigrants Act wives already living in the UK were normally allowed to have their husbands join them in this country, though the women had no automatic right to confer residence on their husbands, and immigration officers could refuse entry to men who were medically unfit, had any criminal record or were not thought capable of maintaining their families. But in 1969 British women were no longer able to have their Commonwealth husbands join them in the UK, and in 1971 the Immigration Act refused entry to all non-British husbands (Atkins and Hoggett 1984: 185). After the 1968 Commonwealth Immigrants Act, vouchers were granted to a quota of Commonwealth UK passport holders who were 'heads of households', but since women were scarcely ever recognised as heads of the family, they could not enter Britain in their own right. The 1968 Act was criticised by some MPs for being discriminatory against women (as well as for its racial discrimination) and two women MPs, the Conservative Dame Joan Vickers and Labour Mrs Lena Jeger, tabled an amendment that would allow widows to enter the country in their own right. They argued that widows should qualify as 'heads of households' and that women were no longer 'just appendages of their husbands'. The Minister responsible denied there was any sexual discrimination, and the amendment was rejected (House of Commons 1968: 1619–27).

Rules on nationality and immigration vitally affect women who marry foreign husbands, or women immigrants and women who come to work in Britain. All women are affected by the taxation system and the way in which social security is administered. Both have assumed the dependence of married women on their husbands, but whereas the tax rules specified the wife's subordination to her husband, the insurance regulations denied her various rights to benefit.

Single women have been treated by the Inland Revenue in the same way as single men, but the position of married women has been peculiarly anachronistic and the rules for taxing married couples anomalous. The basis of the Inland Revenue's calculations was that man and wife should be treated as a single unit. Under the 1918 Finance Act the husband was granted a married man's allowance for his wife; if she worked he was given an additional allowance to offset against her earnings. The tax laws assumed that wives were totally dependent upon their husbands, who were solely responsible for filling in tax forms and paying extra tax, and who were also entitled to receive all tax allowances and rebates on the wife's earned or invested income. The 1918 Act had in fact classified married women with 'incapacitated persons and idiots' in the category of those unable to deal with their own taxes, and the 1952 Income Tax Act reaffirmed that the wife's income should be considered to belong to the husband. This procedure meant that wives had to disclose all their income to their husbands, who were under no obligation to reveal their own income to their wives.

The rules governing National Insurance payments and entitlement to benefit were based on the Beveridge Report and took as their starting-point the assumption that most women would be economically dependent on men. The rules assumed that a woman's role was to look after children and the elderly or sick, and that she would be supported by a man whilst doing so. Single women with no dependants who worked all their lives were treated as honorary men, acquiring the same benefits, though they paid rather lower insurance contributions than men on the grounds that a man would normally expect to provide for a family. But the great majority of women, those who married, forfeited all their previous contributions towards a pension. Married women who stayed at home to raise a family became wholly dependent on their husbands paying in full the required insurance contributions. Married women who went out to work could choose between paying a minimal industrial injuries cover, which gave them no right to sickness or unemployment benefit, or paying contributions at the single women's rate, which only entitled them to sickness or unemployment benefit at lower levels than enjoyed by single women and men. Married women had difficulty in acquiring a pension in their own right if they married late, or spent a long period at home looking after children, since they had to pay insurance contributions for at least half the period between marriage and retirement. Married women at home also had no entitlement at all to benefits to cover long-term illness and disability, nor could they claim any allowance for looking after their own husbands or their old and sick relatives.

But the main problems encountered by women seeking social security, and the strongest sense of humiliation and injustice, occurred when women were unable to earn an adequate wage and were not supported by their husbands. Where the husband himself was not at work for some reason other than actual disablement, or where the woman was better able to act as breadwinner, the system made no provision for the woman to claim for her dependants. Women who were particularly vulnerable were single, separated, divorced or widowed mothers with children. The Finer Report on one-parent families estimated that in April 1971 there were 620,000 such families, 520,000 of them fatherless, and concluded that 'very large numbers of lone mothers have to apply to the Supplementary Benefits Commission'. These women faced, however, the built-in assumption that women are normally dependent on men, which has combined with the punitive attitude still inherent in the administration of social security to create one of the most notorious and discriminatory features of the social security system: the cohabitation rule. The operation of this rule, which stems from a clause in the 1966 Social Security Act, has meant that many single mothers have been deprived of their benefit simply on suspicion of cohabitation, and much larger numbers have been investigated. Women could be charged with being kept by a man if they let rooms to a single lodger, acted as a housekeeper to a man, had an occasional or regular lover who might contribute no money at all, if they went on holiday with a man or simply allowed a male friend to make temporary use of a room. Many commentators have also criticised the nature of the investigations, which often involved questioning neighbours, keeping a woman under observation, questioning the man or his workmates or his landlord, questioning the woman's children or interrogating the woman herself in a way which many found humiliating. During 1971 10,521 women were investigated for cohabitation, 4,712 had their allowances stopped or reduced, £887,000 was saved on benefits withdrawn and the investigations were estimated to cost £400,000 (Lister 1973: 1).

The way in which women have been treated when seeking social security benefits is of considerable importance because women have depended on social security much more heavily than men: as single parents, as daughters with dependent relatives, as widows and as pensioners. The fact that women normally retire at 60, five years earlier than men, was quite often cited to suggest that women enjoyed a favourable position in relation to men. But in practice it meant women's earning power was curtailed earlier, although on average women lived longer than men, so they had to rely much longer on a state pension. Since women normally earned much less than men whilst at work, and were much less likely to qualify for an occupational pension, many elderly women lived in poverty; and many also failed to apply for the social security benefits to which in fact they were entitled. Women's greater need for social security was due to their inequality in the work-place, whilst the treatment of many women seeking state assistance to escape from poverty indicated how official attitudes still embodied long-standing prejudices about the irresponsibility and irrationality of women.

WOMEN AND FINANCIAL INSTITUTIONS

It is not therefore surprising that these attitudes were also held by financial institutions like banks and building societies. When doubts about women's responsibility in monetary matters were allied to institutional conservatism and to an awareness of women's generally inferior earning power, they resulted in a policy of refusing to treat women as financially responsible agents. So banks were reluctant to make loans to women, and building societies and insurance companies often refused to grant mortgages to single women, especially younger women, and usually discounted the earnings of married women when offering a mortgage to their husbands. This kind of discrimination was generally taken for granted in the 1950s and early 1960s, and systematic surveys of the extent of it therefore tend to date from the early 1970s, when public awareness of women's rights was much greater and when attitudes had already begun to change. *Money Which?* for example, carried out a survey in 1971, which included examination of how women were treated when they applied for mortgages. It found that 25 per cent of insurance companies surveyed would only give single women mortgages in special circumstances - if for example they were over 30 and professionally qualified - and 10 per cent would not consider them at all. The rest claimed to treat single women the same as men, a claim made by all the building societies questioned. *Money Which?* sent out a woman investigator who was treated helpfully by a building society, but suggested that societies were likely to be particularly helpful to older women with professional qualifications (Dec. 1971, pp. 181-91). Statistics show that only 3 per cent of mortgages granted by building societies in 1969 went to women as the sole applicants, though it is not clear how many women who applied were turned down (EOC 1978-79: 16).

Women often found it difficult to enter into hire-purchase agreements in their own right. A married woman would normally have to obtain her husband's signature to the agreement, even if she had an independent income; and even divorced, separated or single women might be asked by hire-purchase companies to produce a male guarantor, who would be legally liable for any payments if the woman defaulted. Readers of *Money Which?* were asked to send in accounts of any experience of shops discriminating against women buying goods on credit, and received replies indicating that it was still normal for women to be asked to provide their husband's signature or backing from some man (Coote and Gill 1974: 265-7).

WOMEN IN POLITICS

One reason why women are discriminated against in the policies of both public and private bodies is that women have very seldom been involved in policy-making at the top. This was one of the arguments used by campaigners for votes for women, who believed that once women had the vote their special interests and legitimate claims to equality would be recognised in legislation and government action. Indeed in the 1920s this expectation seemed to be fulfilled by a number of laws granting women their rights (see Introduction); and although women only broke slowly into Parliament, by 1929 - the first election in which all women had the vote - there were some 69 women candidates, 14 women MPs elected and the first woman Cabinet Minister was appointed in a Labour Government. But subsequent progress was slow. The total number of women MPs did rise to 24 in

1945, when 21 Labour women were swept to power in the Labour victory, but 25 years later in 1970 there were only 26 women MPs, about 4 per cent of the total membership of the House of Commons. Since the Labour Party tended to field more women candidates, though the number of Labour candidates fell in the 1960s, the total number of women MPs fluctuated depending on the outcome of elections, but the general pattern of women's representation in this period was uniformly low. The major parties put forward few women candidates: there were 28 Conservative women candidates in 1950 and 42 Labour women; by 1970 there were 26 Conservative women and only 29 Labour (Labour Party Study Group on Discrimination 1972: 45). Moreover, the main parties awarded women few safe seats. The main gain made by women in Parliament in this period was to have the right to sit in the House of Lords, as life peers when these peerages were created in 1958 and as hereditary peers in 1963; and this could be seen as a very belated recognition that women had attained political rights, rather than a significant extension of women's political power, though a few women in the Lords soon gained minor government office.

Within the political parties themselves women were again under-represented in policy-making roles, even though women are very active at constituency level in fund-raising and the voluntary work required to run election campaigns. The Labour Party Constitution reserved places for 5 women members on its National Executive Committee of 26, and one or two more women might be elected for trade union or constituency party seats. But out of 1,352 conference delegates in 1970 only 143 were women, and from 1950 to 1970 only 6 women had acted as annual chairman of the Labour Party. The Conservative Party has a much larger Executive Committee of almost 200, which included nearly 50 women in 1971, and a General Purposes Committee of about 60 of whom 9 were women; but only 4 out of 27 members of the more important Policy Advisory Committee were women.

It might be expected that women would be better represented at local than national level in politics, because being active locally is easier to combine with family responsibilities, because local government is concerned with services in the local community in which women tend to have a direct interest, and because men may regard local government as a more fitting sphere for women than the grand affairs of state, so women might hope to encounter less prejudice in trying to enter local politics. Moreover, it has often been argued that women dislike the ethos of Parliament as a man's club, and are less likely than men to be attracted to the prestige of being an MP, so they may see more scope for real if limited achievements in local government. During and after the First World War politically active women did tend to concentrate on local activities – education boards, boards of guardians under the Poor Law, health and sanitation, administration of insurance and labour exchanges – and the Women's Labour League encouraged this kind of local specialisation. Local government had considerable powers in areas directly relevant to women, for example under the 1918 Maternity and Child Welfare Act, and was a means of politicising women and involving them in public affairs. In fact, since the Second World War women have been rather better represented in local government than in Parliament, but the Maud Report (the first attempt to check the number of women on local councils) showed that in 1967 only 12 per cent of councillors were women, while a Labour Party study of women in local government revealed that only 19 per cent of committee chairmen in county councils and county boroughs were women and that women were usually excluded from chairing finance, planning and general purpose committees (Labour Party Study Group on Discrimination 1972: 36).

The reasons why women were thin on the ground in local and national politics are somewhat similar to those which account for the paucity of women in top jobs. There was no doubt some prejudice against women, especially at the parliamentary level. Michael Rush, who did a detailed study of selection procedures for parliamentary candidates, concluded that selectors in many local parties did have doubts about the capacity of women to be effective Members (Rush 1981: 43). Certainly selection committees are likely to have been influenced by the belief that the electorate was less likely to vote for a woman, a belief that would have seemed well founded in view of the fact that a Gallup poll in 1965 found that only 78 per cent of those questioned said they would be willing to vote for a woman. Subsequent research has suggested that in an actual election the difference made by a woman candidate was sometimes non-existent and at most 1 or 2 per cent of the vote (Hills 1981; Rasmussen 1983), but selection committees would have been more aware of a generalised resistance to women candidates. Nevertheless, women's own reluctance to come forward as candidates has clearly been another important factor – Rush suggests the small supply of women prospective candidates was at least as significant as prejudice on committees, if not more so, in explaining why so few stood in elections. Women have hesitated because of family commitments, lack of self-confidence, lack of ambition for a political career, expectation of prejudice and probably perception of the House of Commons as a male club. Thirdly, the fact that few women entered the professions or business meant that very few had the kind of career that marked them out as likely parliamentary candidates, and few women were engaged in professions which can most easily be combined with being in Parliament, such as law and journalism.

There was an even clearer relationship between women's under-representation at the top of industry, commerce and the professions, and their under-representation on the public bodies and commissions which play a significant role in British public life. A table of the members of public boards of a commercial character, i.e. the Gas and Electricity Boards, the Coal Board, British Rail and other transport bodies, showed that at the end of 1970 there were 420 men who were full-time members of such boards and only 5 women (Labour Party Study Group on Discrimination 1972: 44). The National Council of Women commented in their evidence to the Lords Select Committee on the Anti-Discrimination Bill that they had lobbied unsuccessfully for the inclusion of women on the regional economic councils when these were first formed, and that the South-East Economic Council of thirty-seven members contained only one woman. The National Council of Women also noted that very few women were appointed to the industrial training boards set up in 1964. Their efforts to get more women included met with the response 'that very few women are in the position in industry from which Board members are appointed' (House of Lords 1972–73, Vol. 1: 126). Women have been more numerous on boards closer to traditional 'feminine' concerns, for example a 1964 study of four regional health boards found they had 19 per cent women members, but even here they were substantially under-represented (Currell 1974: 34, 49).

WOMEN IN TRADE UNIONS

The position of women in trade unions is relevant to their role in public life, since union activism and holding union office is one form of politics; and women's low earnings might be seen as a product in part of the absence of union pressure to raise their wages. Not surprisingly, women's membership of trade unions in the early years after the war was low, only 18 per cent of trade-unionists in 1948 were women (Ellis 1981: 11). The steady influx of married women into jobs during the 1950s led to some increase in women's membership of trade unions; by 1961 they constituted 20 per cent of the membership.

At this time only about a quarter of the female labour force was unionised compared with about half of the men at work. But a major change occurred because of the significant growth of white-collar unionism in the 1960s, especially in the public sector. Occupations in which women were numerous were systematically organised into trade unions for the first time. As a result over 2.7 million women were unionised by 1970, 25 per cent of total union membership, and according to DE figures around one-third of the women at work. These government figures cover all unions, the numbers of women in unions affiliated to the Trades Union Congress (TUC) was slightly lower (Coote and Kellner 1980: 26–8).

The reasons why many women have not joined trade unions can be divided into those related to the type of work they do (which influences union membership among both men and women), those directly related to women's own attitudes and social role and those related to the trade unions themselves. Thus women have been grouped in the types of employment less likely to be unionised – in service industries which were only brought into unions on a large scale during the 1960s, in small establishments which have always been harder to organise and in part-time work. They also change jobs more often. But, in addition, women's domestic role in the home has created practical and psychological barriers to involvement in unions, and women in general do not seem to have identified with the ethos of trade-unionism. Trade unions have been primarily concerned to protect men's wages and conditions, have reflected masculine working-class attitudes and have not been welcoming to women.

By 1970, however, the domestic commitments of married women, and women's unwillingness to be deeply involved in the masculine world of trade-union politics, may have had more influence on their lack of activism within unions than on their actual willingness to hold a union card. The evidence on the degree of activism among women unionists up to 1970 is limited, and partly dependent on the views of male union officials about women's passivity. But there are figures to show that women were poorly represented on TUC educational courses: 23 out of 475 full-time and voluntary trade union officials attending the TUC training college in 1970–71, and under 5 per cent of those attending day-release courses for shop stewards were women (McCarthy 1977: 166–7). Women were, therefore, scarce in prominent union positions: only 5 per cent of the delegates at the 1970 TUC were women and there were only two women, in the seats reserved solely for women, on the TUC General Council in the early 1970s (Labour Party Study Group on Discrimination 1972: 35).

Increasing unionisation of women did not, on the evidence about wage and salary levels, have much immediate effect on the economic position of women. There were two reasons for women's lack of power within the union movement: the fact that unions were traditionally masculine organisations with policies designed to promote the interests of their male members, so they had no incentive to challenge management policies which discriminated against women; and the lack of militancy among women workers, which meant there was no immediate pressure on union officials to take note of women's interests or to recognise women as fellow unionists. Nevertheless, the trend towards growing union membership among women did have long-term implications for the unions, who could not wholly ignore the fact that women constituted an increasing proportion of their membership. In addition, there was growing evidence by the end of the 1960s that at least some women were becoming actively dissatisfied and willing to become more militant.

CONCLUSION

The main difference in the position of women by 1970 was not in their objective economic or political power or in their legal rights – by these criteria women remained second-class citizens – but in their consciousness of discrimination. Compared with 1950 many more women were aware of their low status and earning power and their legal inequalities, and in varying degrees resented their inferior standing. This consciousness was stimulated by the new feminist literature and protests which arose at the end of the 1960s and gave women's rights a new saliency. But the new feminist activism was itself partly a product of longer-term trends: the rise in married women going out to work and women's greater prominence as wage-earners, which made their economic inequality more evident and more evidently unjust, and which also brought more women into the trade unions.

The other trend which enhanced women's consciousness of their lack of rights was the opening up of higher education to women in the mid 1960s. A rise in the number of young women with higher education automatically widened the pool of highly qualified young women available to enter the professions and created conditions in which more women might seek a wider range of careers. Higher education also tends to raise political consciousness and enhance personal self-confidence; so creating more women graduates had potential political consequences. The general tendency of women to take part more actively in politics as their educational levels rise may of course be offset by other economic or cultural or political factors: the college-bred generation of the 1950s had often accepted the feminine mystique, especially in the United States. But the generation of women emerging from the universities and polytechnics by 1970 had experienced exceptional radicalism, and were receptive to feminist ideas.

Chapter three

THE FORCES FOR CHANGE 1968–1979

INTRODUCTION

The most dramatic change that occurred in the 1970s was not in the actual position of women but in social attitudes, both among women themselves and in treatment of women in the serious press, television and fiction. Although only a small minority of women actively identified themselves with the new Women's Movement, the majority tended to become more confident in expressing belief in their rights, and the expectations of women, especially of younger women, tended to be higher. Public support for the principle of equality was embodied in a range of legislation passed during the 1970s, which marked the most significant advance for women's rights since the 1920s.

Political agitation and parliamentary measures were, however, only part of the picture. Women's lives were changing too in response to the new social and sexual attitudes generated in the 1960s, which stressed sexual freedom and fulfilment and made divorce, abortion and homosexuality more socially acceptable. The cultural as well as the political radicalism of the late 1960s also influenced the ideas and attitudes of the Women's Movement, and encouraged women to define their rights in personal and sexual terms as well as legal and economic terms. Women's Liberation did not, however, simply reflect and respond to fashionable attitudes. It also involved reassessing the present and past position of women in society and developing a feminist critique of existing political, psychological and other social theories.

WOMEN REBEL: THE EMERGENCE OF WOMEN'S LIBERATION

Women's rights achieved widespread publicity in Britain as a result of the writings, demands and demonstrations of a new generation of feminists who came to public attention at the end of the 1960s. Whilst they promoted much greater awareness of discrimination against women, their immediate political effectiveness depended on cooperation with existing campaigners for women's rights and organisations representing women's interests. Individual women MPs had used Private Members' Bills and other parliamentary devices to try to extend women's rights: Joyce Butler started trying to introduce a sex discrimination bill in 1968. Women's organisations in the Labour Party and trade unions had campaigned consistently on various issues, in particular equal pay, which the Labour Party had been formally committed to introducing since 1964. In addition, bodies dating from the original struggle for women's suffrage, like the Fawcett Society, and organisations representing women's professional interests took the lead in pressing for legislation to end sexual discrimination, though they were joined by new feminist groups in the early 1970s. (For more detailed analysis of the campaigns for the Equal Pay Act and Sex Discrimination Act, see Chapter 5.) Nevertheless, the Women's Liberation Movement did act as a catalyst to campaign for women's rights, and in addition focused attention on a much wider range of issues affecting women's daily lives.

The new feminists saw themselves as part of a movement, and this perception was essentially correct: there was a shift in consciousness among many women, an intense exchange of ideas, a diversity of organisational initiatives, a commitment to change society and a feeling of sisterhood with other women activists. The sense of spontaneity and the willingness to engage in Utopian thinking were also characteristic of a movement rather than a narrower campaign, or of a pressure group. But there are problems in identifying precisely what is meant by the Women's Liberation Movement, because it never had a centralised organisation or clear ideology. Individuals and groups who took up issues relevant to the concerns of the new feminism – for example women's health – sometimes but not always identified themselves with Women's Liberation. Among those who did see themselves as part of the Women's Liberation Movement there were unusually diverse and sometimes conflicting beliefs and attitudes. These differences were reflected in debates at the annual national conferences between 1970 and 1978, which provided one organisational focus for the movement, and in the wide range of new feminist journals and papers that sprang up in the 1970s.

The Women's Liberation Movement was a product of longer-term trends, like the increasing number of women going out to work, and changes in social attitudes, which created a new militancy among many women who did not identify themselves as feminists. On the other hand, dissemination of feminist ideas and campaigning demands through the new women's press and women's groups and protests, and the widespread awareness of militant feminism created by the national press and by radio and television, gave greater saliency to women's concerns and opened up new areas of debate. Many women were alienated by the radical image projected by committed members of the Women's Liberation Movement – particularly perhaps by what they saw as an attack on the family – but then went on to voice much stronger demands for women's equality than had been common before the late 1960s. So the new feminism with its emphasis on individual and communal 'liberation' helped to make the more traditional claims for full legal and economic rights appear moderate and reasonable.

New feminist thinking was first promoted by a number of widely read books. The best known was probably Germaine Greer's book *The Female Eunuch* (Greer 1981), which explored the emasculation of women's personalities by the social and sexual roles assigned to them. Greer became a public representative of the iconoclasm and sexual radicalism of the new feminism, though she never identified closely with the organisations or activities that were part of the Women's Liberation Movement. The novelist Eva Figes explored in *Patriarchal Attitudes* (Figes 1978) the changing social position of women in various historical periods and how women were treated in Freudian psychoanalytical theory. Juliet Mitchell, who had first raised the 'woman question' in the pages of the intellectual Marxist journal *The New Left Review* earlier in the 1960s, spoke for a specifically socialist feminism in *Women's Estate* (Mitchell 1981). At a non-theoretical level Hannah Gavron had articulated the discontents of *The Captive Housewife* in a book first published in 1966, but reprinted by Penguin in 1968 (Gavron 1966). These writings strongly influenced women who joined local groups inspired by the new feminism, but also had a much wider impact in publicising feminist concerns. In addition to these books published in Britain there were a number of extremely influential books emanating from American feminists.

The British Women's Liberation Movement was in part a response to the development of a new feminism in the United States. The American Women's Movement was ahead of its British counterpart in terms of ideas and organisation in the late 1960s. Betty Friedan's *The Feminine Mystique* first published in 1963, but most widely read and reprinted in Britain between 1968 and 1972, had a considerable impact (Friedan 1982). Friedan represented middle-class professional women – her book was based partly on a survey of her former classmates – and the National Organisation for Women she set up, NOW, campaigned for women's economic, legal and political rights. Friedan belonged to the moderate equal rights tradition of feminism, but gave it new life; and she did link up with the wider concerns of the new feminism by examining the social conditioning of women into excessively narrow feminine roles. The impetus to radical feminism in the United States came from the experience of women on the Left who felt humiliated and subordinated by the macho stance adopted by Black Power groups and within the student protests and campaigns against the Vietnam War after the mid 1960s.

A radical feminist theory was expounded by Kate Millett in *Sexual Politics* (Millet 1985), which elaborated the concept of patriarchy and the view that 'the personal is the political' – both ideas that became central to the Women's Liberation Movement. Shulamith Firestone in *The Dialectic of Sex* (Firestone 1979) developed the most extreme attack on woman's traditional role as wife and mother, denouncing not only the family but the physical process of childbearing and looking towards a solution in genetic engineering. At an organisational level the American Women's Movement developed the practice of 'consciousness raising', by women's sharing their experiences and anxieties in small discussion groups. American feminists dramatised their objection to women being treated as sexual objects by demonstrating at the 1968 Miss America Contest, when they threw bras, girdles, false eyelashes and cosmetics into a dustbin. This demonstration, treated with hilarity by the press, gave rise to the bra-burning image that dogged all mention of Women's Liberation for years (Freeman 1975: 112).

The British Movement was primarily young and middle class, drawing on students and women just entering the professions. But some of the earliest groups were set up by young married women suffering frustration and isolation as housewives, and there were groups formed by working-class women as well. These local groups sprang up spontaneously among friends and acquaintances and had a fluctuating membership; they enabled women to share their problems and relate their sense of anger or inferiority to a broader awareness of the position of women. The groups therefore emphasised mutual support and consciousness-raising, and tended to exclude men. Initially, some local groups met with husbands present, but found the men usually dominated the meetings. Consciousness-raising did not, however, become as central to the British as to the American Movement in Sheila Rowbotham's view, and many local groups engaged in protest related to local issues – for example in Liverpool opposing Catholic pressure to ban abortion (Rowbotham 1978: 95–8). The local groups set the pattern for the mode of organisation in the new movement, of autonomous decentralist groups or independent *ad hoc* bodies created to campaign on particular issues and only allowing women to take part in meetings.

The Women's Liberation Movement had a new political style, and it attracted women with no previous political experience, especially as it grew. But it nevertheless had its roots in the political life of the Left in Britain in the 1960s and included from the outset women who were already politically committed. It reflected too the varieties of the Left in this period. Some of those who were active were members of different Trotskyist groups, or were Maoists or identified themselves more loosely as socialists. Indeed the idea of holding the first National Women's Liberation Conference arose out of an informal meeting at the Ruskin History Workshop, set up to re-create working-class history and develop socialist perspectives. Others came from a libertarian background, more influenced by the anarchistic ideas of the May Days in Paris in 1968, or associated with experiments like the Anti-University or were involved in the hippy counter-culture of the period. There were also women who had taken part in the protests against the Vietnam War, a number of whom were Americans living in Britain. These very varying backgrounds explain the ideological diversity of the Women's Movement, even though women committing themselves to feminism often did so in reaction against male-dominated organisations on the Left. For example the best-known feminist periodical, *Spare Rib*, was founded by women working for the alternative press, but unhappy with the way the papers like *Oz* and *IT* portrayed women. The origins of the Women's Liberation Movement in the political culture of the 1960s were, however, reflected in the tone and rhetoric of its manifestos and slogans, with an emphasis on absolute individual rights, including a right to happiness, and an expectation of immediate change.

The first statement of common aims for the Women's Liberation Movement was formulated at the initial National Liberation Conference held at Ruskin College, Oxford, in February 1970. But the intention was to find common ground for action, not to develop a comprehensive policy, which would have been impossible given the extent of disagreement on many issues. Rowbotham has suggested that this conference marked the beginning of a real Women's Movement, though feminists had protested in 1969 at the Miss World Beauty Contest and joined a demonstration for equal pay, and as we have seen there was already a kind of organisational base in the autonomous local groups (Campbell and Coote 1982: 20–3). The Conference agreed to formulate four demands for the national movement: (1) equal pay; (2) equal education and opportunity; (3) twenty-four-hour nurseries; and (4) free contraception and abortion on demand. The first three demands took up issues pressed for a long time by older feminist groups and women's organisations, though the language in which they were framed made clear that the new Women's Movement did not just want equality with men, but to change the nature of the male-dominated society. The fourth demand could be seen as an extension of the work of earlier feminists, who had believed women's ability to control the number of their children was essential to emancipation, but the way it was formulated reflected the new claims to total sexual freedom and a belief that women had an absolute right to control their own bodies.

The Ruskin Conference tackled the problem of how the new movement should be organised. The new feminism was opposed in principle to centralised and hierarchical organisations and favoured decentralism and autonomy for local groups, but there was clearly a problem about maintaining some kind of national focus between annual conferences. The Ruskin Conference set up a Women's National Coordinating Committee, but it was dissolved at Skegness by the Conference in 1971 on the grounds that it had been taken over by one political faction. The Manchester Conference in 1975 decided to create a national fortnightly newsletter, *WIRES*, as a national information service and to focus discussion between conferences, but it soon ran into problems over its precise role (*Spare Rib*, May 1978, pp. 18–19). Women's groups did, however, manage to mobilise round key issues like sex discrimination bills and in opposition to attempts to curtail abortion.

The main instrument of communicating ideas and information was a flourishing internal press. Local women's groups produced their own newsletters, and *Shrew* – one of the better-known women's papers – began as the newsletter of the Tufnell Park Group in 1969. It lapsed in 1972 but was revived four years later and each issue produced by a different group. There were a number of magazines representing groups on the political Left, Communist, Trotskyist and anarchist, socialist feminist magazines like *Red Rag*, and several lesbian magazines. In addition, and more central to the Women's Movement as a whole, were non-sectarian magazines containing a diversity of discussion articles and news about feminists and women's issues in general. One of the most important was *Women's Report* set up in 1971 with help from the Fawcett Society, which was published every two months and five years later was selling about 2,800 copies. *Spare Rib*, which was designed to reach a much wider audience and to appeal to women reading the commercial women's magazines, achieved the highest circulation of all the women's papers, selling about 21,000 copies in 1979.

WOMEN REBEL: WORKING WOMEN DEMONSTRATE

The new young feminists were anxious that the Women's Movement should not be seen merely as a product of 1960s radical chic, or a form of middle-class self-indulgence, a charge sometimes levied at them by men on the Left. Socialist feminists in particular were concerned to link up with the traditions of working-class activism and not to be isolated from the labour movement. This concern was absent in the United States, where since the Second World War middle-class radicals have not looked for allies in the trade unions and working class. But many women who were getting involved with feminist groups and issues in the late 1960s in Britain were greatly encouraged by evidence of strong discontent among some sections of working-class women, and evidence of new militancy. The early examples of such militancy occurred quite independently of the emerging Women's Liberation Movement, but did demonstrate that there was a desire for a change in the position of women that extended to women of different classes and generations.

The most dramatic example of anger among women trade-unionists was the strike of 300 sewing-machinists at the Ford Motor Company at Dagenham in 1968, which won widespread publicity. The women were demanding that their job should be regraded on the grounds that their skill was being undervalued, and that they should be treated as semi-skilled workers. The strike lasted three weeks, and the women extended their demands to the general principle of equal pay – they received only 85 per cent of the pay given to men in the unskilled grade they were in. As a result of the strike, which was declared official by the women's trade union, the National Union of Vehicle Builders, Fords conceded the principle of equal pay and set up a court of enquiry into the grading system which found that the system did not discriminate against women. The Ford sewing-machinists therefore won only a partial victory, but they did inject new militancy into demands for equal pay by women trade-unionists and put the Labour Government under pressure to translate support for the principle of equal pay in their 1964 Election Manifesto into practice.

The Ford strike was not an isolated incident. Other examples of militancy among working-class women in 1968 were the strike by London women lavatory cleaners claiming the 'rate for the job', the well-publicised demands by some bus conductresses that the union should allow them to become bus drivers, and the campaign by wives of Hull trawlermen to improve the safety of their men's working conditions. During 1969 there were further strikes by women demanding equal pay in Skelmersdale, Manchester, Coventry and Dundee. All these cases were spontaneous expressions of anger, frustration and anxiety by the women concerned.

The prolonged campaign by women night cleaners for their own union organisation as a branch of the Transport and General Workers' Union (TGWU) was on the other hand a product of direct cooperation between the cleaners and the Dalston Women's Liberation Workshop. The campaign was initiated by May Hobbs – a night cleaner who had been trying unsuccessfully for years to unionise women cleaners – in October 1970. The cleaners were vulnerable to exploitation by employers, as they were isolated in different office blocks, and forced to work at night, often because they were single mothers with children to care for during the day, or because they were doing another job during the day and needed to work nights as well to maintain their families. Many cleaners were immigrants and therefore especially hesitant to demand their rights or ignorant of what they could claim. They were therefore paid very low wages for physical drudgery. Nearly two years after the unionisation campaign had begun, with limited success, cleaners at the Ministry of Defence went on strike for better pay, staffing and equipment; women cleaners in other government buildings followed their example, and the Civil Service Union backed the strikers, who won a wage increase, though one contractor sacked the striking women. The TGWU was consistently unhelpful, according to the women involved, and the cleaners came up against the reluctance of many male trade-unionists to support women workers (Alexander 1974: 309–25).

GOVERNMENTS LEGISLATE

The result of the new militancy among working-class women, growing pressure from women inside the Labour Party and trade unions and agitation by the new feminist groups was to persuade the Labour Government to act on equal pay. It was also under pressure to legislate by the European Economic Community (EEC), which was committed to implement this principle in the member countries. The demand for equal pay had first been voiced in Britain in 1888, had been the focus of a continuous campaign by women unionists since the Second World War and had been conceded to women working in public service by 1963. The TUC put equal pay at the head of the six-point charter of *Trade Union Aims for Women* which it published in 1963, so both the trade unions and the Labour Party were committed to equal pay on paper. After the Ford women's strike a new campaigning body was set up to campaign within the union movement for equal pay: the National Joint Action Committee for Women's Equal Rights, which organised a demonstration for equal pay by women trade-unionists in May 1969, though it was almost moribund by 1970. The Ford women themselves were met by Barbara Castle as the new Secretary of State for Employment, and she introduced her Equal Pay Bill in Parliament in autumn 1969. The Bill was rushed through to ensure its passage before the election, called in May 1970. As a result, as Barbara Castle commented later, during a Commons debate on a Private Member's Bill to ban sex discrimination in 1972, there were loopholes in the Act finally passed. But it was the first major piece of legislation on women's rights since the 1920s.

The Equal Pay Act passed in 1970 was intended to ensure equal pay for the same kind of work and to outlaw explicit discrimination against women in their terms and conditions of employment. It allowed employers a five-year period before the provisions of the Act came fully into force in December 1975. The Act covered not only basic pay, but overtime pay, allowances and benefits, sick pay, holidays and hours of work. There were, however, a number of exceptions to the Act which allowed for women to be treated differently in relation to protective legislation, maternity leave, retirement and pensions. So women still retired earlier and did worse out of occupational pension schemes.

The major criticisms of the Act have focused on its central provisions and the difficulty of enforcing them. In order to claim a right to equal pay a woman had to show she was doing 'like work' to a man, or was doing a job evaluated as 'equivalent' to a man's job. In practice, therefore, employers had ample scope to continue grading women's work differently and to contest interpretations of 'likeness' and 'equivalence', whilst women grouped in low-status jobs often could not compare themselves directly with men working in their enterprise. If a woman did contest her pay under the Act before an industrial tribunal, the burden of proving that she was doing 'like work' to a man fell upon her.

The passing of the Act did appear to have some positive results for women in the short term by narrowing differentials between the basic rates of men and women, particularly for women doing manual jobs. Judgement of the effectiveness of the Act is complicated by the fact that the Labour Government which came to power in 1974 introduced an incomes policy designed to help the lower paid, so women benefited in any case from narrowing of differentials under this policy. But a study by the London School of Economics (LSE) Equal Pay and Opportunity Project covering the period 1974–77 found women did, in addition, make gains under the Act. Between 1970 and 1977 women's earnings as a proportion of men's rose from 63.1 per cent to 75.5 per cent (the calculations exclude the effect of overtime, which would widen the gap between men and women since more men work overtime), but 1977 proved to be a year of peak improvement, and women's earnings then dropped slightly in relation to men's (Snell 1979).

The other major piece of legislation for women's rights was the Sex Discrimination Act passed in 1975. This Act was the culmination of a number of attempts by back-bench MPs to get an anti-discrimination Bill through Parliament. These attempts met with no success in the House of Commons until 1973, when Willie Hamilton's Anti-Discrimination Bill got as far as being examined by a Select Committee before it was lost through lack of time. The Liberal peer Nancy Seear had introduced a Private Member's Bill in the Lords the previous year. The Lords decided to set up a Select Committee, which sat for nearly a year and heard extensive evidence on discrimination suffered by women (some of which was cited in Chapter 2). The Committee returned a strengthened draft of the Anti-Discrimination Bill to the Lords in the spring of 1973. The Conservative Government decided, however, not to support either the Seear or Hamilton Bills, but published their own more limited proposals for legislation in a Green Paper during 1973. Against this background the new minority Labour Government formed in February 1974 (and re-elected in October that year with a narrow overall majority in the House) committed itself to introduce its own Bill, which became law in December 1975.

The passage of the Labour Government's Sex Discrimination Act could be seen as a victory for the women within the Labour Party who had exerted continuous pressure for reform since the late 1960s, for the professional women's organisations and older feminist groups who had lobbied for legislation, and for the new Women's Liberation Movement which had created a much greater public awareness of the discrimination still suffered by women. The Act symbolised public acceptance of women's claim to equal rights and was intended to prohibit discrimination in all areas of public life.

The most important provisions of the Act concerned employment, and were designed to supplement the Equal Pay Act, by outlawing discrimination in recruitment, training, promotion, redundancy and dismissal, and in provision of fringe benefits. Discrimination was made illegal not only for individual employers, but for employers' organisations and trade unions, employment agencies, vocational training bodies and bodies grading qualifications for particular types of employment, and in job advertisements. Private households and firms employing five people or less, were exempt from the Act, and some jobs were excluded: the armed services and ministers of religion being two of the main exceptions. The Act still allowed women to be treated differently in certain respects, in provisions for pregnancy and in provisions for death and retirement, so it did not cover discrimination in occupational pension schemes. The Act did extend to education, to financial institutions and to accommodation, transport and entertainment, although allowing certain exemptions.

Despite the scope of its provisions the Act did not immediately appear to be a very effective measure for changing the actual practices of employers since it proved difficult to enforce. In the first two years after the Sex Discrimination Act came into force only 472 cases were referred to tribunals, compared with 2,439 cases under the Equal Pay Act. Women often found it difficult to know, and even more difficult to prove, that discrimination had occurred in areas like appointments and promotion – pay rates are at least more tangible. Moreover, complaints of discrimination tend to apply to individual women and not to categories of workers as under the Equal Pay Act. Nevertheless the Act did result in at least partial public compliance in matters like job advertisements.

The body charged with primary responsibility for monitoring how both the Equal Pay and Sex Discrimination Acts worked in practice, for suggesting amendments to them, and for investigating suspected cases of discrimination, was the Equal Opportunities Commission (EOC). The Commission, set up under the Sex Discrimination Act, was also given legal powers to require organisations to obey the anti-discrimination legislation, and if necessary to take them to court; it was further empowered to help individuals contesting discrimination with advice and to take their cases before tribunals and courts. Finally, the Commission was given a rather broader brief to explore forms of discrimination not covered by the two main Acts, to suggest amendments to other laws and to encourage research and education in areas relevant to women's rights. During debates on the Bill the Conservative Opposition had complained that the powers of the Commission were too wide. So the role adopted by the Commission would clearly be important in determining the vigour with which the Acts were enforced, though ultimately the enforcement responsibility lay with tribunals.

Commentators on the Commission have generally agreed that its early achievements were modest. Because the Commission was set up in a hurry after the passing of the Sex Discrimination Act, it took time to recruit senior staff, several of whom were not in place until the end of 1976. The Commission was also unexpectedly deluged with individual inquiries from women seeking advice – 3,000 in the first five weeks and over 10,000 by early 1968 – so energy was diverted from pursuit of the broader objectives envisaged for the Commission. But despite these early difficulties, the main reason for the lack of impact made by the Commission in its early years was undoubtedly the nature of the Commissioners themselves and their view of the appropriate strategy to be adopted. The Commission was appointed by the Home Secretary, and the institutional interests of the CBI and the TUC were strongly represented, and it adopted a strategy which stressed conciliation and high-level, behind-the-scenes negotiations rather than confrontation or direct attacks on discrimination (Byrne and Lovenduski 1978). But in assessing the record of the EOC it is important to take account of the weight of institutional resistance to the anti-discrimination laws and the impact of general economic policies and trends on women's pay and employment. A much more detailed assessment of how much can be achieved by legislation, the role of the EOC itself, the interpretations of tribunals and courts and the problems inherent in the actual provisions of the Acts, is given in Chapter 6 of this book.

The Labour Government passed other welfare and employment legislation in the mid-1970s that served to plug some of the loopholes in the Equal Pay and Sex Discrimination Acts. Women's lack of entitlement to occupational pension schemes was remedied by the Social Security Pensions Act of 1975, which required employers to grant women equal access to pension schemes, though it did not require them to grant equal benefits to women. The right to maternity leave – a central issue for women trying to combine having a family with a job – was covered by the Employment Protection Act of 1975, which required employers to grant six weeks' paid maternity leave, and to hold open the job for twenty-nine weeks after the baby was born so that the woman was guaranteed a right of reinstatement. This right was qualified in various ways by length of previous employment and by the woman's willingness to work for the first six months of her pregnancy and at that stage only applied to full-time workers.

Women who worked part-time were least well protected by legislation, and were also the worst paid and worst treated in terms of fringe benefits. Part-time workers did in principle come within the scope of the Sex Discrimination and Equal Pay Acts, but they lacked protection against unfair dismissal, and had no rights to maternity leave, redundancy pay or sickness pay. Since increasing numbers of women were working part-time, the proportion increased between 1971 and 1976 by 30 per cent, their exclusion from employment rights was of considerable importance. Their problems were partially met when the Government amended the Employment Protection Act in 1977 to extend the definition of full-time work, and so extended the rights guaranteed to full-time workers to all those working a sixteen-hour week, or over an eight-hour week if they had been in the same job for five years. Whilst this still left quite a few women unprotected, for example many cleaners and school dinner ladies, it did mean that a considerable number of the estimated 40 per cent of women workers who did less than the standard week gained employment rights.

Inequalities in the treatment of married women under the social security rules were partially remedied under the Social Security Pensions Act of 1975. The option for married women to pay lower insurance contributions, and therefore lose various rights, was to be phased out after 1977, and from 1978 married women gained the right to employment and sickness benefits at the same rate as men. Women also became entitled to a state pension for periods when they were at home looking after children or sick relatives, provided they had been employed and paid full insurance contributions for twenty years. In addition the Act abolished the half-test rule for married women, which restricted their right to pensions. The main criticism levelled at the Act was that it nevertheless still assumed men were the breadwinners in the household, as a result women who were for various reasons supporting their husbands and families were not able to claim extra benefits to cover their dependants unless their husband was actually disabled. Married women were, moreover, precluded from claiming certain allowances to help them look after sick relatives or on account of their own disablement. These omissions resulted in many women suffering hardship, frustration or humiliation, as investigations by the National Council for Civil Liberties (NCCL) Women's Unit and the EOC revealed. (For details see Chapter 4.)

New laws were passed in the early 1970s to strengthen the rights of married women. They dealt with two topics which were central to the early struggles for married women's rights in the Victorian era, property and the guardianship of children. The Matrimonial Proceedings and Property Act of 1970 was a recognition of the problems facing women whose marriages broke up, if they could not claim a right to a share in the family home. A number of court cases in the 1960s had shown the uncertainty of the wife's position in an area governed by judicial conceptions of property rights and open to differing interpretations. Unless she had joint legal title to the house, a specific contractual agreement with her husband or had made direct financial contributions towards buying the house, a woman had difficulty in persuading the courts she had any rights to a share in the proceeds of the sale of the family home. In the eyes of the law a wife who gave up her job to look after her children full-time had made no 'contribution' to the home at all; and even if she had earned money which contributed to the housekeeping, children's clothes or furniture the courts might not deem this indirect contribution sufficiently 'substantial' (*Tulley v. Tulley* (1965) and *Gissing v. Gissing* (1969)). Moreover, if her husband left her, she had no right to go on living in the house; this issue was dramatised by a case in 1965, when the House of Lords ruled that if a husband deserted his wife and then sold or mortgaged the house, the new owner could rightfully evict the wife (*National Provincial Bank v. Ainsworth*, 1965). The new Matrimonial Proceedings Act specified that a woman's contribution to the family by working at home should count in entitling her to a share in the house.

The Guardianship Act of 1973 brought in by Mr Heath's Conservative Government was designed to grant mothers full legal equality with fathers in deciding how their children should be brought up. It superseded the 1925 Guardianship of Infants Act, which had left legal custody with the father, though the mother could go to court to acquire the right to custody. Two Conservative women MPs had attempted to alter the law on this issue, Joan Vickers in an unsuccessful Private Member's Bill in 1965, and Irene Ward, who withdrew her own Private Member's Bill on this topic in favour of the Government's Bill which was entering the Lords. When introducing the Bill in the Commons, Mr Carlisle commented that it might come as a surprise to many to hear that 'in the 1970s the rights of a mother over her child are, at common law, non-existent' (House of Commons, 1973d: 426). The father technically had sole responsibility for deciding on a child's education, religion, control of a child's property and taking important decisions (for example medical decisions) on a child's behalf. In practice, of course, most couples did take these kind of decisions jointly, but the Act was brought in to end the wife's legal inequality and to ensure her full rights and responsibilities if disputes did arise.

Increased public awareness of the discrimination suffered by women and the justice of their claim for legal equality in all spheres was reflected in another measure affecting women's rights as British citizens. The Labour Government amended the law on nationality and citizenship in 1974 to allow foreign husbands of British women to live in Britain, although the husbands could not acquire British nationality until they had been in the country for five years. The previous position, whereby women could confer no rights at all upon their husbands, was reversed.

The 1970s therefore saw what was on paper an impressive amount of legislation, which removed many previous inequalities and anomalies and also set out, in the two central Acts on Equal Pay and Sex Discrimination, to remove the long-standing structural inequalities suffered by women in public life and in particular in the work-place. Despite the criticisms which could be levied against these Acts, and the omissions which still allowed some forms of discrimination, women appeared to have made significant progress towards equality of rights and respect.

CHANGING SOCIAL AND CULTURAL ATTITUDES

There was a significant shift during the 1960s in social attitudes, affecting personal and sexual relationships and also reflected in social manners, dress and popular culture. It was a revolt against the social and sexual restraints of the 1950s, espousing an ethic of personal exploration and enjoyment and a belief in expanding possibilities, that was normally summed up as 'permissiveness' but also implied 'liberation'. Some elements of the permissive society like the drug culture had no direct relevance to women's attitudes and position in society, but the new attitudes to sexuality did have a very direct relevance to women and influenced both the Women's Liberation Movement and women's beliefs and behaviour more generally. It is important not to oversimplify the nature and extent of social change. A public relations image of 'swinging London' did not reflect the reality of most people's lives in London itself, and the fashions adopted in the capital reached other parts of the country more slowly, if at all. The attitudes and behaviour of older generations may change comparatively little, even if the young do flout previous conventions; and the culture of the 1960s was predominantly a youth culture. Moreover apparent changes in sexual behaviour may have been exaggerated, because more people acknowledged previously hidden sexual relationships. Nev theless, there was a significant change in attitude involving greate tolerance of all forms of sexuality, and an emphasis on the need for sexual self-fulfilment, which did result in important changes in the law and did have repercussions on behaviour. Since women are in general much more constrained sexually when society requires a strict sexual code of behaviour, because of the traditional double standard for men and women, the sexual freedom they began to gain in the 1960s was understandably seen as a vital element of liberation by many in the Women's Movement.

Changing social attitudes were reflected in the trend towards higher divorce rates. Greater belief in the importance of individual self-fulfilment and happiness, and less commitment to the concept of duty and the sanctity of family life, encouraged individuals to seek divorce and meant greater social tolerance for divorced women. The annual divorce rate almost doubled between 1951 and 1968, rising to 50,000 in 1968 (CSO 1970: 57). Social acceptance of the desirability of ending unhappy marriages and awareness of the difficulties and bitterness created by divorce procedures led to the passing of the Divorce Reform Act in 1969, which made divorce legally and financially much simpler. It also abandoned the previous criteria of innocence and guilt and enabled divorce by mutual consent after a separation of two years. Making divorce easier naturally tends to increase the number of divorces, and by indicating social approval of divorce may also increase the readiness of couples to consider it as a solution to difficulties in their marriage. Certainly the divorce rate soared during the 1970s and 160,000 divorces were granted in 1980 (CSO 1983: 31).

Whether making divorce easier benefits women has been controversial in the past. Whilst women's rights campaigners have always supported a woman's right to divorce a cruel or irresponsible husband, and demanded equality between men and women in claiming grounds for divorce, women's organisations have not usually campaigned for easier divorce. The Women's Cooperative Guild representing working-class women was unusually radical when it argued the need to cut the costs of divorce, and suggested to the Royal Commission on Divorce Reform, set up in 1909, that divorce by consent should be granted after two years' separation (Gaffin 1977: 132–3). As late as 1963 the Married Women's Association opposed Leo Abse's attempt to introduce a Bill simplifying divorce procedures, whilst Edith Summerskill also opposed what she saw as a 'Casanova's Charter' (Banks 1981: 198).

Opposition to easier divorce may of course spring from religious or

ent to maintaining marriage, or from concern about
children. But the specific fear that easier divorce will
been based on the belief that women are more likely to
lly and socially from divorce: because marriage has
tral to women's lives, because older women seemed
much less likely to remarry than older men and because women living
alone tended to be socially isolated. These arguments do not, however,
take account of the fact that many women in the past may have
tolerated unhappy marriages because of legal and financial difficulties
in getting divorced, and that changing social attitudes which have
removed the stigma from divorce might make divorce more attractive
to women. The evidence of the last two decades suggests that
increasing numbers of women have wanted divorce – seven out of
every ten divorces granted in 1981 were granted to wives. Moreover,
although more divorced men than divorced women do remarry, the
remarriage rate for women doubled between 1961 and 1980 (CSO
1983: 30). Increasing economic independence, higher personal
expectations and greater self-confidence may have influenced women's
willingness to leave their husbands. The Women's Liberation
Movement was not therefore likely to favour restricting divorce,
though the issue on which many radical feminists and more
conventional women's organisations agreed was that divorced wives
with children were still financially very vulnerable and needed
support.

Women's claims to sexual freedom and fulfilment and greater social
tolerance of sex outside marriage, both of which probably contributed
to the divorce rate, were also reflected in other social trends. More men
and women were living together outside marriage, and more children
were being born out of wedlock. Whereas only 6 per cent of all live
births in England and Wales were illegitimate in 1961, the proportion
in 1981 was over 12 per cent. Children were most likely to be conceived
out of marriage by girls under 20, and there appears to have been much
greater pressure in the past for pregnant girls to marry. The number of
illegitimate babies would presumably have been very much higher
during the 1970s if it had not been for the increasing availability of
contraception and contraceptive advice, and for the 1967 Abortion
Act.

The long battle by supporters of birth-control to give information
on methods of contraception to all women who needed it, and to
provide cheap or free supplies of contraceptives to women in all social
classes, was not won until the late 1960s. Voluntary efforts to promote
birth-control became widespread in the 1920s, and in 1930 a Labour

Minister of Health responded to pressure from birth-control and women's organisations and issued a circular to local authorities enabling them to provide advice on contraception, but only on the medical grounds that further pregnancies would damage the health of the women involved. By the 1950s the Family Planning Association ran 500 clinics in conjunction with local authorities, who often provided premises, and had achieved public respectability and governmental recognition, but no central government support. A Bill to enable local authorities to provide advice and contraceptives to all women was brought in by Merseyside MP, Edwin Brooks. His National Health (Family Planning) Act of 1967 authorised local councils to assist women with contraception on social as well as medical grounds. But local authorities were not required to respond, and a year after the Act was passed only a quarter were providing a full family planning service. During the 1970s increasing demand for contraception, and public acceptance of its desirability, resulted in free contraceptive advice being made available to all women on the National Health Service (NHS) in 1973. When the Labour Government came to power in February 1974 it introduced free contraceptive supplies under the NHS, a policy which had been strongly supported by Opposition Parties and by the House of Lords, but resisted by the Conservative Government, the previous year. When in 1975 GPs began to provide family planning services under the NHS the long struggle for contraception was complete. Political pressure during the early 1970s had been mounted by groups concerned both about women's rights and about the separate but topical issue of population control.

Abortion was made more readily available to women in the same year as an unrestricted contraceptive service was authorised by Parliament, and the 1967 Abortion Act also originated as a Private Member's Bill and was the outcome of a long period of campaigning. The terms of the 1967 Act still required two doctors to agree that abortion was necessary to avoid harm to the pregnant woman or the risk of a damaged baby being born, and interpretation of the terms of the Act left doctors considerable discretion. As a result, abortion is more readily available in some areas than others, depending on the attitudes of the medical profession to abortion. But the Act did for the first time authorise abortion not only for narrowly defined physical or psychological reasons, but on general grounds of the woman's physical or mental health and allowed social circumstances to be taken into account. In practice quite a few doctors have been prepared to interpret the Act liberally, and between 1971 and 1979 over 50,000 women a year received abortions on the NHS, though married women have found it much easier to get NHS abortions. The numbers who had legal abortions by paying for them in private hospitals and clinics rose steadily from 41,000 in 1971 to 65,000 in 1979; in this year 52 per cent of the total abortions were for single women compared with 47 per cent in 1971 (CSO 1983: 35).

Abortion has always been a key issue for the Women's Liberation Movement on the grounds that women have an absolute right to control over their own bodies. Although many supporters of legally available abortion would not accept so uncompromising a stance, and may be more concerned about the proven dangers of driving abortion underground, in practice feminists have combined with liberal and medical opinion to protect the 1967 Abortion Law. The National Abortion Campaign was formed in 1975 to defend the 1967 Act against attempts to restrict abortion by new Private Members' legislation in Parliament, and mobilised opposition to the Bills brought in by James White in 1975 and William Beynon in 1976 designed to eliminate alleged abuses of the 1967 Act and to make abortions harder to get. Both Bills lapsed, but a third Bill to limit entitlement to abortion was introduced by John Corrie in 1979, and was the focus of a major campaign by opponents and supporters of abortion. Women's groups gained the support of the TUC, which organised a mass demonstration against the Corrie Bill, and campaigners outside Parliament were assisted by women MPs who mounted strong resistance to the passage of the Bill, including a filibuster at the committee stage. Although the Conservative Government was moderately sympathetic to the Bill, it was allowed to fall for lack of time.

The other piece of major legislation which symbolised the new sexual liberalism of the late 1960s, the 1967 Act legalising sexual acts between adult men, did not directly affect women. But it did have implications for women both sociologically and ideologically. Whilst lesbianism had never been illegal, it had been treated as a psychological deviation and subject to social hostility and ridicule, so the legalising of male homosexuality and the emergence of the Gay Liberation Movement did buttress the position of lesbian women as well. It also made it easier for the Women's Movement to espouse respect for lesbianism as a central tenet of the movement. Acceptance of lesbianism followed logically from a number of feminist positions: claiming women's right to explore and develop their own sexuality had to include homosexuality; rejecting marriage as the sole ideal, and rejecting the tendency of society to define women solely in relation to men, implied that lesbianism was a valid alternative; whilst awareness of the male domination involved in many relationships between men and women also suggested that lesbian partners might enjoy a more equal union. Commitment to organisational separatism, and belief in the creative and peaceful values of women as opposed to the competitive destructiveness of men, led to both organisational and sexual segregation among some feminists.

The relationship between the new feminism and the sexual and cultural permissiveness of the 1960s was complex. The increased freedom for individuals and greater tolerance of diversity did seem to benefit women. The greater freedom of dress in the 1960s also harmonised with feminist rejection of the dictates of fashion and of an ideal feminine figure. But the new permissiveness had its own traps: a requirement of chastity might be replaced by men claiming a right to sex; and women normally had to take responsibility for contraception and found the new popular methods (the pill and intra-uterine devices) could have dangerous side-effects. The ending of censorship in the theatre and the acceptance of nudity and soft porn could lead to further exploitation of women as mere sexual objects, and did encourage much more explicit and titillating use of the female body in advertising. Women in the movement protested about the use of women's bodies to market commodities early on, and showed increasing awareness of possible abuses of the sexual freedom associated with the 1960s.

WOMEN PROTEST ABOUT VIOLENCE AGAINST WOMEN

If the Women's Movement developed to some extent out of the sexual and cultural freedom of the 1960s, and played only a contributory role in securing its original legislative gains, the movement did take the initiative in the 1970s in seeking protection of women in a number of key areas like rape, sexual molestation and domestic violence. These important issues transcended the cultural trendiness associated with the late 1960s, affected women of all social classes and ages, and were issues on which new women's groups could link up with the established and more conventional women's organisations, enlisting the sympathy of many men. At the same time, violence against women highlighted the radical feminist critique of existing society, since the violence was largely hidden and ignored, and when cases of violence came to light the tendency of public, police, social workers, psychologists and courts was to blame the woman.

Rape became a central problem for feminists during the 1970s. It demonstrated in extreme form men's tendency to treat women as sexual objects, male hostility to women and women's vulnerability to male violence. Feminist criticism also focused on social attitudes to rape, which often assumed that the woman must have led the man on. Feminists attacked too the police practice of starting from the suspicion that a woman who complained of rape was lying, and the conduct of rape cases in the courts, which resulted in humiliating cross-examination of the woman about her own sexual history and in these details being widely reported in the press. Feminists pointed to the sexual double standard involved in judicial procedures, which divided women into the sexually pure and the sexually promiscuous, and assumed that raping the latter was not a crime. They also stressed that the ordeal undergone by many raped women at the hands of the police and courts, which often seemed to turn into a trial of the woman, not her attacker, prevented many women from reporting rape. Feminist pressure and partial acceptance that court proceedings in rape cases were unfair to the woman led to a Private Member's Bill, the Sexual Offences Amendment Act, being passed in 1976, with the aim of protecting the anonymity of women in rape cases. Recognition of the trauma suffered by women who were raped, and the sense of shame and reticence normally imposed upon them, led to the setting up of rape counselling centres, where women could get both psychological help and legal and medical advice.

Apart from gaining some potential protection from press publicity, women who were raped did not appear to get much better treatment from either the police or the courts, who both still reflected the belief that women claiming rape were often irresponsible liars. Nevertheless, it did seem that more women were reporting rape than in the past after the 1976 Act, perhaps because they felt legally rather better protected, and probably also because women were becoming more self-assertive and angry about perceived discrimination. It is impossible to tell whether the statistical increase in rape in the late 1970s was entirely due to more women going to the police, or whether it also reflected a real increase in the incidence of attacks on women. The number of rapes and indecent assaults reported in London in the first quarter of 1978 had doubled compared with the same figures for 1977, and senior police officers expressed alarm and were advising women against going out alone at night (*Guardian* 23 Oct. 1978).

At this time feminists were becoming increasingly angry at the sexual violence suffered by women, and the danger of walking along the streets alone. The first demonstration to assert women's right to go out at night unmolested occurred in November 1977 under the slogan of 'Reclaim the Night', when women paraded in Soho and the centres of several other big cities. Concern about women being driven off the streets at night by fear of attack became acute during the period when the 'Yorkshire Ripper' killed a total of thirteen women in northern cities, mostly prostitutes, but in an especially well-publicised case in November 1980 a girl student at Leeds University. The organisation Women Against Violence Against Women held its first national conference in Leeds in late 1980.

The Ripper case focused attention on two other issues already raised by women's groups: social attitudes to prostitution, which assumed that women who were prostitutes must expect to be targets of sexual assault and physical violence; and the role of pornography in encouraging sexual violence. Peter Sutcliffe, the Ripper, was found to have had a large store of pornographic material. Some women saw pornography, and especially hard porn depicting sadistic acts, as encouraging male fantasies of humiliation and assault on women; and there were a number of feminist demonstrations outside cinemas showing blue movies.

A cause espoused early on within the Women's Movement was the cause of women who suffered violence inside the respectable bounds of marriage. Like many contemporary feminist issues, this problem had been taken up by supporters of women's rights before: John Stuart Mill wrote about the violence inflicted by men on their wives within the despotic framework of the Victorian family, in his book on *The Subjection of Women*. But when Erin Pizzey opened the first centre for battered women in Chiswick in 1972 she drew attention to the fact that the impulse of some men to assault women had not ended with the Victorian era. Most women who suffered from being beaten by their husbands had tried to hide the fact, out of shame and perhaps out of fear of further violence. Women beaten by their husbands were in a similar position to rape victims, aware that their neighbours were likely to blame them for 'asking for it'; and police were reluctant to intervene between husband and wife. Psychological thinking tended to reinforce popular prejudice by assuming battered women 'wanted' and provoked male violence. Moreover, in practice most wives had nowhere to go with their children, so they had little choice but to go on enduring violence in silence.

The opening of the Chiswick Centre and widespread media coverage drew attention to the extent of the problem. By 1980 the Women's Aid Federation had set up 200 refuges for battered wives and their children, but the refuges were overcrowded, and despite some central and local government aid were under-funded, and did not meet the need for accommodation for women with violent and dangerous husbands. A Commons Select Committee on violence in the family recommended in 1976 that there should be a place in a women's refuge for one in every 10,000 women, but by 1981 there was only one place for every 60,000 (*Guardian* 21 Oct. 1981). The campaign to assist battered wives had some legislative success when Labour MP Jo Richardson got through her Domestic Violence Act in 1977. The Act enabled women to apply for an injunction to prevent their husbands assaulting them or their children without having to start divorce proceedings, and empowered a judge to arrest a man who had inflicted 'actual bodily harm' and was likely to hurt his wife again. But a year after the Act was passed a conference of those involved in the problem of domestic violence – social workers, lawyers and members of the Women's Aid Federation – expressed concern about the way the Act was being implemented. There were long delays in granting injunctions and some judges were unsympathetic to the women concerned, and did not regard anything short of broken bones as 'actual bodily harm' (Coote 1978b: 184). Shortage of housing exacerbated the difficulties facing a woman with a violent husband, since local councils were reluctant to allocate housing to women in this position.

THE FEMINIST CRITIQUE OF SOCIETY

The Women's Movement did succeed in focusing public attention on the problems of rape and wife-battering and in bringing some change in public and official attitudes as represented by legislation. How far social stereotypes about women who suffered rape and beating were altered is difficult to assess – deep-seated beliefs and attitudes take a long time to change – but by creating counselling centres and refuges the movement has enabled the women to seek help and to discard their own sense of guilt. Simultaneously, feminists were attacking the orthodoxies of psychological and social theory and encouraging further research into the causes of rape and violence against women and a re-evaluation of women's own position.

The process of questioning social practices and sexual stereotypes was extended by feminists to most areas of life, but considerable emphasis was given early on to the treatment of women by medicine and psychiatry. Women complained that specifically female problems like painful periods and the menopause were not taken seriously by male doctors. Many feminists resented doctors assuming total omniscient control over women's bodies, especially in the hospital routine of controlled childbirth, and their withholding information about medical problems from the patient. Women also charged that doctors tended to treat women as inherently irrational and neurotic, that GPs often dismissed physical symptoms as signs of neurosis and that a routine response to anxiety or depression was to issue tranquillisers, which drug company advertising has regularly presented as being designed particularly for housewives.

Prevailing attitudes and practices in psychiatry were clearly important since more women than men end up at some time in mental hospitals; the figures for 1970 were 104,065 women compared with 72,098 men admitted into hospitals in England and Wales (Fransella and Frost 1977: 168). Women are physiologically vulnerable to mental disturbance at certain times – post-natal depression and the menopause are the obvious examples – but research findings suggest the social context is more important than purely physical factors. Moreover, women do not seem especially prone to mental illness in all cultures – research in Finland covering 130 years found women fairly consistently less likely to end up in mental hospital: in total 44 per cent of women compared with 56 per cent of men.

Feminists have argued that women may be especially prone to depression because the standard psychological criteria of normal femininity, including passivity and unassertiveness, are very close to those of depression. So excessive identification with a 'womanly' role may lead to characteristics of depression. On the other hand, women who refuse to conform to this role may also be seen as unbalanced or even mentally ill. Psychoanalytic theory in particular has often suggested women must learn to conform to the social role of wife and mother, then 'feminine integration is completed' (Kestenberg, cited in Holland 1981: 18). Michele Barratt and Helen Roberts studied a sample of doctors and their patients, and found examples of women's adjustment being viewed in terms of their purely domestic role, for instance willingness to do housework (Barratt and Roberts 1978: 46). They also argue that the fact that both doctors and psychiatrists are predominantly male influences their attitudes to women, and that doctors were likely to side with the husband in a family conflict and assume the wife was being unreasonable.

Feminist critiques and campaigns have had a considerable impact on medicine and on practices in hospital, especially in relation to childbirth. Changes that have occurred are not entirely due to the Women's Liberation Movement. The campaigning groups that grew up in the 1970s to promote women's medical interests sometimes reinforced the work of existing organisations, and to some extent coincided with changing attitudes towards alternative medicine and a partial shift of attitudes within the medical profession. The National Child Birth Trust, for example, had been formed in 1956 to promote natural childbirth methods, and Sheila Kitzinger has through her work as a tutor for the Trust and through numerous books been especially influential in changing medical practice in childbirth. The ideas of the French physician Dr Leboyer, who criticised hospital techniques of delivery for causing babies unnecessary shock, have also had some impact. But the activities of local groups set up in the 1970s to campaign for home deliveries and higher status for midwives, and concern within the Women's Movement for women to control their own bodies and to oppose hierarchical attitudes in medicine, certainly boosted support for organisations already engaged in trying to improve maternity services or change hospital practices.

These campaigns raised controversial issues: whether the preferences of the mother for a natural birth might conflict with the doctor's judgement of what would be best for the baby; whether hospital births were not safer for both mother and child than home deliveries, especially for poorer women living in bad housing; and whether women might not prefer a high-tech and relatively pain-free birth. But they did challenge doctors and hospitals to take account of women's own views.

The most distinctive contribution made by the Women's Liberation Movement to health care was the development of self-help groups, as part of a process of encouraging women to learn more about their own bodies and to share their knowledge and experience. A number of feminist books on women's health and on self-help were also published, and a National Conference on Women and Health was held in 1974.

The feminist movement has had less observable impact on the diagnosis and treatment of mental illness than on ordinary medicine. Some women psychiatrists and psychotherapists, and some women who had experienced mental breakdown, wrote critically about standard treatment, and a Woman's Therapy Centre opened in London in 1975. But feminist concern about the social factors in mental illness and about the definition of madness has run parallel to radical critiques of orthodoxy by R. D. Laing and T. S. Szasz and so formed part of a wider attack.

At a theoretical level feminists have been interested in uncovering the history of medicine and women's active role as healers and midwives until displaced by a masculine medical profession. Feminists have also argued that the tendency to treat women in hospitals like unreliable and dependent children, and that common medical and psychological assumptions about women's nature, are deeply revealing about the place women have occupied in society as a whole, and about the mechanisms of social control. This critique has been extended to the treatment of women in other institutions, for example in prisons, and to the general attitudes towards women evinced by the law, by the press and in general social theory.

Contemporary feminism has been rich in new ideas and encouraged critical reassessment of orthodox theories and approaches, not only in medicine and psychology but in politics, economics, sociology, history, literature, art and language itself. One part of this enterprise has been to rediscover or redefine the role of women as a social group in political and economic activity by looking for example at women's apparent political apathy and greater conservatism, or at the economic role played by women in the home and women as consumers. Feminism has stimulated a new look at women's previous historical roles, for example the phenomenon of witchcraft and the history of medicine, once a largely feminine preserve. In addition feminists have explored women's forms of creative activity like embroidery, and have uncovered the works of individual women artists whose achievements have they believe been ignored by male historians who automatically tend to see women as mistresses or wives, models or assistants to great men. Similar research has been undertaken on the work of individual women scientists who may also have been overshadowed by their male colleagues.

Feminist writers have had a significant impact on social theory, promoting critiques of liberal and socialist theory, developing a conception of patriarchy, challenging the heritage of Freud and raising questions about the connections between masculinity, hierarchy and organised social violence. Feminists do not agree on all these issues; interpretations of the relevance of Freud for feminism differ; psychological analyses of rape as inherent in male aggression are countered by anthropological evidence of rape-free societies; some feminists believe women can only be free under socialism, others see the sexual struggle as more basic than the class struggle and look for a new vision of society.

The tone and style of some feminist writings are alien to the usual forms of academic discourse, but feminist ideas and researches have percolated into orthodox academic studies, both by inducing some awareness of the issues raised and as a result of specific campaigns for 'women's studies'. The success of feminism in the realm of ideas is indicated by the prominence given to books dealing with women or on feminist themes in publishers' lists, and on the shelves of libraries and bookshops. Feminists have also been active in promoting their own publishing houses, distribution networks and research centres. The best known and most successful women's publishing house has been Virago Press, founded in 1976, which combines publishing once well-known but forgotten women authors with commissioning new works on a wide range of topics from nuclear weapons to sex education. Five other women's presses founded since Virago continued to flourish into the 1980s, indicating that a wide market for books dealing with feminist issues remained, even if the movement itself appeared to lose momentum by the end of the 1970s. Some socialist feminists were in the early 1980s expressing disquiet about increasing fragmentation and growing sectarianism and intolerance among 'true feminists' (Heron, *New Statesman* 1 April 1983). But the issues raised by the second wave of feminism starting in the late 1960s clearly transcend the organisations or internal politics of the Women's Movement.

Chapter four

WOMEN IN THE EIGHTIES

INTRODUCTION

In this chapter we look at the position of women in the 1980s after a decade of legislation for women's rights and of political pressure for change. Our aim is to examine women's general levels of pay and their situation at work, the opportunities now open to them and whether more women are getting to the top, and also to explore how far explicit forms of discrimination against women have ended. We also summarise the evidence on women's present degree of representation in public life, consider how far general social attitudes are changing and note some continuing feminist campaigns. Finally, we ask whether the gains women have made are permanent or liable to be undermined by economic trends or reversed by political action, and to assess the impact on women of the Conservative Government's policies since 1979.

Before looking at statistical evidence we need to clarify what we are looking for. Ten years after the major laws to ban sexual discrimination have been passed, or come into effect, it is reasonable to expect to see an end to direct and overt discrimination. It is not realistic to expect fundamental shifts in work patterns, mass promotion of women into top jobs or a great increase in the number of women in positions of political power, since all these require changes in inherited behaviour and attitudes and could hardly be expected within a few years. But if the political measures of the 1970s are to be judged at all effective there should be evidence of significant long-term changes under way, to ensure genuine equality of opportunity and access to status and power for the present and future generations of young women.

Figures which demonstrate women's low representation in various crafts or professions, their tendency to cluster at the bottom of the pay scale and job hierarchy within occupations, and their often token position in political bodies, indicate continuing inequality. But there is a need to discuss the implicit message contained in such statistics. One possible interpretation is that ideally men and women ought to be represented in all jobs and in all positions of power equally. But apart from being over-schematic, this goal would ignore completely the likelihood that some jobs will continue to appeal more to men and others to women, and the possibility that there may not be an equal number of women seeking political office. There are underlying questions about how society is being changed by various long-term trends, or should be changed to reflect women's interests and values more directly than at present (to be discussed in Chapter 7), but the issue here is what changes within the present economic and political structure are desirable and reasonable.

There are four kinds of argument for the more equal representation of women in all trades and professions and in political life, but these arguments have somewhat different implications. The first aim is to ensure genuine equality of opportunity for women to enter all occupations, which is not available so long as certain kinds of training and jobs are almost totally dominated by men, so that women meet with active prejudice and are treated as oddities. It may well be that only relatively few women will choose to become carpenters, mechanics, engineers or physicists, but until these careers include enough women to make such a choice seem normal, genuine freedom of choice for girls will not exist; and it is impossible to know in advance how popular such 'masculine' subjects may prove to be.

The second aim is to ensure that there are enough women in key professional and political positions to protect women's special interests. Medicine, psychiatry and the legal profession are three obvious areas where women may find greater understanding and get better service from other women, especially as they are also professions at present marked by a strong tendency to patronise and distrust women. At the political level there are good grounds for thinking more women in government or Parliament would tend to ensure more serious and sympathetic consideration of women's rights or particular interests than is often the case at present. The small number of women MPs have over the years played a central role in bringing forward legislation in favour of women, and in resisting measures they see as inimical to women's interests, and have often cooperated across Party lines to do so. Major legislation depends on mass pressure being exerted outside Parliament, but women MPs promote the interests of women's groups in a much more continuous way (even though some have understandably tried to avoid concentrating too exclusively on women's issues) and often do so in the face of indifference or ridicule inside the House. There is in addition a more general argument that so long as assessment and promotion of women is predominantly in the hands of men there will be greater obstacles in women getting to the top. If this is true, it does of course constitute an argument for more women at the top of all occupations, in order to counter bias and also perhaps to offer more positive encouragement to diffident women, who do not recognise their own abilities.

There are qualifications to be made to this second set of arguments. Some men have strongly and generously espoused women's interests over the last 100 years, and some still do. Conversely, some women who embrace the feminine role may be more hostile to women's rights than many men, or show more prejudice against individual women – for example those subjected to male violence. Nor are women who have themselves had success in a man's world always very willing to support other women to do the same. Nevertheless, on balance women do tend to have more sympathy with other women, and even those women who disavow any belief in feminism often in practice strongly support women's rights in some, if not all, spheres. The presence of more women in positions of authority, and where they can influence what happens to others, is probably important not only in countering the more open and extreme forms of prejudice, but even more in discerning and opposing the more subtle and often unconscious discrimination by men, who may believe they are judging quite dispassionately, but are influenced by socially ingrained beliefs that women on average are less able than men. Women themselves are by no means immune from this unconscious bias, but are on the whole more sensitised to it.

The third argument for more women in well-paid, responsible and authoritative positions relates to how the overall structuring of society and its hierarchy shapes the way people think. So long as most women remain at the bottom, and men dominate all major institutions, beliefs about the inferiority of women are reinforced by their inferior economic and political position. In order to counteract this belief women need to be visibly successful and powerful. In the professions where women predominate it would be reasonable, to expect them to be most numerous in the managerial positions and in the relevant trade unions. Where they are a minority it is still reasonable that some should get to the top.

Fourthly, if women are virtually excluded from many kinds of work then society may be failing to make use of a reserve of skills and talent. This argument can be divided into two rather different claims. The first is simply that there must be women who at present do work below their potential, who might with different training and opportunities have become doctors, physicists, engineers, architects or managers and that this pool of talent should be tapped in the future. This approach assumes there is a significant (but not necessarily total) overlap between the skills of women and men. The second claim is that women by virtue of difference in personality, behaviour or perception (and perhaps because they evoke different responses from men) may make a special contribution that men could not. For example women police might be better able to defuse some potentially violent situations than their male colleagues, or women managers might be better at ensuring good personal relations with their workers. If this claim is formulated in these limited terms it is compatible with the first. But if the belief that women have a unique contribution to make to society is taken to its logical conclusion, as it is by some feminists, then it becomes an argument for a social revolution to introduce a new society based on womanly values, not an argument for equal rights.

How to get more women into masculine occupations, or into top jobs or political power in the first place, is of course the major problem, but is not the theme of this chapter. As in the earlier struggles for women's rights, the initiative and determination of individuals to break new ground, political pressure and legislation backed by the courts are all indispensable. Some of the efforts made by women during the early 1980s are touched on in the course of the general analysis of women's present position.

WOMEN'S ECONOMIC POSITION

The three central questions to be answered, when assessing the effects of the Equal Pay and Sex Discrimination Acts on women's general economic position, are: how much have women's average earnings in relation to men risen since 1970, how far are most women still segregated in certain types of low-status work and have more women managed to reach the top jobs?

Women's pay as a proportion of men's did rise between 1970 and 1980, if we concentrate on the earnings of full-time workers. Women's average gross hourly earnings, excluding overtime, were 63.1 per cent of men's in 1970 and 73.5 per cent of men's in 1980. If overtime is taken into account, the fact that many more men work overtime widens the gap: women earned 54.5 per cent of men's total earnings in 1970 and 64.8 per cent in 1980.

But improvements in hourly pay peaked in 1977 (as noted in

Chapter 3) and then fell back slightly; since 1978 there have been minor oscillations from year to year, but women's hourly earnings seemed by 1985 to have stabilised at around 74 per cent of men's on average. The pattern in relation to overtime pay is less clear cut – women's total weekly earnings as a percentage of men's have risen slightly since 1977 to about 66.90 between 1981 and 1985 – but this presumably reflects the fact that in a time of recession men have been doing less well on overtime, not that women have been doing more (EOC 1986: 32–4).

The main problem in achieving equal pay is of course that men and women often do not do exactly the same jobs, and within a given industry men's and women's jobs are often graded differently. The Equal Pay Act did cover work evaluated as being 'of equivalent value' to a man's by a job-evaluation scheme, but employers often used grading schemes which evaluated women's work less highly than that of men, for example by giving more weighting to jobs which involved physical strength or shift work. Many women did have their pay raised, because of a clause in the Act which required that women's rates should not fall below the minimum rate paid to a man within a collective agreement or pay structure, but their earnings still remained lower on average than men within that industry. The continued importance of the grading issue was ironically demonstrated by the fact that the Ford women workers, who went on strike in 1968 to demand equal pay and regrading, were on strike again in the winter of 1984, still demanding that their work should be upgraded. The women had lost their regrading claim at the inquiry held immediately after their first strike, and had taken the issue unsuccessfully to Ford's Grading Grievance Committee in 1970, 1974, 1981, 1982 and 1983. Male shop stewards at Fords were prepared to agree that the women had a good case, but pointed to other grievances under an elaborate and out-of-date grading scheme. The striking Dagenham sewing-machinists' shop steward told the press that the strike was not only for more money, but to force the company to recognise women's skills. 'The reason we are in this grade is simple, it is because we are women' (*Guardian* 7 Dec. 1984). The women finally won their case for regrading as skilled workers before an industrial tribunal in April 1985 (*The Times* 26 April 1985).

Pay comparisons based on full-time workers do not, however, give the full picture of women's earnings, since increasing numbers of women went into part-time work during the 1970s and were estimated to be over 40 per cent of the female work-force by 1980. During the 1980s the proportion of women in part-time jobs has risen even higher.

All the evidence suggests that part-time women workers earn less per hour than those in full-time jobs. The Low Pay Unit discovered in 1977 that 74 per cent of part-time women workers were earning under £1.20 an hour, compared with 47 per cent of women who were full-time and 13 per cent of men who were full-time. Part-timers, however, often worked unsocial hours with no extra payment and had no paid holidays (Hurstfield 1980: 8). In addition it is estimated that possibly as many as 660,000 women are engaged in a hidden sector of the labour market – working at home (Carr 1984: 9). Some homeworkers may now be operators of the new technology and may for example work with computers. But most are thought to be engaged in low-paid areas of female labour like the clothing industry or toy-making. Most of those who work at home do so because they have to care for young children or for elderly or sick relatives, or because they themselves are disabled or are old age pensioners; quite a few homeworkers are women from ethnic minorities. A number of surveys in the 1970s, for example by the Low Pay Unit, suggested homeworkers were especially badly paid and were exploited by employers. A DE survey published in 1982, which used a sample based on the records of Wages Council inspectors in London, contested this generalisation, suggesting that homeworkers often got the same rates as women who went out to work and did the same jobs, if the hours worked were calculated rigorously. But this survey did note that a rather high proportion of homeworkers (19 per cent of the sample) might for various reasons be less competent, and so work long hours for very low rates; and conceded that homeworkers not covered by Wages Councils, for example those who addressed envelopes, might be paid very little (Hakim and Dennis 1982).

Since women's segregation into certain industries and services, and certain types of job within them, is a major reason for low pay among full-time women workers, it is disturbing that during the 1980s such segregation seems to have increased. During the mid-1970s there were signs that this segregation was beginning to break down: between 1973 and 1977 there seemed to be a statistically significant increase in men and women moving into jobs traditionally reserved for the other sex, though assessment is complicated by the fact that there was a change in the job classification used by the Labour Force Survey in 1979. A DE study of the impact of sex discrimination legislation in twenty-six organisations between 1974 and 1977 showed that in a quarter women did move into men's jobs, and to a lesser extent men moved into female preserves. The momentum for change appeared, however, to be short-lived; between 1978 and 1979 the broad trend was reversed. The most obvious reason is that the recession hit job opportunities for women. (Hakim 1981). A TUC Report on *Women in the Labour Market* (TUC 1983: 8–9) concluded that by 1981 women had become increasingly concentrated in a small number of industries, being more segregated than in 1975, and were still grouped in a relatively few occupations like clerical and secretarial work, assisting in shops, catering and cleaning, and certain routine assembly-line jobs. A survey of National and Local Government Officers' Association (NALGO) women members, published in 1982, showed that the proportion of women in administrative, technical and professional grades had actually fallen significantly in 1981, compared with 1974, and the proportion of women who were typists, secretaries and clerks had risen marginally to 99.6 per cent of the secretarial grade and 82.0 per cent of the clerical grade (*New Statesman* 18, June p. 3).

In the professional sphere by contrast there was a tendency for young women to break into occupations where they had been only nominally represented before. For example the proportion of women among university graduates entering accountancy rose from 8.2 per cent in 1970/71 to 27.5 per cent in 1980/81. More women graduates from both universities and polytechnics were entering industry and finance and other previously non-feminine occupations like civil engineering and architecture in the late 1970s (EOC Annual Reports 1983: 81–2). Women were at last breaking into the legal profession; the number of women solicitors rose from 619 in 1967/68 to 2,132 in 1976/77, and the total of women barristers rose from 99 to 336 between 1965 and 1977, (EOC 1978: 14 and 19). This trend reflected an absolute increase in the number of women graduates, but suggests too, some change in the career expectations of highly educated young women and in the attitudes of employers. During the 1980s there has been a further increase in women entering the professions. Nevertheless, women remained a small percentage of the total membership of all but a few professional bodies: the figures for 1985 show women ranging from 41.0 per cent of the Institute of Personnel Management to 19.2 per cent of the Institute of Bankers, 14 per cent of the Law Society and only 0.8 per cent of the Institute of Mechanical Engineers (EOC 1986: 42).

Women's progress towards the top jobs in the professions, industry and commerce during the 1970s and early 1980s has been slight. If job status is measured by earnings, then two sample surveys showed that women made up 2.1 per cent of high earners (defined as the top 2–3 per cent of all full-time employees) in 1968 and 1.85 per cent in 1979. If the earnings band is extended downwards to cover less well-paid jobs where women are more likely to rise to the top (like teaching), then women made up 5.7 per cent of the total top 20 per cent of earners in both 1968 and 1979 (Fogarty, Allen and Walters 1981: 6–7).

Even where women are numerous at the bottom of a profession there may be very few at the top. There were, for example, still under 1.0 per cent of women bank managers in 1977, and in the Civil Service no women permanent secretaries and only four deputy secretaries (EOC 1978/79; 47–8). Two groups to campaign for women's rights were formed in the Civil Service in 1978, in the higher administrative grades and in the executive and lower grades, and by 1978 three departments within the Civil Service were found by Fogarty, Allen and Walters (1981: 86–7) to be actively concerned about the promotion of women, but they concluded that the overall Civil Service approach was 'low key'. After Dame Evelyn Sharp retired in 1966 no woman was appointed a permanent secretary until 1984. In the BBC the number of women in the top posts actually declined between 1968 and 1979, because the generation of women who used the opportunities created by the Second World War to prove their managerial skills had retired and not been replaced. There had been some slight improvement in women's representation at lower levels of management and in professional grades, but progress was not impressive despite the campaigning efforts by Women in Media to widen the career opportunities for women, and despite the fact that the BBC, like the Civil Service, is an institution relatively favourable to the promotion of women.

Women do rather better in the less prestigious world of teaching, but are still under-represented at the top. Whilst women made up 69 per cent of primary teachers in 1980, only 43.6 per cent of heads of primary schools were women; at secondary levels women constituted 45 per cent of teachers, but only 16.3 per cent of head teachers (EOC Annual Reports 1983: 88). A survey carried out by the National Union of Teachers (NUT) of about 3,000 women teachers found that women were serious about their own careers, over 75 per cent thought it was as important as that of their husbands and 7 per cent said it was more important, so lack of motivation did not explain lack of promotion. The fact that fewer women teachers were graduates, and the break in the career of married women with children, were both partial but inadequate reasons for women's failure to get on. Women graduates did proportionally much less well than male graduates, and single women with no career break also did worse on average than men, though better than married women. The survey concluded that women tended to suffer from three types of discrimination: general sex discrimination, specific discrimination against married women and discrimination against older teachers, which in practice penalised married women returning after a break to bring up children. (NUT 1980: 9–11, 29, 51–54).

Women have been less numerous on university staffs than in schools, but the proportion has risen from being about 9 per cent of all academic staff in the late 1960s to about 15 per cent in the 1982–3 academic year. But only 2 per cent of professors are women and there are no women vice-chancellors; the only two women who have held this post have done so where it rotates, in London and in Cambridge (Blackstone 1984). Women make up over a quarter of university researchers, but almost half of them are in the lowest grade; and whilst 44 per cent of the staff in university libraries were women, only 8.5 per cent of them were in the higher grades III and IV, compared with 27 per cent of the men (EOC 1982: 8, 12)..

Women managers have on the whole been confined to small-scale managerial posts in female-dominated occupations, for example among sales staff and clothing workers, or running hotels and restaurants, laundries and hairdressing salons. They have been very scarce in top-level industrial management: figures for 1979 show that only 2 per cent of the Institute of Directors were women (Holland 1981: 16). A later survey of careers of 1,882 managers by the British Institute of Management found that proportionally more of the 412 women in the sample had postgraduate diplomas or higher degrees than the men, though men had other professional qualifications slightly more often, and that 39 per cent of the women were single, divorced or widowed, compared with 8 per cent of the men. The survey concluded that women managers in industry and commerce have to be better qualified than men, have to be more ambitious and willing to change jobs frequently if they are to get to the top (Nicholson and Metcalfe 1985).

Detailed examination of changes between 1968 and 1979 suggests that some companies did demonstrate a change in attitude and practice, but others did not. Fogarty, Allen and Walters (1981) found that one of the two companies surveyed, but not the other, was recruiting a higher proportion of women as management trainees, putting more women on to promotion lists, allowing them greater scope in jobs and showing less evidence of direct discrimination. However, the proportion of women in this company between 1968 and 1979 rose only from 2.7 per cent to 3.3 per cent, though the actual number of women managers doubled from 104 to 208. The women interviewed were not optimistic that there would be a significant opening up of job opportunities at the top. Most women managers were in junior grades and were relatively young women with no children. The typical career pattern was still geared to men and did not allow for women to take time off for children; and job opportunities at the top by 1979 seemed to be contracting with reorganisation and the impact of recession.

To sum up what economic gains were made by women as a result of the campaigns and legislation of 1970s, those who benefited most were a small minority of highly educated and professional women, who did gain from an expansion of opportunities if they were young and might have slightly higher prospects of promotion in mid-career. There are signs here of a long-term trend towards opening up of jobs for women in the professions and in administration, though even at this level opportunities were also being foreclosed by economic recession. The great majority of women benefited much less from legislation and pressure for change. Although a very small number of women did break into manual jobs previously reserved to men, to become lorry-drivers or garage mechanics for example, the general trend was towards narrowing the job opportunities open to women. Whilst the pay of full-time manual women workers did rise in relation to men's pay, the total position of women at work in terms of pay, conditions and security of employment deteriorated sharply in the 1980s. Although there were loopholes in the laws designed to equalise women's earnings and opportunities at work, the greatest obstacle to progress has been mass unemployment and the economic trends related to it. There is in addition a considerable danger that in the future automation and the new communications technology will relegate most women to marginal jobs.

TRAINING

The possibility of women entering a much wider range of jobs depends to a considerable extent on their education and training. The general picture in the early 1980s is that girls and women are more often acquiring good educational qualifications, but only to a limited extent in science, mathematics, engineering, technology or computer science. Their chances of acquiring craft skills or day-release training are still very slim.

Whilst the proportion of girls taking GCE O levels changed very little between 1970 and 1980 – almost exactly half the O-level passes at grade C or above went to girls – noticeably more girls went on to take A levels: by 1980 45 per cent of A-level passes went to girls. As a result of this increase in girls with A levels and of the growth in the number of degree places, the percentage of girls who went on from school to take degree courses rose from 4.3 per cent in 1967 to 6.8 per cent in 1981, whilst the percentage of boys barely increased, though it remained higher and was 9.3 per cent in 1981 (CSO 1983: 42). So at university level women who had made up only 27.6 per cent of undergraduates in 1965/66 constituted 39 per cent by 1980/81. There was as well a marked rise in the number of women doing higher degrees, and by 1980/81 women were 30.5 per cent of postgraduate students (EOC Annual Reports 1983: 69). At polytechnics, however, the proportion of women doing degrees was quite a bit lower than in universities.

The cutbacks imposed by the Conservative Government in the early 1980s on the total number of students at university appeared likely to curb the number of women, especially as the main cuts were being made in arts and social science courses where most women still apply. But although student totals began to fall after the 1981/82 academic year, the number of women entering university rose absolutely until 1983/84; and the percentage of women undergraduates has gone on rising even as total numbers fall, and was 41.5 per cent in 1984/85 (EOC 1986: 17). The Department of Education was persuaded in 1984 to revise its forecast for future student demand to take more account of the rise in girls taking A levels, and of the increased number of mature women becoming aware that they had been deprived of higher education opportunities in their youth (*Guardian* 13, July 1984).

Girls were gradually moving into the traditionally masculine subjects at school and university. Statistics show a consistent growth in the proportion taking physics, maths and computer science at O level and A level, and doing science and engineering at university. But there were still only 18 per cent of girls getting A-level passes in computer science (though 30.8 per cent in maths) in 1984, and only 10.1 per cent of students taking engineering at university in 1984 were women, though those taking science totalled 33 per cent. (EOC 1986: 8, 17). But a study published in 1986 found that there was 'still a cause for serious professional concern' about under-representation of girls in science subjects, and blamed the conservative attitudes of pre-dominately male teachers of maths, physical sciences and technical subjects as a major cause (School Curriculum Development Committee 1986).

Whereas access to higher education for girls has expanded considerably, the picture for further and vocational education is more complex. The reduction in the number of teacher training colleges has meant a big drop in the number of women with teaching qualifications during the 1970s, although women's enrolment on advanced further education courses in languages, literature, health and welfare has increased. Therefore the proportion of women acquiring advanced further education fell from 50.3 per cent of all students in 1970 to 43.6 per cent in 1980. However, the proportion of women taking non-advanced full-time and sandwich courses has risen, especially in social, administrative and business study courses (EOC Annual Reports 1983: 68). Women's enrolment in both non-advanced and advanced further education courses has continued to increase during the 1980s (EOC 1986: 15).

Women do worst when it comes to industrial training and apprenticeships, where there is no evidence that women's job opportunities are being significantly widened. The total numbers on day-release courses have been dropping since 1979, and by 1982 the proportion of young men on such courses had fallen more than the proportion of young women, but women still only comprised 18 per cent of all day-release trainees in 1982 (EOC Annual Reports 1984: 70). Girls have taken an increasing part in youth training schemes (41.6 per cent of all trainees under the national Youth Training Scheme in December 1983), but are mainly concentrated in typing and clerical courses, and in skills like hairdressing and food preparation. Very few women were being trained in carpentry, construction, engineering or information technology. This picture was confirmed by a survey published in 1985 that found girls on the Youth Training Scheme were still being channelled into traditional women's jobs (*The Times*, 30 Jan. 1985).

CONTINUING DISCRIMINATION AGAINST WOMEN

One of the most obvious forms of discrimination against women before the Sex Discrimination Act was passed was their unequal access to pension schemes and their difficulty in getting financial institutions to treat them as persons in their own right.

Occupational pension schemes are the most important benefit attached to a job and an important index of how far treatment of women workers has changed. There has been some improvement, which began in the 1960s but accelerated in the 1970s, although the rise in women qualifying for pension schemes has been more consistent in the public than the private sector. The total number of women enjoying membership of occupational pension schemes rose from 1.7 million in 1963 to 2.4 million in 1971 and to 3.3 million in 1979; the total number of men in such schemes fell slightly from 9.4

million in 1963 to 8.5 million in 1979, due to a sharp drop in the private sector. As a result the proportion of women among all those enjoying occupational pension rights rose from 15.3 per cent in 1963 to almost 28 per cent in 1979 (EOC Annual Reports 1981: 76). So women workers are still much less likely than men to get occupational pensions – only about 35 per cent of the female workforce compared with 65 per cent of the male. This discrepancy is partly due to the exclusion of part-time workers from the majority of pension schemes, though there are moves to encourage nationalised industries and local government to include part-timers. But even where women do have pension rights they often have them on unequal terms. Whereas virtually all pension schemes allow men to pass on pension rights automatically to their wives, only a minority allow women to pass on their rights automatically to their husbands. The precise figures vary in recent surveys: according to an EOC study published in 1985 under a third of the schemes gave such a right to women, and in 54 per cent the husband could only receive the pension if he was totally dependent on his wife (McGoldrick 1985).

The other most important form of financial discrimination against women is their access to mortgages. The EOC undertook a survey in 1978 to discover how far building societies and mortgage brokers discriminated against applications for a joint mortgages by refusing to take the wife's earnings properly into account. The survey found that 36 per cent of building society branches discriminated in some way against couples where the wife earned more than her husband, and that discrimination was more likely by smaller building societies (EOC). After publication of the survey the Commission noted a drop in the number of complaints it received about mortgages, but a small trickle continued, and the Commission observed (EOC Annual Reports 1984: 2) that when it pursued complaints it discovered that some major companies still seemed ignorant of the sex discrimination laws.

Refusing women credit unless they obtained the signature of male guarantors was a common form of discrimination before it was made illegal under the Sex Discrimination Act. Soon after the passage of the Act the Commission backed a court case by a woman who was told that when she applied for some furniture on credit that her husband must act as guarantor. Mrs Quinn lost her case initially before the court, but when she took it to the Court of Appeal the Master of the Rolls found that requiring – or even advising – a woman to get her husband to sign the guarantee form was unlawful discrimination. (EOC Annual Reports 1981: 6). Nevertheless the Commission continued to receive complaints about retail credit, and found that some credit companies still had openly discriminatory policies and refused credit to married women (EOC Annual Reports 1984: 22–3). During 1984 new systems of credit scoring for applicants led to a big increase in complaints to the EOC (EOC Annual Reports 1986: 12).

WOMEN AND THE STATE

The treatment of women by the state was not covered by the Sex Discrimination Act and the picture has remained rather confused. Women have gained some right as citizens, but lost others as immigrants. There has been no real change so far in the area of taxation, and some extension of women's rights under social security, but a general policy of tightening up on benefits which tends to hit women most severely.

The new Nationality Act of 1981 did give women the right for the first time to pass on their citizenship automatically to children born abroad; and whereas in the past British men conferred immediate British citizenship on foreign wives whilst foreign husbands had to wait five years before they could even apply for naturalisation, under the new law both wives and husbands had to wait three years. This formal equality was granted to British women as a concession to the strong opposition expressed to the Conservative Party's original policy of preventing all foreign husbands from settling in Britain in order to restrict immigration. (NCCL, *Rights* Winter 1983, p. 5).

But the practical value of this formal concession was undermined in reality by the Immigration Rules, which took away rights granted by the Labour Government. The 1980 Rules prevented women living in Britain, but not born here, from bringing foreign fiancés and husbands into the country. Even husbands of women who were born in Britain were on probation for a year to see if the marriage was still in force. One case taken to the European Court of Human Rights by the NCCL concerned a Ugandan Asian woman settled in Britain, who was unable to apply under the Rules to have her fiancé, who she had met while studying in India, join her in Britain (NCCL 1980: 13). The Rules treated women unequally in other ways, by giving women with work permits, or women students, no right to have their husbands stay with them, whereas men in a similar position could confer the right to stay on their wives. Indeed, a woman entitled to live in Britain because she was working here could lose that right if she married a man with only temporary permission to stay in Britain, since she was then regarded solely as his 'dependant' (NCCL, *Rights* July–August, 1981, p. 11).

The new Immigration Rules which came into force in 1983, when the new Nationality Act was implemented, were according to the EOC 'fundamentally sex-discriminatory' in approach and terminology, except where they dealt with EEC nationals. Foreign men settled in Britain kept the right to have their wives with them, whilst non-British women in the same position did not. The EOC also complained that foreign husbands or fiancés of British women were subject to special tests (EOC Annual Reports 1983: 21).

The tax system continued to treat married women as dependants of their husbands. It has been possible for a wife to opt for separate assessment and so split the total tax bill, or for a wife to opt to pay tax separately on her earnings, though her unearned income would still be credited to her husband who would pay tax on it. But both schemes have meant the husband can have access to all his wife's financial transactions, and for the second the husband's explicit consent is required. The EOC commented that:

> There are few areas where Whitehall has clung so tenaciously to the assumptions of the Victorian Era ...

and objected to the wife's lack of privacy and subordinate status in dealing with the tax authorities (EOC 1977: 4).

The EOC Report noted that Inland Revenue's procedures were increasingly at odds with the trend for more married women to go out to work, and the tendency for more couples to reverse roles and the woman to become the chief breadwinner. The Report included examples of humiliating and unfair practices involved in tax rules: one woman who had paid the mortgage on a house could only claim the tax relief on it with her husband's permission, and another woman who had started divorce proceedings against her husband found that a tax rebate of over £200 on her earned income had been sent to her husband (EOC 1977: 26-7).

The EOC report evoked a strong response, both from individuals and organisations who wrote direct to the Commission, and in the press. The Commission published a second report summarising some of the complaints it had received. One issue raised was the financial loss suffered by women who were no longer earning, who had their investment income credited to their husband, often resulting in a high rate of tax. One correspondent explained that the interest on her building society account, which she had saved for her retirement, was being taxed at about £1,000 a year. Another woman pointed out that although she was paying a considerable amount of tax on her savings through her husband, she was not able personally to sign a deed of covenant and had to ask for her husband's signature. (EOC 1979b:

8–9). *Woman's Own* and the *Sunday Times* both campaigned for changes in the tax law, and over 30,000 people signed a statement in favour or reform in the latter.

The Labour Government made some minor reforms in 1978, when the Inland Revenue was instructed to correspond directly with married women instead of addressing all letters to their husbands, and wives became entitled by law to receive their own tax rebates on earned income taxed at the basic rate. (NCCL, *Rights*, July–August, 1981). But despite a Green Paper published in 1981 by Conservative Chancellor Geoffrey Howe, suggesting more radical changes, which received support from many women's organisations including women in the Conservative Party, the Government has done nothing except raise the married man's allowance. Four years later the Chancellor, Nigel Lawson, promised at the time of the Budget another Green Paper on tax reform, which would propose individual assessment for husbands and wives which would grant privacy to both, and would probably abolish the married man's allowance in its existing form. The Green Paper was eventually published in the spring of 1986 and proposed that an unemployed wife or husband could transfer her or his tax allowance to the wage-earner. This solution was opposed by feminists who feared it would create a disincentive for wives to return to work, and ran counter to the views of a House of Lords Committee which had examined how to achieve equality in taxation. It recommended in December 1985 that husbands and wives should be taxed quite separately on their earned income, and that if one gave up work (for example to look after children) the family income should be supplemented by cash benefits, not by a transferable tax reduction.

Most consistent progress in equalising the rights of married women has occurred in the rules governing social security. The 1975 Social Security Act had given wives the right to unemployment and sickness benefits, and to pensions under certain conditions; but the rules covering benefits still assumed men were the main earners, and so penalised those women who kept their families. This position was changed by the Conservative Government's 1980 legislation, which responded to an EEC directive requiring equal treatment of women in welfare by enabling married women and common-law wives to claim for their dependants. The new law, which came into effect in 1984, did, however, leave two exceptions to full equality which were both the subject of a campaign by the EOC – treatment of disabled wives and of married women caring for relatives. Disabled wives could only claim a non-contributory invalidity pension if they could demonstrate to the Department of Health and Social Security (DHSS) that they were not only unable to go out and work (which was what men and single women had to prove), but unable to do the housework that was deemed to be much easier. The EOC Report cited examples of women certified unfit for clerical work assessed as being capable of housework, and of women with arthritis or multiple sclerosis who were not considered disabled if they could perform some tasks like peeling vegetables sitting down, or if they could get up stairs on their knees (EOC 1981a). Secondly, married women could not claim an invalidity care allowance for looking after their relatives, because it was assumed they would be at home anyway, even though in many cases they had given up their jobs to care for their disabled children, elderly relatives or sick husbands, and in the latter case were often in dire poverty. The Commission received over 10,000 letters of complaint when it advertised in women's magazines about these two rules.

The Government took action to changes the rules governing invalidity pensions when it announced its intention in 1983 to create a new severe disablement allowance which would cover married women in the same way as single women and men. This new allowance was phased in during 1984 and 1985. The Government made no response to the pressure to grant married women an invalid care allowance, but Mrs Jacqueline Drake, who had to care for her elderly mother, took the issue to the European (EEC) Court, arguing that the refusal to pay her a carer's allowance was in breach of an EEC social security directive. She won the case, which received widespread publicity, in a judgment delivered on 24 June 1986. The British Government is obliged to respond to the Court's ruling.

No action has been taken to improve the position of single mothers who receive welfare and get caught up in the inquisitorial 'cohabitation rule'. Indeed the Conservative Government's desire to cut welfare benefits, and its greater emphasis on investigating alleged benefit frauds, has encouraged harassment of women suspected of being kept by a man. In addition, as a result of Derek Rayner's inquiry into cutting social security costs the Government adopted one of his recommendations, which denied single parents the right to claim unemployment benefit unless they could show that they had made provision to look after their children. Since single mothers or fathers might well be too poor whilst out of work to pay for their children to be looked after, this was a classic catch-22 regulation (Rogers 1983: 34–41).

WOMEN IN PUBLIC LIFE

Recent changes in policy have been presided over by a woman Prime Minister. But Mrs Thatcher's success has not been matched by other women entering Parliament in significant numbers. Indeed, women have made little progress in achieving parliamentary representation since 1945: only 19 women were elected in 1979 and 23 in 1983, one fewer than in 1945, but in 1987 the number of women rose to 41. The lack of women MPs still reflects a low proportion of women candidates – 11.8 per cent in 1979 – and the fact that women are more likely to be selected for unwinnable marginal seats (*New Statesman* 22 June 1979, p. 899). At the European level, where a seat is less highly prized, 11 of 81 British members of the EEC Parliament are women (EOC Annual Reports 1984: 95). The desire to improve women's parliamentary representation led to the setting up of the 300 Group in 1980 with the aim of encouraging and helping women in all political parties to become candidates. The group was launched with some fanfare and with prestigious support, but ran into political difficulties, partly because of its all-party basis. The group's founder and key organiser was a former Liberal candidate, and after a few months Liberals remained most closely involved (*New Statesman* 30 Jan. 1981, p. 3). But the 300 Group has remained an all-party body, has acquired members and regional branches and continued to organise training sessions for women interested in entering politics and to monitor women's progress in elections. It was cooperating in 1986 with the Fawcett Society to get more women appointed to public boards and committees, by clarifying the criteria for appointment and collecting information about possible women candidates to make available to those responsible for nominations.

Women have made greater gains at the local level, where the proportion of women among local councillors has risen from about 12 per cent in 1964 to 15.8 per cent after the 1974 reorganised local government elections, and to 18.4 per cent in 1982. Women do better in non-metropolitan than metropolitan areas, better in England than in Scotland or Wales and better in the South than the North (EOC Annual Reports 1984: 95). The 1985 local council elections showed more women candidates coming forward, and women made up 19.2 per cent of councillors elected (EOC 1986: 39).

Representation of women on public bodies is another index of how far women have positions of importance in public life, and the proportion of women has increased slightly, though women were primarily to be found in consumer, child-care, health and welfare bodies, and there were hardly any at all in industrial, agricultural or financial areas. Though there was a slight overall increase between 1977 and 1981, the policies of government departments responsible for nominations varied: the Departments of Trade and of Industry appointed slightly fewer women in 1980 than in 1979 for example (EOC 1981b). Analysis of the first full set of figures given to the EOC in 1983 (earlier statistics for some departments had excluded outside nominations) showed that women were 17.4 per cent of the total appointments (EOC Annual Reports 1984: 96). This low representation reflected continued inequality and segregation at work. By 1985 there had been a marginal increase to 18.5 per cent.

One sphere of public life where women's interests are often directly affected is the law. Until the 1970s there were extremely few women solicitors and barristers, but as we have seen there has been some expansion of women in the legal profession. But there have been virtually no women holding judicial office of any sort. There were no female Lords of Appeal or Lord Justices of Appeal by 1977, only 2 High Court judges out of 72 and 7 circuit judges out of 285. There had been a slight increase in circuit judges since 1972 and also in the number of recorders, but there were still only 8 out of 370 recorders who were women (EOC 1978: 23). The position of women at the top of the legal profession had improved marginally by 1983 – the number of High Court judges had risen to 3, of circuit judges to 12 and of recorders to 12 (Lovenduski 1986b: 218) – but given the small numbers of women with sufficient experience and the conservatism of the judiciary no rapid change is to be expected. Women's representation among magistrates is much better and has improved significantly in the last ten years: in 1975 there were about 6,500 women justices of the peace in England and Wales compared with 13,000 men; in 1985 there were 11,250 women to about 16,000 men (Letter, Lord Chancellor's Department, 15 Oct. 1985).

One important step was taken in 1974 which gave women much greater access to juries than before. The Criminal Justice Act waived the property qualifications for jurors, which had restricted the possibility of jury service to about 11 per cent of all women, and opened jury service to all those on the electoral roll. There has also been a change in attitudes towards women jurors. Previously judges could and occasionally did choose all-male juries for trying certain cases, and women jurors could be challenged purely on grounds of being women. The Magistrates Association expressed the view in 1965 that normally the majority on a jury should be men, though they did include the proviso that an accused woman should have the right to ask for a majority of women (Currell 1974: 174). It is now normal for juries to include a number of women, and this extends to important political trials like the Clive Ponting Official Secrets Trial in 1985, where there were four women on the jury.

WOMEN IN TRADE UNIONS

Political and economic life intersect for women in trade unions, where they have made some limited gains. Women's progress in the unions can be measured by four rather different criteria: the extent of their membership, the extent of their active participation, how well they are represented in trade union posts and how far male trade-unionists and officials take seriously women's concerns.

Women's membership of trade unions was rising during the 1960s, as we have seen, because more married women were returning to work and white-collar jobs were being unionised; both trends continued into the 1970s, and the proportion of women among unionists rose from 25 per cent in 1971 to 31 per cent in 1981 (EOC Annual Reports 1984: 97). The proportion of women at work who were in trade unions was of course rising too, and stood at 38.9 per cent in 1979 (Ellis 1981: 11).

The evidence on how active women unionists are is much more patchy. Certainly women do go on strike, not only for their own rights at work but on broader issues, for example in the struggle over pay beds in the NHS hospitals. Women workers, moreover, played a part in the wave of factory occupations and setting up of workers' cooperatives, at the Lee Jeans factory at Greenock and at the Fakenham shoe-factory. On the other hand, the general picture appears to be of fairly low levels of union activism. Two MORI polls in 1976 and 1979 indicated that women were less likely to attend branch meetings, to vote in union elections, to go on strike or join pickets than men, and more likely to take no part at all in union activities: 33 per cent of women polled in 1976 compared with 17 per cent of the men had done nothing in the union (Coote and Kellner 1980: 33). The comparative apathy of women may be due in part to factors that also influence activism among men: the fact that most do unskilled and uninteresting jobs and that they are much more likely to change jobs, and so may have to switch unions, and are less identified with their work. Two small-scale studies of women in skilled jobs in the Association of Scientific, Technical and Managerial Staffs (ASTMS) and the Association of Cinematograph, Television and Allied Technicians (ACTT) indicate that there women are slightly more inclined to attend branch meetings than the men – the exception was a laboratory branch of the ACTT (Ellis 1981: 14). Part-time working also inhibits union involvement. But women face additional problems in being active in unions because of their commitments as wives and mothers. Married women who have to shop, do the housework and laundry and look after children find it impossible to attend union meetings after hours or to spend time with fellow workers discussing their grievances. Women often find union matters complicated, and lack confidence to take part in union affairs, as a study in Hull confirmed (Coote and Kellner 1980: 14–15).

Lack of active participation is of course one reason why fairly few women become shop stewards or branch officials; but it is not a total explanation. Women seem to be assigned to subordinate positions even when they are active. A survey carried out by NALGO in 1974 found that the only posts often held by women were branch secretary and to a lesser extent welfare officer; women were hardly ever in the chair. The NALGO study concluded: 'Posts like assistant secretary are presumably held by women so that they can do the branch typing work' (quoted by Ellis 1981: 15). The small-scale ACTT study also found that women in the television branch served on shop committees fractionally more often than men, but nearly always as secretaries, not as union representatives.

There has been some improvement in women's representation at higher levels of the unions, especially during the 1980s. A detailed study of the thirty largest unions carried out in 1976 found only two unions where the proportion of women on both the Executive Committee and among full-time officials was more or less the same as the proportion of women members: the Society of Civil and Public Servants and the Professional Civil Servants (Ellis 1981: 17). By 1985 NALGO, which has 52 per cent women members and has as a union shown concern for women's interests, had women constituting 32 per cent of its National Executive and 13 per cent of its full time officials – in 1981 only 19 per cent of its National Executive were women. By contrast in the Union of Shop, Distributive and Allied Workers (USDAW) with a female membership of 61 per cent, women still only made up 19 per cent of the National Executive by 1985, and in the powerful TGWU with a 16 per cent female membership women formed only 3 per cent of the National Executive, but these figures still represent an increase (EOC 1986: 44). Preliminary evidence in 1986 from union elections suggests that the 1984 Trade Union Act, requiring union executives to be elected by secret ballot of all members, is boosting numbers of women on executives in unions with a high female membership (*Marxism Today* June 1986, p. 5). In general, women are somewhat better represented on national executive committees than among full-time officials. Two women have so far been selected as general secretaries: Diane Warwick in the Association of University Teachers in 1983 and Brenda Dean in the print union, Society of Graphical and Allied Trades (SOGAT '82), in 1985. The TUC agreed in 1980 to raise the number of women's reserved seats on the council from two to five.

If women have not got very far in achieving office in the trade unions, they have gained much greater attention for their concerns within some unions, which have established women's advisory committees or equal opportunities committees to monitor women's rights at work. The TUC itself has published a number of reports considering women's problems, and the TUC Conference in 1979 adopted a Charter on Equality for Women in Trade Unions. The Charter recognised the principle that equal pay should cover work of 'equal value', and encouraged unions to set up advisory committees, to provide women's seats on executive bodies and to promote women's participation at local level by holding union meetings in working hours, and providing child-care facilities where needed at meetings. Special efforts to get women to attend training courses were urged by the Charter, and the TUC and some individual unions had begun by 1980 to organise courses for women only. The unions in addition gradually became more active in promoting cases of individual women under the Equal Pay and Sex Discrimination Acts, although they were not inherently enthusiastic about the use of legislation, preferring generally to rely on collective bargaining (Ellis 1981: 38–9). The TUC Women's Conference, too, gained in importance: by 1984 it was receiving much more attention from the media than had been the case in the mid 1970s.

The visible change in the unions' public attitudes to women's rights does constitute progress, but as the unions themselves have conceded it is progress from a starting-point of having almost totally ignored women workers and their problems. A TASS booklet on *Women's Rights and what we are doing to get them* (p. 19) noted that trade unions had belatedly recognised:

> That their women members have been shamefully neglected and many of them are trying to make up for lost time (quoted Ellis 1981: 47).

The pace of change within the unions is still fairly slow, due to force of habit, union bureaucracy and the continuing disposition of many men to denigrate 'women's issues'. The chances of women making major advances through the unions are further limited by the growing weakness of the trade union movement as a whole in an era of mass unemployment and restrictive union legislation. Nevertheless, the change of attitude towards women's rights does have long-term significance and indicates the much greater social acceptability of arguments for women's equality.

What has been particularly interesting has been the willingness of the unions to take up some issues espoused by feminists and outside the normal trade union remit. The most important example was TUC support for women's right to abortion on demand, passed at the TUC Conference in 1975, and followed by TUC opposition to the Corrie Bill. More recently the TUC has given its support to the campaign, first launched by the NCCL Women's Rights Unit, to end sexual harassment at work. Many women trade-unionists attended a conference on this theme in 1982, and NALGO took up the issue and circulated leaflets on the problem to its members. A number of unions, including the Society of Civil and Public Servants, have adopted TUC guidelines, which seek to make sexual harassment a disciplinary matter. This is an issue where trade union action may combine with legal action in cases where serious sexual harassment has led women to lose their jobs, either because they could no longer stand the strain and left, or because they have reacted vigorously against advances by their employer and been dismissed.

SOCIAL ATTITUDES TO WOMEN'S RIGHTS

The fact that sexual harassment has been taken seriously by unions and industrial tribunals – the EOC won two cases about it in 1983 under the Sexual Discrimination Act – despite initial ridicule, especially in the popular press, suggests that feminist concerns have become more publicly acceptable. There are other signs of responsiveness to feminist criticism – for example in the treatment of women who have been raped. Though there is disturbing evidence that only a small minority of women feel able to report rapes to the police (Hall 1985) and continuing criticism of treatment of the women by police and the courts, the police have begun to respond. The Metropolitan Police in London began in 1985 to give special training to women officers to interview women who report being raped, and have tried to make the experience of being interviewed and medically examined less harrowing (*Guardian* 21 Nov. 1985 and 16 Oct. 1986).

Other issues of central concern to women's groups in the 1970s are still being pressed by women's groups and surface in the press and on television. Public concern was expressed over the continuing failure of police to follow up cases of domestic violence where wives are at risk from their husbands. A Metropolitan Police working party concluded that women found the police very unhelpful if they complained of being assaulted. The report was finished in January 1986 and leaked to the press by a Labour MP in November that year when it had not been published or acted upon by police or government (*Guardian* 4 Nov. 1986). The case of Wendy Savage, a doctor who was accused of incompetence by some of her male colleagues, and who championed the right of mothers to have their wishes taken into account during the process of childbirth, received prolonged publicity in 1985 and 1986. She was strongly backed by mothers and by the GPs in the working-class area of Tower Hamlets in London where she worked, and was cleared of incompetence by a professional inquiry in July 1986, but had to engage in a further struggle to regain her position as a consultant obstetrician at the London Hospital. Her case dramatised conflicting attitudes to the proper relationship between doctors and patients, and Mrs Savage publicly championed in television interviews and in campaigning activities the right of women to choose the kind of health care they received. (Savage 1986).

One of the most interesting shifts in attitude has taken place in the Church of England, after a prolonged campaign to allow women to be ordained as priests. The Synod voted in November 1984 to set in motion the process which would allow ordination of women, but this had still to be confirmed by a two-thirds vote by the bishops, clergy and laity. The voting in 1984, though it fell short of this requirement, did show a move in favour of women priests compared with voting in 1978 among all three categories, especially among the clergy represented (*Guardian* 16 Nov. 1984). Synod took a smaller but significant step in July 1985, when it voted to allow women to be ordained as deacons. Until then only the lay position of deaconess had been open to women. Women can now become members of the clergy (*Daily Telegraph* 3 July 1985). The Synod moved further towards the ordination of women when it endorsed in February 1987 a report proposing legislation in the 1990s to permit women priests. The Church of England debate has been complicated by concern for Christian unity with the Catholic and Orthodox Churches (where women priests are still unthinkable) and influenced by a general reluctance to change a familiar institution. But it clearly touches on fundamental beliefs about the nature of women, the opposition reflecting unwillingness to accept women in positions of religious authority; there is still deeply felt resistance to the ordination of women.

Assessing attitudes is always complex and the evidence sketchy. Some institutions are more resistant to accepting women on an equal basis that others; the Stock Exchange opened its doors with reluctance in the 1980s, and working men's clubs which allow women to accompany their husbands often refuse to allow them in if their husband dies. Individual attitudes tend to vary with age, class and politics, but it would be rash to attempt to correlate men's views on women's rights closely with these factors, since there are bastions of male privilege in both working-class and upper-class contexts. What has clearly happened, however, is that support for women's rights has become officially respectable, and men are therefore much more likely to accept the principle of equal rights than they would have been twenty years ago. This is a European-wide trend, as an EEC survey of attitudes to women indicated (*Guardian* 10 Sept. 1979).

Since the main aim of the Women's Liberation Movement was consciousness-raising among women it is especially relevant to ask how far women in the 1980s believe in women's rights. If the women's magazines are taken as an index of what it is socially respectable for women to do and think, then there has been a significant change since the 1950s and early 1960s. In part the magazines have reflected the new attitudes to sexuality of the late 1960s, and have become much more explicit about divorce and sex outside marriage. From the mid 1970s the magazines have laid less emphasis on marriage as the main goal for women and recognised that most wives go out to work; they have also given space to issues of women's rights. Indeed *Woman's Own* has actually campaigned on the tax issue and child-care facilities. Perhaps it is indicative of a new attitude among women themselves that the circulation of the women's magazines had dropped (Ferguson 1983).

Only quite a small minority of women have been active in the recent wave of feminism and many disclaim support for Women's Liberation. Those who have been most willing to identify with feminism, and who have gained most, are the highly educated younger generation of women; and as earlier discussion has suggested this group as a whole seems to have wider career expectations and to be rather more ambitious than previous generations of professional women. Young working-class women seem to have limited expectations from work and so centre their ambitions on marriage and motherhood: Sue Sharpe came to this conclusion in a study in the mid 1970s, and the trends of the 1980s have probably accentuated this attitude among many girls (Sharpe 1976). Working-class girls inherit low expectations both because of their class and their sex, and unless they are academically clever the training opportunities open to them remain limited. On the other hand, the signs of rebellion and self-assertion among working-class women were not limited to the late 1960s and early 1970s. The most obvious example has been the militancy of the miners' wives during the year-long 1984–85 strike; given the macho attitudes associated with the mining communities the prominent role of the women in organising support, joining the picket lines and going on demonstrations has marked a significant new militancy. Taken in conjunction with greater support for women's participation in the unions, there does seem to be a slow but real change under way in the attitudes of working-class women, and of their men.

The trend towards women desiring and men accepting a genuine equality for women has, however, come under attack in the 1980s, from a new emphasis on right-wing ideology, from the policies of Mrs Thatcher's Government and above all from the economic realities fostered by the Government. Since the early 1950s saw an association between conservatism and the idealisation of domestic femininity, the 1980s might seem to presage the same pressures on women to renounce liberation along with sexual permissiveness. The fact that two of the best-known advocates of the Women's Movement in the 1960s, Betty Friedan and Germaine Greer, have both published books in the 1980s which seem to reverse their earlier claims for liberation and stress the glories of traditional femininity and motherhood, lends apparent support to the impression that there has been a swing away from radicalism and feminism. But this interpretation would be superficial reading of Friedan and Greer, and more importantly a simplistic assessment of the social and political mood of Britain and of women's own activities and attitudes, and underestimates the continuing vitality of many feminist groups. Nevertheless, the election of Mrs Thatcher in 1979 has marked a clear break with the liberal welfare consensus of British politics since the war, and has given more weight to both traditionalist and populist conservative views which are hostile to the liberal conception of equal rights for women.

THE IMPACT OF CONSERVATIVE GOVERNMENT

Prominent members of Mrs Thatcher's circle have associated themselves with the view that women ought to take up their natural duties as wives, mothers and daughters and abandon their claim to be workers and citizens. Patrick Jenkin, who became Secretary of State for Social Services after 1979, had made the quotable remark:

> If the good Lord had intended us all having equal rights to go out to work and behave equally, you know he really wouldn't have created men and women (Coote and Campbell 1982: 87).

Sir Keith Joseph on becoming Secretary of State for Education also urged women to leave their jobs and look after their children. Feminist fears that the Government sought to save public money by forcing women to look after the ill and elderly unpaid in the home was strengthened by the leaks from the Government's Family Policy Group in 1983, which suggested families should reassume responsibilities taken on by the state. In addition the extolling of market freedoms, which characterises Mrs Thatcher's brand of conservatism, presaged an attack on the rights of all workers, which in practice might well fall particularly on women in low-paid, part-time or temporary jobs. It was clear after 1979 that some of the gains of the previous years might well be reversed.

The 1980 Employment Act was seen as the first setback for women, and was criticised by the EOC and the NCCL Women's Rights Unit. The Act specifically weakened the previous provisions for maternity leave for working women, by exempting small firms with less than six employees from granting women the right to return to work after having their babies, if the firm could show it was not 'reasonably practicable' to do so, and by allowing larger firms to offer women different jobs, which they had to accept or risk dismissal for 'unreasonable' rejection of a suitable alternative (Atkins and Hoggett 1984: 45–6). In addition the Act required a more elaborate procedure for women to notify employers of their need for maternity leave and their wish to return to work afterwards: a woman who failed to fulfil the detailed requirements, by failing to write the three separate letters required or not confirming she was returning to work within the specified time limit, could lose her right to return.

Whether statutory rights for women with babies to return to work significantly affect how many women return in practice was contested by some research undertaken in the late 1970s (Daniels 1981); but the NCCL (1981) noted that they had been inundated with queries about maternity rights, and stated that some employers were refusing to allow women to return to their jobs.

The 1980 Employment Act also reduced protection against unfair dismissal; workers in firms employing twenty or less employees had to have been in jobs for two years before qualifying, a clause more likely in practice to affect women.

The Conservative Government made clear its unwillingness to strengthen the rights of women at work when Jo Richardson presented a Private Member's Bill on Sex Equality to the Commons at the end of 1983. The Bill was designed to plug some of the main loopholes in the Equal Pay and Sex Discrimination Acts by redefining equal pay for equal work to cover work of 'equal value', and by making it easier for women to bring cases of discrimination to tribunals. It also contained provision to allow for positive action by employers to train and promote women, included sexual harassment as a form of discrimination, and established leave for fathers as well as mothers after the birth of a baby (NCCL *Rights* Winter 1983, p. 3). When the Bill was introduced in the House of Commons it received support from Labour and Alliance MPs, and also from two women Conservative MPs who expressed broad agreement, especially on the issue of equal pay for work of equal value. But it was opposed by the Government's junior Employment Minister, Alan Clark, who argued that the Bill was unrealistic and unfair to employers, and the Bill fell when 198 to 118 MPs voted against it (*Guardian* 10 Dec. 1983).

Apart from the Government's lack of enthusiasm for women's rights and its commitment to the economic freedom of employers rather than the rights of workers, its other ideological attitudes were in practice inimical to women. Anxiety to restrict coloured immigration resulted, as we have seen, in renewed discrimination against women. Hostility to social security and commitment to cut central and local government spending and to privatise health and welfare provision where possible all had important implications for women. During 1980 two separate pieces of legislation on social security cut entitlements to benefit and the amount of benefit, which the Child Poverty Action Group (CPAG), the National Women's Aid Federation and the NCCL all criticised for their damaging impact on women in need (NCCL, *Rights* Sept.–Oct. 1980, p. 9). The EOC commented circumspectly that social welfare measures could result in 'indirect discrimination' if they bore more hardly on women (EOC Annual Reports 1981: 22). Cuts in existing services, like provision of child-care facilities and children's school meals, and cuts in hospital and community provision for the old and the sick, all passed more responsibility and in many cases more work on to women.

The impact of Mrs Thatcher's Administration between 1979 and 1983 was, however, less dramatic than statements of its political theory and goals might suggest. There are a number of reasons why not. The moderates within the Party itself have opposed what they regard as extreme policies, and electoral considerations discouraged drastic cuts in the NHS or the Welfare State. Women in the Conservative Party have also resisted measures which would seriously undermine women's rights or their welfare. Moreover, both conventional and radical organisations representing women's interests outside Parliament have continued to exert pressure for the protection and extension of women's rights.

Another important factor is that the trend of EEC Directives, EEC Parliamentary inquiries and decisions by the (EEC) European Court of Justice have been in the direction of requiring the British Government to modify its domestic legislations to avoid discrimination against women. One important example was the 1978 EEC Directive requiring member states to accord men and women equal treatment, which led the Government in 1980 to extend the rights of married women. Especially interesting was the ruling by the European Court in 1982 that the Equal Pay Act did not meet Treaty of Rome obligations because it did not cover the right to equal pay for work of equal value. The Government responded by bringing in regulations to amend the European Communities Act in 1983. Although the Minister who introduced them in the Commons, Alan Clark, made clear that the Government was unwillingly doing the minimum required by European law, and the Equal Pay and Opportunities Campaign commented that the draft order seemed to represent 'a grudging attempt to comply with the letter of the European Court judgment', the Government was accepting its European commitments (*Guardian* 28 Mar. 1983).

The European Court has not always upheld the complaints of women who bring their case to it: for example in the 1986 case of a woman police officer in the Royal Ulster Constabulary (RUC) in Northern Ireland, who had lost her job because the Chief Constable would not allow women to carry firearms, the Court found that sex might be a determining factor in police work where there was serious internal disorder (*The Times* 16 May 1986). But the general tendency of EEC Directives and EEC Court decisions has been to promote women's rights. The Court ruled in February 1986 that women had a right to retire at the same age as men in a case brought by a former nurse, who had been forced to retire at 62. The British Government responded to this judgment by amending the Sex Discrimination Act to require employers to set equal retirement ages. The state retirement age was not changed. (See Chapter 6 for further analysis of the role of European Court rulings and their impact on women in Britain.)

Finally, the view that women should revert to a primarily domestic role as wives and mothers and return to the home is totally at odds with the social pattern of rising divorce and the steady long-term trend for more married women to go out to work. The number of single-parent families, which are almost all headed by the mother, has been growing steadily and was estimated at 900,000 in 1981 by the DHSS (TUC 1983: 5–6). The Royal Commission on the Distribution of Income and Wealth calculated in 1978 that without the wife's earnings three times as many families would be below the poverty line, and that 54 per cent of women with dependent children work. Moreover, the Government's own economic policies are forcing more wives to become the family breadwinner – one of the Ford women strikers in 1984 pointed out to the press that she was in this position. As male unemployment has risen steadily as a result of the contraction of manufacturing industry, employers have been seizing the opportunity for a part-time, low-paid and often temporary workforce composed largely of women.

Large numbers of women are unemployed too – just under 1 million according to the official figures for 1985 (EOC 1986: 24). This is certainly an underestimate, because as a result of several adjustments by the Government to methods of registering unemployment only those eligible to claim unemployment benefit and registered as available for work (which includes proving they have child-care facilities) are counted, thus excluding all those who do not fulfil these criteria. Even before the methods of counting were changed many women were known not to be registered as unemployed, because they were not eligible for benefit or because they had given up hope of a job. But many of the new jobs created under the Conservative Government have been part-time jobs, often taken by women. The pattern in the mid 1980s was a continuing loss of full-time jobs and at the same time a rise in the number of part-time jobs. The results for women are mixed: their right to go out to work and the importance of their economic role has been strengthened, but the work the majority have to take up is unskilled and ill paid.

The overall effect of government policies since 1979 has been to weaken labour legislation designed to safeguard workers' rights and to reduce welfare rights. High unemployment, cuts in the money available to local councils and privatisation of cleaning and catering services have further undermined the position of the poorer and more vulnerable sectors of society. The Government was dissuaded in 1985 from abolishing the Wages Councils, which exist to protect non-unionised workers in such areas as catering, shops, laundries and hairdressing and clothing manufacture, but did curb the Councils' powers and removed workers under 18 from their protection. As a result of privatisation of cleaning in hospitals many women cleaners have been forced to accept even lower wages than before, and in a number of cases have gone on strike in protest. High unemployment makes it easier for employers to forbid their workers to join trade unions – a Low Pay Unit survey in the West Midlands uncovered Victorian conditions in some small firms, particularly in clothing factories (Morton 1984). Cuts in council funds reduce the ability of local government to subsidise the large number of voluntary bodies that aid women and usually depend at least in part on council grants, such as refuges for women beaten by their husbands.

New social security legislation, previewed in a Green Paper in 1985 and introduced into Parliament in 1986, was strongly attacked by both women's rights bodies and the poverty lobby, especially for proposing to abolish the maternity grant to all but the poorest women, cutting back the state pensions scheme introduced in the 1970s to fill the gap for those who did not have adequate occupational pension schemes, and abolishing the Family Income Supplement (usually paid to the woman) by a family credit to go to the head of the household (NCCL *Civil Liberty* July 1985, Feb. 1986). A Conservative back-bencher tried to amend the Bill in committee to pay family credit direct to the parent looking after the children, but government whips got the amendment narrowly defeated. There was in addition concern that the amount of child benefit was to be frozen, despite reports published in 1985 demonstrating how strongly mothers valued this benefit, which they could claim direct and which involved no means testing (*Guardian*, 2 Nov. 1985). The CPAG coordinated a campaign started in November 1985 to save child benefit, and won support from the Mothers' Union and the National Federation of Women's Institutes. The Government responded by agreeing to raise the benefit slightly in July 1986 (CPAG, *Poverty* Spring 1986, p. 3). The increase was 10p a week.

Black women have suffered particularly from the cumulative effects of government policies and from unemployment. Black women are at an inherent disadvantage in British society, since they automatically have to contest both racial prejudice and prejudice against women, and in addition the majority of them are the poorest sector of society. They have been therefore particularly vulnerable to unemployment – for example the unemployment rate for all women under 25 between 1980 and 1981 rose by 58 per cent, but for black women it rose by 64 per cent (TUC 1983: 14–15). They also tend to get the worst paid and least desirable jobs like cleaning. Many of the women in the sweat shops in the West Midlands are Asian women. Problems of language and cultural constraints may lead women in ethnic minorities to become homeworkers, where they may enjoy no legislative protection of their wage rates.

It would be wrong, however, to see working-class women and black women purely as victims of economic stringency, lack of protection and of prejudice. There is evidence, too, of considerable resiliency and willingness to fight back. When councils in Clwyd and Liverpool announced cuts in nursery provision, vigorous local campaigns were launched by women not normally involved in local political activity (*Spare Rib* July 1979, p. 9). Women caught up in the results of privatisation have protested not only at the injustice they themselves have suffered, but at the deterioration in services provided as a result of cost cutting. Women have, moreover, been active in one of the more positive recent developments in the economy, the formation of small-scale cooperatives, a number of which are run entirely by women. Women's groups have been set up within various ethnic communities in Britain, and came together at a National Black Women's Conference held at Brixton in March 1979. The groups have tended to take up a range of issues affecting women in the local community, and affecting black people in general, for example immigration laws or the role of police, and Third World problems.

CONCLUSION

The total picture of women's gains and losses during the first half of the 1980s is therefore complex. There have been positive developments in opening up previously male-dominated professions to women, extension of higher education and some increase in the number of women taking subjects like maths and science at A level and university. More women are, moreover, attaining positions of power in public life – except so far in Parliament itself. Although progress has been gradual it appears to be a fairly consistent trend, supported by continuing campaigning efforts by women's groups and the expectations of a younger generation of women. Although only a privileged minority of women immediately benefit, these trends are of longer-term importance for all women for reasons discussed at the beginning of this chapter: to ensure equal opportunities in the future, to strengthen protection of women's interests by those with professional or political influence and power, and to change social attitudes to women and girls' own expectations. Indeed the accession to power of a woman Prime Minister, despite feminist criticisms of Mrs Thatcher for failing to promote women's interests, has almost certainly had an important impact on how girls and young women view the possibilities open to them in our society. More women moving into the sciences and acquiring mathematical and computer skills may be especially important to the position of women at work in the future. At present the evidence suggests there is a great danger that automation and the new communications technology will leave women in routine jobs making use of computers and word processors, and on the margins of the economy, but that they will be excluded from a central role.

There has in addition been a significant shift in attitudes towards greater acceptance of equality, despite abundant evidence of continuing prejudice, inertia and discrimination; and there are indications of a greater willingness to respond sympathetically to women suffering sexual harassment or physical violence from men. But the role of groups and individuals committed to achieving equal rights and fair treatment is clearly still essential.

On the other hand, this chapter has documented in some detail how the economic position of many women has deteriorated, some being forced to accept lower wages and many losing protection of their rights at work. High unemployment, changing job patterns and Conservative Government policies have meant that the position of working-class women has tended to worsen since the 1970s, when there was some improvement in average wages for full-time workers. What is happening in the economy now is a combination of short-term factors and longer-term developments due to increasing automation and new information technology.

In the future the economic position of the majority of women will depend on how jobs are created and allocated in the new economy that is emerging, and how Government distributes welfare and assists provision for increased leisure. How society adjusts to the new technology will affect everyone. The evolution of post-industrial society could, however, crucially affect the future position of women, and mean either a genuine liberation for many previously tied to routine and low-paid jobs or a new subordination in a masculine-dominated high-technology society in which women's roles and concerns are treated as peripheral. It is therefore vital that women help determine the nature of this society.

Part two
THE PROBLEMS OF WINNING WOMEN'S RIGHTS

INTRODUCTION

The previous four chapters have traced how the social and economic position of women has altered since 1945, and how their legal rights have been extended. They also indicated some of the social processes and political pressures which have combined to bring about these changes. Let us now look in some detail at how women's rights have been promoted. Chapter 3 concentrated on the role of the new Women's Liberation Movement in raising women's consciousness, changing public attitudes and focusing on problems like rape and domestic violence. Here we focus on the pressure-group activity and lobbying that preceded two central pieces of legislation for women's rights, the Equal Pay Act and the Sex Discrimination Act, examine the role of individual MPs and Cabinet Ministers and consider the influence of the trade unions and of the CBI. This discussion includes some examination of what political factors encouraged inertia or prompted government action.

In addition to considering the politics of achieving specific laws to promote women's rights, it is important to ask how far women are achieving their goals through the established political parties, and whether women's influence and power is increasing within them. This assessment involves consideration not only of party policies and the degree of prominence women have achieved in the party, but also of how far party tradition and ideology is sympathetic to women's rights and the possible electoral incentives for change. Will women voters reward a party with a strong programme of women's rights? A summary of the evidence about women's voting behaviour is needed to provide the basis for an answer.

THE POLITICS OF LEGISLATING FOR EQUALITY

Legislation is the main political instrument for bringing about social and economic change, so passing laws is a central focus of campaigning for pressure groups and movements seeking change and one test of their effectiveness. It is, in addition, interesting to see how parties and governments respond to pressure for new laws and what makes them take action. The two most central laws designed to promote women's rights were the Equal Pay Act of 1970 and the Sex Discrimination Act of 1975, and it is the politics of passing these two Acts we compare here.

Although they were only separated by five years, and the Equal Pay Act did not become fully operational until 1975, these two Acts reflected differing pressures for reform and a significant change in the attitudes of political parties to the demand for women's rights. The Equal Pay Act was the culmination of a slow but steady progress towards accepting the formal equality of women at work – equal pay had already been implemented for white-collar workers in public services and in the professions by the early 1960s. The Act reflected international endorsement of the principle of equal pay by the International Labour Organisation and the EEC and was a product primarily of long-term pressure within the trade union movement. Demands from women trade-unionists became more vocal in the 1960s when the Labour Government delayed taking action, and the Act followed manifestations of working-class women's militancy in 1968–69; but the Labour Government's decision to legislate in 1969 owed little to the emerging Women's Liberation Movement. The Sex Discrimination Act by contrast did reflect a greatly heightened public awareness of women's lack of rights, due in part to the new feminism, and was adopted after several years of increasingly active lobbying and attempts by MPs to introduce Private Members' Bills. It was influenced, too, by the precedent of legislation against racial discrimination and by the American approach to enshrining equal rights in law.

The Labour Party had included a promise to introduce equal pay for women in its 1964 Election Manifesto, after the previous Conservative Government had turned down a request from the TUC to legislate on equal pay on the grounds that this was a matter for employers and trade unions to resolve, not for governments. The Labour Party support in principle for legislation reflected an abstract commitment to women's equality, but its failure to introduce an Equal Pay Bill until its last year in office clearly showed that women's rights had a very low priority. Repeated resolutions for equal pay at National Labour Women's conferences did not have any obvious effect.

There are some obvious reasons for the Wilson Government's

reluctance to put equal pay high on the agenda. During its first term of office, from October 1964 to March 1966, it only had a majority of four MPs in the House of Commons, it had immediately to deal with a sterling crisis and other economic problems, and it was committed to introducing mainstream Labour measures like higher pensions, strengthening rights of tenants against landlords, buttressing trade union powers and renationalising steel. The threat of inflation led the Minister of Labour, Ray Gunter, to impose strict controls on prices and incomes. He chaired a committee set up to examine the implications of equal pay for women, and told the TUC Secretary in 1965 that introducing equal pay would raise too many difficulties at a time when there was a pay norm of $3\frac{1}{2}$ per cent (Meehan, 1985: 65). When Labour was returned to power after March 1966 with a majority of nearly 100 MPs it was in a much stronger position to carry out its full domestic programme, and it did re-examine the question of women's pay. But a study group on which both unions and employers were represented was unable by 1967 to agree on the costs involved in implementing equal pay. The reluctance of the CBI and further economic difficulties again led the Government to postpone action.

The role of the trade unions in promoting equal pay for women has been ambiguous. When women's entry into traditionally male jobs threatened to undercut men's wage rates, for example during the Second World War, the unions did press for equal pay. The TUC and relevant unions did also back the demand for equal pay in the public service after the war, whilst the TUC raised the basic issue again in the 1960s. But trade unions as a whole did not (as we have already seen) have a good record of backing the interests of their women members – the majority after all had failed to raise equal pay in negotiations with employers. The leadership of the Amalgamated Union of Engineering Workers did commit itself to seek rapid implementation of equal pay in 1964, but most union leaders did not press the issue, and women trade-unionists became increasingly impatient during the 1960s. The Women's Advisory Committee of the TUC drew up the Working Women's Charter in 1963, calling not only for equal pay but equal opportunities for promotion and for training and special provisions for women workers, and the TUC endorsed it at their 1963 Conference. Women complained at the 1966 Women's TUC Conference about the lack of urgency shown by the TUC over equal pay, and in 1968 criticism became more vociferous both at the TUC Conference and at a special TUC Conference on Equal Pay.

Two factors are usually cited to explain why the Labour Government did at last introduce an Equal Pay Bill in 1969: the strikes by women workers in 1968 and the appointment of Barbara Castle as Secretary of State for Employment in 1968 to replace Ray Gunter. Both were certainly important.

The Ford women's strike in 1968 hit the newspaper headlines, held up £50 million worth of exports and led to a march on the House of Commons. The strike dramatised an increasing sense of anger and injustice among working women, which in turn influenced trade-unionists. One result of the strike was that the Ford women's union, the Vehicle Builders Union, backed the creation of the National Joint Action Campaign Committee for Women's Equal Rights, which demonstrated in Trafalgar Square for equal pay in May 1969, a demonstration joined by members of old and new feminist groups. By 1969, therefore, equal pay had become a more salient public issue, which it was harder for the TUC leadership and the Labour Government to relegate to the indefinite future when economic difficulties had been overcome. Public concern was not so strong that the Government had to act, but it was possible to believe, as apparently Barbara Castle did, that equal pay would be popular and a potential vote-winner in the forthcoming election.

Barbara Castle's personal role was decisive. Several commentators have suggested that the Equal Pay Act would not have been pushed through if there had not been a woman as Secretary of State for Employment, and this is probably true, though Barbara Castle's feminism should not be exaggerated. Her *Diaries* indicate that she did not wish to involve herself closely with women's issues (Castle 1980: 141, 278). But she did have an interest in women's role at work and in improving the position of working-class women, who would be the most immediate beneficiaries of an Equal Pay Act, and she had joined an equal pay demonstration in the 1950s. Moreover, she had met a deputation from the Ford women during the strike and publicly promised that equal pay would be introduced in November 1968. Richard Crossman suggests in his *Diaries* that after Barbara Castle had lost a battle to impose legal sanctions on trade unions to prevent unofficial strikes she needed a success (Crossman 1977: 678). Crossman speaks of the Government being landed with the Bill, and later clashed with Castle because his department was opposed to her attempts to include pensions and social security in the Bill, and he was in competition with her for scarce parliamentary time to pass legislation before the 1970 election (Crossman 1977: 789, 919, 921). So his testimony was biased. But he does make clear the opposition within the Cabinet from several ministers who saw no point in pursuing equal pay, and from Roy Jenkins who did believe in the principle of equality but as Chancellor of the Exchequer opposed it on grounds of cost (Crossman 1977: 627). The passing of the Bill depended therefore on Barbara Castle's skills and determination in piloting the Bill through the Cabinet and Parliament, circumnavigating obstacles raised by the CBI, and ensuring that although many items on the 1969–70 legislative agenda failed to become law when Harold Wilson decided to go to the country in May 1970, the Equal Pay Act did get through. Barbara Castle succeeded because she was an able and energetic minister, keen to make a success of whatever she turned her hand to, and usually good at getting her own way. The Act reflected compromises she accepted under pressure: she was unsuccessful in getting pensions and social security covered, and refused to try to include discrimination in areas like recruitment and training. But passage of the Act did have considerable symbolic importance as well as some practical effects in the mid 1970s, and it paved the way for further legislation on women's rights.

The main obstacle to equal pay during the 1960s was the widespread assumption that women's issues were unimportant, at least in the political arena. Although there was potential ideological opposition on the Right among those who still believed woman's place was in the home, and on the Left from those who saw feminism as a diversion from the central class struggle, within the liberal consensus that embraced the majority of Conservative and Labour Party members and supporters the principle of equal pay was unexceptionable. Indeed, Robert Carr for the Conservative Opposition welcomed the Equal Pay Bill and even noted that it did not go far enough to be really effective (Meehan 1985: 65). Objections centred primarily on costs and secondly on whether legislation was appropriate when reasons for opposing action were given. Much of the resistance seems, however, to have stemmed from a feeling that it was unimportant and there were other priorities. Continuing lack of interest, even in 1969–70 when women's protests and press coverage had created a much greater sense of urgency, is indicated by low attendance at parliamentary debates on the Bill (Randall 1982: 183) and by very cursory references in Wilson's own account of his Administration (Wilson 1974: 907, 987). Even awareness of the fact that if Britain succeeded in joining the EEC it would be bound by an article in the Treaty of Rome on equal pay, which the existing member states had agreed in 1961 to implement in stages, does not seem to have been an incentive to either Conservative or Labour Governments trying to negotiate entry to act on equal pay.

Whereas equal pay had been on the public agenda since 1945, broader measures to ensure equal opportunity had been canvassed by feminists without attracting much attention. When the Equal Pay Act was introduced there was recognition in debates in Parliament that supplementary measures were needed, but a general law against sexual discrimination was a new idea stimulated by the 1960s experiment in legislating against racial discrimination. It was, moreover, inherently more controversial than equal pay, since it raised questions about the desirability of trying to change attitudes through the law, problems about the scope of such a law and difficulties about what women wanted or needed. So it is interesting that the Sex Discrimination Act was passed after only a few years' agitation. One reason must be the spread of feminist ideas and feminist activism between 1969 and 1975, accompanied by a change in attitudes to women's rights by the press, radio and television and among many of the public. There was certainly a marked increase in sympathy and interest among MPs in that period. It could more cynically be argued that the major obstacle to equal pay – fear of increased wage costs – did not apply to the Sex Discrimination Act, since the costs to employers arising from it were less clear cut. But CBI evidence to the House of Lords was markedly unenthusiastic about a Sex Discrimination Act, so there was some employer resistance.

The pattern of the campaign to achieve a Sex Discrimination Act was a series of Private Members' Bills, backed by increasingly well-organised and visible support outside Parliament and cross-bench support inside it. All these Bills eventually failed, but the Conservative Government felt impelled to produce a Green Paper in 1973, even though feminists dismissed it as a token gesture, and the Labour Government got an Act passed in 1975.

Joyce Butler, the Labour MP for Wood Green, sponsored the first Private Member's Bill against sexual discrimination in 1968, and did so again each year until 1971. She used the device of the Ten Minute Rule which allows back-benchers to introduce a Bill and speak on it for ten minutes at the end of Question Time in the Commons on Tuesdays and Thursdays. Even if a Bill introduced in this way is allowed to proceed, it is extremely unlikely under parliamentary procedures that it will reach a second reading. But it is a useful way to publicise an issue, and had been used previously to promote campaigns for abolishing capital punishment and legalising homosexuality.

Joyce Butler was not only hampered by the exigencies of the parliamentary timetable but, in addition, by lack of expert advice on how to frame an anti-discrimination Bill. Although a number of bodies including the Liberal Party and the NCCL had published reports in the mid 1960s on the inequalities still suffered by women, and a range of women's organisations cooperated to try to make women's equality at work and in social security and taxation an election issue in 1966, the campaign was still rather diffuse (Meehan 1985: 44–6). The Fawcett Society, which had been formed in 1866 to campaign for votes for women, but had been since the 1920s concerned with the full range of women's rights, is credited with playing a key role in the late 1960s in bringing together other feminist groups (like the Six Point Group set up in 1921 to press for full equality) and organisations representing professional and married women. The Fawcett Society, to which a number of women MPs belonged, was also active in helping formulate an anti-discrimination Bill in 1971 and coordinating support for it. The society worked with the new parliamentary group on women's rights, formed by Joyce Butler and Edward Bishop, on the contents of the Bill; and liaised not only with the established women's organisations but the new Women's Liberation Movement through the Women's Lobby, formed by members of the new movement committed to campaigning for legislation.

A more promising focus for a campaign than a Ten Minute Rule Bill occurred when Willie Hamilton, the controversial Labour MP for West Fife, won a place in the ballot for Private Members' Bills in the 1971–72 Parliamentary Session, and agreed to put forward the Bill already drafted by Joyce Butler and Edward Bishop. Private Members' Bills are debated on Friday afternoons and are the likeliest way for back-benchers to get a law passed, though the Bills are still liable to be talked out at their second reading and do not usually reach the statute book unless they are totally non-controversial or the Government makes extra time available for them. Banning sexual discrimination was potentially an appropriate topic for a Private Member's Bill, since it was not a question on which MPs divided on strict party lines, and could be seen as falling into the category of moral and social issues traditionally covered by such Bills. Moreover, it was not as controversial as divorce and abortion reform or abolition of theatre censorship or legalising homosexuality, which had all been the subjects of successful Private Members' legislation in the 1960s.

There was considerable organised support for a law to ban sexual discrimination when Hamilton introduced the second reading of his Bill in January 1972. Supporters of women's rights sat in the gallery and a lobby of Parliament had been arranged. Hamilton noted in his speech that the National Joint Committee of Working Women's Organisations representing 3 million women had launched a campaign for greater equality for women in education, training, employment and promotion, and that the Women's Institutes had for the first time expressed support for the principles of the Bill. The Conservative Government's response was, however, to query if legislation was suitable and whether there was much sexual discrimination in employment. The Minister of State for the Home Office, Richard Sharples, in a speech widely criticised as inept, claimed most women liked working in traditional female jobs and implied they were suitably employed in work which was an extension of their domestic role. Shirley Williams attacked the Minister for misjudging the mood of both sides of the House and of the country, and commented that he sounded like the white Rhodesian Government speaking of the African majority in that country. Despite a well-attended debate at which the majority of speakers supported the Bill, the Speaker refused to allow a vote on it before Parliament adjourned, on the grounds there had been insufficient time for debate – by precedent two hours was normally required. Discussion of the Anti-Discrimination Bill had been delayed by Ronald Bell, a committed Conservative opponent of legislation on women's rights, conducting a filibuster on the previous Bill. Amid bitter complaints about Bell's role and the Speaker's unwillingness to stretch precedent the Bill lapsed for that session (House of Commons 1972: 1813–46). The only apparent outcome of the debate was that Richard Sharples shortly afterwards lost his ministerial post and became Governor of Bermuda.

A Private Member's Bill introduced in the Lords in 1972 had rather greater success. The Liberal peer, Nancy Seear, who had done academic research into women's position at work, sponsored a Bill on similar lines to Hamilton's draft. The Lords agreed to send it to a Select Committee, which provided an opportunity for women's organisations to submit detailed evidence of discrimination, and over half the evidence received by the Committee came from them (Meehan 1985: 48). The Fawcett Society and Women in Media held a conference in January 1972 attended by eighty organisations to discuss submission of evidence to the Committee. The Select Committee sat for about a year and proved a useful forum for exposing the extent of discrimination. Its deliberations also resulted in an amended and strengthened Bill, which had benefited from the expertise of a former head of the Parliamentary Drafting Unit, Sir Noel Hutton. Although the Bill excluded the church and single-sex schools, feminists welcomed it, approving in particular of clauses banning occupational discrimination on any grounds except ability, banning discrimination based on marital status and penalising single-sex advertisements. Particularly welcomed was a clause enabling a proposed Sex Discrimination Board to investigate discrimination without waiting for individual complaints (*Spare Rib* Aug. 1973, p. 18). This version of the Bill returned to the Lords in May 1973 for further debate.

While Lady Seear's Bill was still in the Lords' Select Committee, Willie Hamilton won another place in the ballot for Private Members' Bills for 1972–73, and reintroduced his Anti-Discrimination Bill which came up for its second reading on 2 February 1973. Attendance by MPs was unusually and impressively high for a Private Member's Bill and the public gallery was crowded with the Bill's supporters. Women's Lobby with the backing of many women's organisations had called a mass lobby of Parliament, and a public meeting was held at the same time in Caxton Hall. The view of the Government, put by Home Office Minister Mark Carlisle, was much more sympathetic in tone than a year previously and indicated backing for the goals of the Bill. Carlisle noted that three Conservative back-bench MPs supported the Bill, Sally Oppenheim, Janet Fookes and Elaine Kellett-Bowman, and referred to action already taken by the Government to promote women's rights, for example to change the law on guardianship of children. Despite a much more polished performance than his predecessor's a year previously, Carlisle indicated Government unease about the far-reaching implications of the clause on education, concern about the proposed enforcement mechanisms and a general desire to delay pending further evidence from the Lords' Select Committee and a Department of Employment survey. Dame Patricia Hornsby-Smith indicated that she supported the aims of the Bill, but stressed a number of problems – for example whether it was in women's interests to make midwifery open to men – and suggested specific legislation on various issues would be better. But the debate was in general favourable both to the Bill and to the cause of women's rights. Both the House and the gallery erupted into protest when at 4 p.m. the Speaker again refused to put the motion to a vote on the grounds the debate had only lasted an hour and three-quarters (House of Commons 1973a: 1850–86).

The meeting at Caxton Hall was addressed by MPs involved in promoting the Hamilton Bill, and afterwards several hundred women marched to Downing Street to protest against the lapsing of the Bill for a second time and to demand that the Government find extra time to allow it to pass its second reading. Despite the fact that the Leader of the House had tried to quell the uproar in the Commons when the Speaker refused to take a vote by promising that the Government would look into possible arrangements for enabling a decision to be made on the Bill, the Government did not respond to the demonstrators' request. But the Labour Opposition agreed to allocate an afternoon of Opposition Party time to the Bill, which again on 14 February and duly passed. The Bill was then Commons' Select Committee.

It became clear, however, by the early summer of 197ɔ ᴛᴴᴀᴛ the Hamilton nor the Seear Bill would be allowed to make further progress. The Government indicated in the Lords in May that it would oppose the Seear Bill, largely because it objected to the proposals on education which it claimed were based on inadequate evidence and would create difficulties for setting up single-sex schools and colleges in the future. The Government was pursuing its own enquiries and planned a Consultative Paper. When the Green Paper *Equal Opportunities for Men and Women* was published in November 1973, Baroness Summerskill argued it was an 'election ploy' to win women's votes at minimum cost to vested interests (Meehan 1985: 67). Critics of the Green Paper focused particularly on the inadequacy of enforcement powers: the proposed EOC was to have only advisory and persuasive powers, whilst enforcement was left to industrial tribunals. Women's groups began to submit detailed comments on the Green Paper, but the Government called a snap election in February 1974 in response to the challenge posed to its authority by the miners' strike.

As a result the Labour Party returned to power, though as a minority government. Despite its precarious parliamentary position the new Government published a White Paper *Equality for Women* in September 1974 along with other legislative proposals, before calling a further election in October. On being elected with an overall parliamentary majority of three, Labour pressed ahead with a Sex Discrimination Bill, which went further than the White Paper on the important issue of including the concept of 'indirect discrimination'. The Bill published in March 1975 proved at that stage to be fairly uncontroversial and was passed that year with few amendments. Although the Conservative Opposition raised some doubts about the scope of the Bill and the proposed powers of the EOC, the strongest criticism came from the Government's own back-benchers seeking to extend the Bill (Byrne and Lovenduski 1978: 137). Only Conservative back-benchers Ronald Bell and Ivor Stanbrook and Enoch Powell, now an Ulster Unionist, opposed the principle of legislating for women's rights in debates in the House. (For more detailed analysis of the Act see Chapter 6.)

The Labour Government acted with a speed and decisiveness on the Sex Discrimination Act that was in marked contrast to its record on equal pay, even though its position in Parliament was even weaker and it had urgent items on its agenda like the repeal of the Conservative industrial Relations Act and other labour legislation (Wilson 1977: 56). There was some pressure from the EEC to promote equal opportunities for women at work – a Social Action Programme was published early in 1974 and debate on an EEC Directive on this theme began in spring 1975 (Meehan 1985: 86). But there are several reasons for doubting the importance of EEC influence on the Labour Government, which had not been similarly responsive on equal pay between 1964 and 1968. The Labour Government was in fact ahead of the EEC in taking action: its White Paper was published before debate on the EEC Directive began and its Act was passed before the Directive was. In addition, continuing British membership of the EEC was still in doubt when the Sex Discrimination Bill was published, since Labour committed itself to hold a referendum on the issue which took place in 1975.

Responsibility for action on the Bill lay with a liberal-minded Home Secretary, Roy Jenkins. But although he certainly influenced the content of the Bill there are no grounds for believing his role was crucial in getting it on to the legislative agenda. Commentators have suggested that interest in the Bill was linked to a commitment to improve the 1960s race relations legislation, passed by a previous Labour Government, which had been found inadequate, primarily because of an absence of enforcement powers. But whilst it is true that the Sex Discrimination Act was used in 1976 as a model for revising the previous race discrimination acts, it is still necessary to ask why the Sex Discrimination Act came first.

The obvious answers are that a lot of the preliminary work had been accomplished through the debates on the Seear and Hamilton Bills, evidence collected and the possible provisions of a Sex Discrimination Bill clarified, and that there was now strong pressure for action and little opposition. There was widespread support for such a measure in the Parliamentary Labour Party and in the Party generally. Although some individual unions, for example the Post Office Workers, supported forms of discrimination against women, the TUC had given evidence in favour of the Seear Bill, with qualifications about the dangers of removing protective legislation. (The 1975 Act reflected the TUC position and did not repeal protective legislation covering women, for example in relation to night shifts.) The Conservative Party had indicated support in principle for legislation, so a major parliamentary battle was not threatened. Above all there was now widespread public support for promoting women's rights. Joyce Butler speaking in the 1973 debate on the Hamilton Bill commented on the enormous change of attitudes between 1968 when she introduced her first anti-discrimination measure and 1973. While her first attempt was greeted with ridicule, treated as trivial by the press and supported with embarrassment even by those who were in sympathy, by 1973 there was a strong sense that justice for women had been too long delayed. Joyce Butler believed that attitudes of both the media and the House had been changed by 'the tremendous surge of public support for the idea of the Bill, the tremendous interest taken by all the established women's organisations and the newer ones that sprang up after the celebration of 50 years of women having the vote' (House of Commons 1973a: 1878). The Fawcett Society maintained pressure on the new Labour Government in 1974, bringing together a range of organisations to call for legislation. So did the NCCL, which published a draft Bill. But the Government was probably responding less to specific pressure than to a general feeling that the time had come for action in a self-evidently just cause.

Both the Equal Pay Act and the Sex Discrimination Act were passed by Labour Governments presided over by Harold Wilson, and his Administration was also responsible for the Social Security Act promoting women's interests and for assisting Jo Richardson's Domestic Violence Bill, so Wilson can claim to be the Prime Minister who has done most for women's rights. Barbara Castle notes in her *Diaries* that he was 'always anxious to promote the status of women', (Castle 1980: 141), and indeed Wilson was responsible for placing Barbara Castle in a number of important ministerial posts which did not fall into traditional feminine categories, including Secretary of State for Employment. Wilson's willingness to appoint Barbara Castle, Shirley Williams and Judith Hart to Cabinet posts and to give quite a number of women experience of a wide range of ministerial jobs does show a positive commitment to encouraging women. References in his own accounts of his terms of office, particularly 1974–76, suggest sympathy for women's rights, but also indicate they were peripheral (Wilson 1979: 15, 123, 126–7). He was clearly not willing to make an issue of equal pay, but happy to respond when changing public attitudes and pressure-group activity made legislative action on equal pay and equal rights appropriate.

Given the large number of groups involved at various stages in lobbying for equal pay or the Sex Discrimination Bills and in presenting relevant evidence it is impossible here to delineate them in any detail or assess the influence of each group. But it is worth noting the diversity of the organisations involved. There were sectional interest groups representing women at work – professional and business women's associations as well as women in trade unions – and organisations promoting the interests of wives and mothers. In addition to women's bodies there were general professional and trade union organisations that gave particular support to women's rights, for example the NUT. There were in addition numerous promotional or cause groups involved. Some of these were set up specifically to agitate for equal pay or for legislation to end discrimination, for example the Women's Lobby, while there were other feminist groups with rather different aims, for example Women in Media whose primary purpose was to contest stereotypes and sexist bias and demand better jobs for women in the media, who took part in the campaign. Apart from specifically feminist organisations, both old and new, one promotional group which played an important role in campaigning for legislation was the NCCL, which had been persuaded during the 1960s to extend its concern with civil liberties to women's rights by a number of women on its council, and which set up a Women's Rights Unit in the 1970s.

Finally, there was pressure from women within the major parties for equal rights; not only from women MPs with the support of some of their male colleagues, but also from the women's organisations within the parties. Sustained pressure for equal rights legislation came primarily from women in the Labour Party, but the Liberal Women's Federation and Conservative Party Women's Advisory Committee were also involved in promoting legislation. It is to the campaigning role of women in the main political parties and their degree of representation and power within them that we now turn.

WOMEN'S ROLE AND INFLUENCE IN THE POLITICAL PARTIES

Women in the Labour Party campaigned for equal pay and equal rights in the 1960s and 1970s primarily through the established channels within the Party. Women have special representation at a number of levels. Locally, women's sections may be set up in wards and send delegates to the constituency general management committee. At the national headquarters of the Party there is a Women's Department headed by a Chief Women's Officer, and since 1951 there has been a National Women's Advisory Committee which works closely with her and which reports direct to the Party's National Executive Committee (NEC). Five places have statutorily been reserved for women on the NEC itself. In addition there is an annual National Labour Women's Conference attended by representatives from local women's sections, trade-unionists, members of the

Cooperative Society and of socialist societies. But resolutions from the annual Women's Conference have not been in any way binding on the Party, or even required serious discussion, and at least until the late 1960s the women's organisation was in every sense peripheral.

Despite their advocacy of equal pay, women in the Labour Party did not, as we have seen, appear to have much influence on the Labour Government's decision-making on this issue. But Labour women did have a much greater impact on the formulation of party policy on legislating to end sex discrimination, and this seems to have been associated with some increase in the influence of the women's organisation within the Party from the late 1960s. The NEC set up a working group to explore the extent of discrimination against women in 1967. The group included Joyce Butler, Margherita Rendel, who was one of the pioneers of women's rights agitation in the 1960s, Millie Miller, who became an MP in 1974 and lawyer Anthony Lester. It produced a preliminary report in 1968, which was discussed at the National Labour Women's Conference, and a further study of women and social security in 1969. The final result of the group's work was the Labour Opposition Green Paper, *Discrimination Against Women*, published in 1972, which forcefully summarised the evidence on the extent of discrimination and made twenty-four recommendations for reform. The Women's Advisory Committee followed up this report by urging a Manifesto commitment to end discrimination. Their demand was accepted, no doubt in part because of the mounting campaign for legislation and changing attitudes documented earlier; but Oonagh McDonald was told that by the mid 1970s the influence of the Advisory Committee had grown (McDonald 1977: 152). During the period 1967–75 Betty Lockwood was the Chief Women's Officer and actively promoted equal rights.

During this period Labour women also began to consider women's position within the Party. The Green Paper had underlined women's poor representation at the National Conference and on the NEC. A proposal to abolish the places reserved for women on the NEC led the Women's Advisory Committee to make strong representations to the Executive that these places should be retained until women had achieved parity in positions of power within the Party, and to produce a statement in 1971 setting parity as a goal. The NEC retained the reserved seats and was willing to consider the longer-term goal, asking for a report on the problems faced by women in politics in 1974. But women's representation and influence inside the Party did not increase significantly for the rest of the decade. Furthermore, women were not making much headway in getting selected as parliamentary candidates:

there were only 10 per cent of women on the Party's list of approved potential candidates in 1979, and only 8 per cent of candidates standing for Labour were women (Vallance 1984 303–4). The majority of those women who were selected were in marginal or unwinnable seats.

Since the Party went into opposition there has been more sustained and partially successful pressure to get women's rights high on the policy agenda, and to improve women's position within the Party itself. The first goal has been somewhat easier than the second to promote. The 1983 Party Manifesto included strong commitments to equal pay, equal opportunities and creating nursery facilities, though these issues did not figure in the election campaign. Pressure for internal changes inside the Party has been undertaken by the campaigning group, Women's Action Committee, set up in 1980 by the Campaign for Labour Party Democracy, which won reselection of MPs and election of the leader by an electoral college of the Party as a whole. The Women's Action Committee drew up a set of demands designed to strengthen the constitutional position of the Women's National Conference, including a proposal that the Conference should directly elect the Advisory Committee (now elected regionally) and more controversially that it should elect the five women members with reserved places on the NEC, now elected by the Party Conference (*Feminist Review* Summer 1984, p. 78). Feminists have had to fight to get their local constituency parties to put women's rights resolutions to the Party Conference, but have made progress during the 1980s. Women's Action Committee demands were first debated at the 1982 Conference, when the trade-union block vote defeated them. Four years later in 1986 the resolution proposing women members of the NEC be elected by the Women's Conference was again defeated, but a resolution requiring consultation on the composition of the National Women's Conference was passed. The main problem is how women trade-unionists should be formally represented at the Conference and the impact of union representation on voting procedures.

Getting more women into Parliament remains a central aim for feminists. There were more women coming forward in 1983: they constituted 15 per cent of the national candidates list and 12 per cent of Labour candidates standing, though in a disastrous election for Labour only ten women got to the House of Commons. But the process of selecting candidates for the next election – especially in safe Labour seats – appeared by 1985 to be excluding women almost totally. The Women's Action Committee launched a campaign calling for general management committees only to short-list women candidates. Although by July 1985 only 12 out of 158 safe seats had gone to women, the Action Committee claimed success for its efforts in two London constituencies (*Guardian* 9 July 1985). By the end of the year 16 women had been picked for safe seats and a further 13 for seats which Labour could win if it did as well as the Conservatives (*Guardian* 13 Dec. 1985). In order to strengthen women's chances of selection by constituency parties, a crucial blockage at a time when more women are coming forward as candidates, the Women's Action Committee called for mandatory inclusion of at least one woman on short lists of candidates. This proposal proved controversial initially, even among Labour women. Renee Short, for example, commented in a survey in 1983 that this kind of proposal was patronising to women (*Guardian* 3 June 1983). But there has been an interesting change of attitudes – the 1986 Labour Party Conference did pass a resolution calling for mandatory inclusion of one woman.

Labour's main claim to be the party of women's rights has rested since 1983 on the proposal for a Minister for Women. Before the 1983 election Michael Foot appointed Joan Lestor as Shadow Minister for Women, but she failed to retain her seat in the election, and Jo Richardson became Labour's spokesperson for women's rights. She came to the conclusion that a Minister for Women's Rights without the backing of a separate government department to promote a consistent programme would find herself powerless. She has therefore taken the initiative in having detailed proposals for a Ministry of Women put to the NEC. The 1986 Party Conference formally endorsed the commitment to create such a ministry and in addition to give the Minister for Women Cabinet status. The proposed Ministry would work with a strengthened EOC, and be responsible for seeing that the Government in its own role as employer, in providing public contracts and in appointing public bodies, would strengthen the position of women. Labour's programme to promote equality includes commitment to a statutory minimum wage and introducing equal pay for work of equal value, and a major expansion of child-care facilities for children under 5. It also envisages encouraging men to play more part in child care through introducing parental leave and shorter and more flexible working hours for men as well as women.

There has therefore been a significant move within the Party to espouse women's rights in general and a gradual response to calls for internal reforms in favour of women. But when the General Secretary, Larry Whitty, was interviewed in November 1986 he admitted that the Party had responded rather less well to the demands of women than the trade unions had recently done (*Guardian* 25 Nov. 1986).

One of the most innovative and most controversial moves to strengthen women's rights was the creating during the 1980s of women's committees by a number of Labour local authorities, most notably the Greater London Council (GLC). The formation of the committees demonstrated the responsiveness of some local Labour parties to feminist and other radical pressure, but once in operation the committees came up against the prejudices of both Labour and Conservative councillors, town hall bureaucracy and predictable vilification by the popular press. The committees have had problems in clarifying their role, and suffered from internal disputes among feminists with conflicting views, and have sometimes offered easy targets for their critics. Women involved in the committees agreed in a round-table discussion that preparation had often been inadequate and that it takes time to integrate into the structure of local government (*Marxism Today* July 1986, pp. 16–20). But the committees and women's officers may consolidate ways of channelling resources to help women in the local community and improve the position of women in the local authority itself.

Women in the Labour Party can draw on a general tradition of sympathy for women's rights, but have at the same time to combat inertia, vested interests and a considerable reservoir of male chauvinism in sections of the Party; Women's Action Committee members complained that their demands prompted an overtly chauvinist response at the 1983 Conference. They have had to contend, too, with the view on the Hard Left that feminism is a distraction from the class struggle. Ideologically the Liberal Party looks likely to favour women's rights more unequivocally than Labour, since liberalism stresses individual rights and modern liberalism is also sympathetic to a degree of state intervention and welfare provision, which in practice are very important in buttressing women's position. Indeed, the Liberal Party took up the question of discrimination against women in the mid 1960s, before women's rights had become fashionable. But the position of women inside the Liberal Party has not been especially strong. Women have been almost totally excluded from the main offices in the Party, and if we look at the less important roles, for example the annual presidency of the National Liberal Federation, only four women held this post between 1945 and 1979 compared with eight women chairmen of the Labour Party in the same period (one of whom held office twice) (Butler and Sloman 1980). Moreover, there has been no woman Liberal MP in the House of Commons since Megan Lloyd George, who ceased to be a Liberal in 1951 and went over to Labour, until Elizabeth Shields entered the

House through a by-election in 1986. Whilst the proportion of women on the national candidates list and of women standing for election was somewhat lower than in the Labour Party in both 1979 and 1983, the percentage of women standing for the Liberal Party rose from 7 per cent in 1979 to almost 10 per cent in 1983.

Recently the Liberals have been concerned to promote women's interests, but seem to have focused on formulating policies favourable to women and increasing the number of women parliamentary candidates, rather than on internal party reform. The Women's Liberal Federation is able to elect members to the Party's 275-member Council, along with other bodies, and has felt the existing channels for promoting its views and getting resolutions considered by the Assembly Committee are adequate. It has strengthened resolutions by submitting back-up papers presenting the case, and by lobbying members of the Committee. But positive action has been considered necessary to bring forward more women candidates. The 1986 Liberal Assembly passed a resolution making inclusion of one woman and one man on all short lists of candidates mandatory. This could not significantly affect the position at the election, since most candidates had already been chosen and the only seats left were those where the Liberals had no hope. But the impact of this measure of positive discrimination in favour of women may be visible by the 1990s, especially as Elizabeth Sidney was appointed Deputy Chairman of the Candidates Committee with special responsibility to help women stand. She is exploring a range of measures, including educational sessions to improve the knowledge of potential candidates about party policies, setting up local networks of politically active women to give each other practical assistance and clarifying the requirements for a good candidate, so that women know what would be entailed and may feel less intimidated.

The Social Democratic Party (SDP) formed in 1981 has from the outset given prominence to its commitment to women's rights, and set a precedent by making inclusion of at least two women on candidates' short lists a requirement immediately. It fielded forty-four women candidates (14 per cent of the SDP total) and had 17 per cent women on its national list in 1983, so giving women better representation than the other major parties. There were obvious reasons why the SDP should adopt a strong policy on women's rights: it was an issue on which the Party might hope to outbid the Labour Party, it could expect to draw middle-class and professional women into the Party, and to have some success in attracting the votes of women voters disillusioned with both Labour and the Conservatives. Moreover, as a totally new party, which drew in quite a few previously uncommitted people, it could more easily plan to include women in policy-making. Finally, its four prominent founding members included a woman, Shirley Williams, and also Roy Jenkins, who had seen the 1975 Sex Discrimination Act through the Commons. Nevertheless, the SDP's attempt to formalise equal representation of women and men on its policy-making bodies at its inception was outvoted by the party membership, when the Constitutional Conference was deadlocked on this point. Moreover, after 1983, when Shirley Williams lost the seat she had won for the SDP in a by-election, there was no woman SDP MP until Rosie Barnes in 1987. But the SDP and Liberal Conferences in 1986 were able to endorse a joint Alliance policy to improve the position of women in relation to taxation, the rights of part-time workers and child care.

The Conservative Party is ideologically least predisposed to support women's rights, embracing as it does old-fashioned patriarchal views and the anti-feminism of the New Right represented by the *Salisbury Review*. But the welfare liberal consensus accepted by the moderate leadership of the Party before Mrs Thatcher meant, as we have seen, acceptance in principle of the case for ending sex discrimination. Mrs Thatcher's philosophy incorporates a strongly individualistic form of *laissez-faire* liberalism, particularly in relation to the role of the state in the economy, which has meant dislike of state regulation of wages and employment conditions and a desire to reduce welfare benefits that is, as we saw in Chapter 4, in practice detrimental to women's rights. This strictly individualistic theory also refuses to recognise structural inequalities in society resulting from social class, race or gender, and so does not see a need for legislation or state action to remedy them. But it does in the abstract recognise individual rights and the right to equality of opportunity. Whilst it is not clear how far Mrs Thatcher's liberalism extends beyond the economic sphere, as it coexists with nationalist and authoritarian beliefs, she is bound by her own success to extend the principle of equal opportunity to other women. So in theory the Party has a limited sympathy for women's rights.

In the past there has been a dichotomy in the Conservative Party between the position of women in the Party in the country, the National Union, and their chances of getting into the Parliamentary Party. In the former they have been comparatively well represented at the level of constituency party chairmen (where they have sometimes held around half these posts) and on the 200-strong Executive Committee of the National Union, where they held a quarter of the seats in 1971. Though they have figured less well at the very top, five women were President of the Union between 1945 and 1979 and ten were Chairmen of the Union in the same period. But the proportion of Conservative women candidates has been lower than in all the other major parties: in the 1979 election, when Mrs Thatcher came to power as Prime Minister, only 4 per cent of the parliamentary candidates were women and only eight women became Conservative MPs.

Women have probably been quite prominent in the National Union, especially at local levels, because upper-class women have traditionally played a part in local life, especially in the countryside, and their social status has extended to party politics, and class outweighed the disadvantages of being a woman in politics. But when it came to selecting women to the seat of power at Westminster, Tory prejudices against the fairer sex meddling in masculine preserves have been more pronounced. In the past it is also quite possible that energetic and able women in the Conservative Party have not felt their place was in the House of Commons, because they have broadly accepted a domestic definition of the role of women, supplemented by voluntary activity in the local community. But the social composition of the Conservative Party has been changing and so have general social attitudes, so Conservative women seem likely to have changing views about their own contribution to the Party. It is, moreover, impossible to ignore the significance of having a woman as a Conservative Prime Minister.

The Conservative Party has shown some concern to increase the number of women parliamentary candidates. In fact the percentage of women standing for the Conservatives in 1983 was 6 per cent, and 10 per cent of those on the national candidates list were women. Two male Vice-Presidents of the Party responsible for candidates, Marcus Fox and Sir Anthony Royle, had tried to raise the number of women on the list to 10 per cent. After the 1983 election Emma Nicholson became Vice-Chairman of the Party with special responsibility for women and has adopted a policy of trying to encourage more professional women to stand as Conservative candidates, organising a series of 'High Flyers Conferences'. But consistent with its own philosophy the Party has not considered introducing any form of positive discrimination to get women on to short lists, and is the only major party not to have done so by the end of 1986. (The minor parties have on the whole a better record of fielding women candidates than the major ones.)

What impact has Mrs Thatcher herself had on the attitudes and role of women in the Conservative Party? She has expressed publicly the wish to see more women become active in politics and public life, but is usually criticised for taking no steps to promote them. Except for a very brief period when Baroness Young was Lord Privy Seal, she has run a Cabinet in which she was the sole woman. On the other hand, as she herself has claimed, she has appointed several women to ministerial posts, and in making Baroness Young a Minister of State for the Foreign Office has not always put them in recognised feminine posts. Her example may well have encouraged more women to believe they could succeed in politics, though it is hard to tell whether the rise in the number of women candidates between 1979 and 1983 was due to Mrs Thatcher, or simply was part of a trend visible in all the parties and a product of wider social changes. It has been suggested that Mrs Thatcher's demonstrable toughness and competence may have reduced men's prejudices against women in power. But the tendency of both Mrs Thatcher herself and of her colleagues to project her as the 'best man available for the job' has the effect of singling her out as a wholly atypical woman, an exception to join a list of strong women rulers who have surfaced in many historical periods. Psychological speculation about deep-rooted male fears of strong and powerful women might suggest that Mrs Thatcher's personality personifies what they fear, and may strengthen resistance to allowing women to get to the top in politics. In practice, however, both the positive and possibly negative influence of Mrs Thatcher is likely to be much less important than more general shifts in attitude, especially among younger women.

In considering the parties' policies on equal rights, and the position of women within them, it is important to ask whether they have been directly influenced by feminism, and whether the electoral pressure to bid for the women's vote has been a significant factor in altering policies. The first is relevant to assessing the impact of the feminist movement of the 1970s, one of the central issues for this book, and the second raises fundamental questions about the potential power of women's votes.

Women who espoused the original equal rights tradition of the suffrage movement have been active in all political parties, and a few women in Parliament upheld this tradition in the 1950s and 1960s. These included notable campaigners for women's rights in the Conservative Party like Irene Ward, as well as Labour women MPs. But in their response to the radical feminism of Women's Liberation there is a sharp differentiation between the parties. Conservatives have been predictably hostile to the ideas and activities emanating from a protest movement. Sally Oppenheim, who sponsored the 1972-73 Hamilton Bill to ban sex discrimination, went out of her way in a speech supporting the Bill to distance herself from the Women's Liberation Movement, and was booed by feminists in the gallery. Mrs

Thatcher attacked 'strident' feminists in a 1979 election speech. Whilst attitudes among Labour women to the new feminism have clearly varied, activists for women's rights like Joyce Butler and Jo Richardson have welcomed the support of a wider protest campaign. The young women who were caught up in consciousness-raising and protest in the early 1970s were in many cases sceptical of any attempt to work through established political channels, but if they were persuaded of the need to achieve political power, then the Labour Party was their natural home. There is clear evidence that during the 1970s younger feminists did begin to become active in constituency parties, and in the 1980s played a role in the Women's Action Committee and in the local authority women's committees. No member of Women's Liberation would dream of joining the Conservative Party, unless she underwent a dramatic conversion to belief in a non-permissive sexual morality and woman's natural domestic duties, as a few individuals did. Whilst the Liberals and SDP were most likely to attract a younger generation taking up a moderate equal rights feminism, and looking for professional and political careers, but only influenced indirectly by radical feminism.

However, the greatest influence of the new feminism on all the parties has probably been through its contribution to changing social attitudes, making women's inequality more visible and prompting a revival of concern about equal rights. Mrs Thatcher was clearly a beneficiary of new attitudes: she was elected to replace Mr Heath in 1975; it would have been unthinkable ten years earlier to choose a woman as party leader. Concern for women's rights seems slowly to have percolated into the Conservative Women's National Conference. *Spare Rib* (Dec. 1979, p. 13) noted sadly the Conference had voted to try to reduce unemployment by encouraging women to return to being housewives, and had opposed women's right to automatic reinstatement at work after maternity leave. By 1986 the *300 Group News* (Autumn 1986, p. 3) found encouragement in the fact that women at the Conservative Conference that year criticised Government proposals on taxation (which involved a transferable tax allowance likely to act as a disincentive to wives working) and on reducing maternity benefits.

Heightened awareness of women's rights as an issue appears to have prompted the parties to a degree of pre-electoral competition in 1986 in presenting policies favourable to women. There are obvious reasons why parties should make some attempt to court women, who make up over half the electorate; especially since allegiances to Conservative and Labour have become weaker during the 1970s and 1980s, and less simply correlated with social class than in the past, and voters more volatile. If there were an identifiable women's vote it could be decisive. But there is no evidence to date that women's voting behaviour has been strongly influenced by awareness of the parties' records or policies in relation to women. This could be because no party has in the past made women's rights and interests a salient issue – though on their past records feminists would judge Labour have done better by women than Conservatives since 1970. But the main reasons are almost certainly that women, like men, are predisposed by class, age, experience and temperament towards differing political attitudes and beliefs, and do not vote primarily as women; and that women as citizens react to major issues like the economy and defence. Women do not, therefore, see themselves as forming a coherent grouping with common interests when it comes to elections, though they may do so when pressure-group activity on specific women's issues is required.

Nevertheless, because the experience of women is different from men's and there is a tendency for women's attitudes to life and social issues to differ too, it is quite likely that women's voting behaviour may be distinctive. In the past political sociologists have believed that women tended to be more conservative than men, and evidence on voting behaviour for the period 1945–74 indicated that women were somewhat more likely to vote Conservative, though the percentage difference was not very great, and estimated at only 2.5 per cent in 1974 (Randall 1982: 49). One suggested reason for women's slightly higher propensity to vote Conservative has been that the old are more likely to vote Conservative than the young, and that there are more elderly women than men. Some detailed research into the 1964 election supported the importance of age as a factor and found young women more likely to vote Labour than young men. Whether older people become more conservative due to age, or are fixed in voting patterns they acquired when younger, is less clear. There is some evidence that voting has been largely determined by political choices made when people first vote: for example those who first voted in 1945 and chose Labour tended to remain loyal to Labour in 1970 (Pulzer 1975: 113). Another possible reason why more women have voted Conservative is that women tend to be more committed churchgoers, and there has been a correlation between active Church of England membership in the past and support for the Conservatives (Butler and Stokes 1971: 100–5). There is an overlap between religion and class, but working-class women in the Church of England might be more inclined to vote Conservative.

Since there has been a strong correlation between voting Labour and trade-union membership, one possible reason for more working-class women voting Conservative might have been that women who were housewives (and indeed women going out to work) were in the past less likely to be influenced by trade-union activity and allegiances. But research by Butler and Stokes (1971: 196) throws doubt on this theory, since they found in their data for 1964 very little difference between male trade-unionists and their wives in voting patterns, except among wives of trade-unionists in supervisory non-manual grades, where working-class identification would be less strong.

Nevertheless, it does seem plausible that women have reacted to government policies and opposition promises primarily as consumers rather than as wage workers, because they are responsible for the household budget. Even when increasing numbers of women were going out to work in the 1970s and joining trade unions, their primary interest was probably the family income. Barbara Castle put forward the view at the beginning of her *Diaries* that the vote during the 1970s was polarising on sex rather than class lines: 'The pursuit of money wage increases is a masculine syndrome; the fight for the social wage is a feminine need.' Women were interested in real wages and levels of social security (Castle 1980: 22). Concern about inflation was suggested by commentators as a reason for greater support for the Conservatives among women in poll findings before the 1979 election, even though Labour had just done a good deal to strengthen women's position (Coote 1978c).

Despite the polls, however, the 1979 election in fact marked an end to the previous built-in advantage to the Conservatives among women, since evidence drawn from the actual voting indicated that 45 per cent of the women voted Conservative against 46 per cent of the men (Crewe 1979). Poll findings for the 1983 election differ. The MORI polls suggested that slightly more women than men favoured the Conservatives, 46 per cent women to 44 per cent men (Kellner 1983: 7). But the BBC-commissioned poll by Gallup found that 46 per cent of men voted Conservative, but only 43 per cent of women, with more women switching to the Alliance. Ivor Crewe, who designed the Gallup poll, drew the confident conclusion that: 'For the first time ... the Conservatives drew less support from women than from men' (Crewe 1983: 5). If we accept provisionally that women's slightly greater tendency to vote Conservative was reversed in 1983 there are possible short-term and long-term explanations. There is some evidence from a Marplan poll published in February 1983 that women were more concerned to avoid cuts in health, education, social services and housing, whilst they were as concerned as men about unemployment as well as inflation (Rogers 1983: 158–9). If Mrs Thatcher benefited in 1983 from the 'Falklands factor' as many commentators assumed, then men may have enjoyed the vicarious thrill of military victory in the Falklands more than women.

There do seem, however, to be wider factors influencing women's voting in much of Western Europe, not solely in Britain. Recent elections in Scandinavia and France suggest women's previous propensity to vote Conservative has been reversed in these countries too (Lovenduski 1986b: 124–6). The emergence of new generations of women with expectations differing from those of their mothers, and influenced at least indirectly by the revival of feminism in the 1970s, is likely to have an impact on political behaviour. But it is not now clear what will influence women's voting in the future. As more women go out to work for the whole of their lives, and as more become engaged in professional and political careers, it could be argued the experience of women and men will converge; that women will be more highly politicised, and that gender differences in voting will gradually disappear. But since women still suffer from economic inequality and their legal rights are by no means fully secured, feminist issues could become more prominent in elections in the future. Though it is unlikely most women would vote solely on women's rights, they might well be influenced by how economic and welfare policies impinge on women. So the political parties may become more explicit about the significance of their policies for women as workers as well as consumers, and the policies on women's rights adopted at the 1986 party conferences may herald a new emphasis on women in future elections.

The 1987 election did not provide any conclusive evidence on the trend in women's votes. During the election the Labour Party stressed unemployment, education and the National Health Service, all likely to influence many women, and both Labour and the Alliance publicised their commitment to women's rights. The MORI poll suggested the same proportions of women and men voted for each major party (*New Society* 19 June 1987). But an age breakdown indicated that women under 35 swung away from the Conservatives to Labour compared with 1983 and were significantly more likely to vote Labour than young men. Women between 35 and 54 were however rather more likely to vote Conservative (*The Times* 13 June 1987). So there did seem to be a gap between generations of women. Efforts to increase the number of women in Parliament did have some effect. The Conservative Party had in the 1987 election 17 women MPs, Labour 21 and the Liberals, SDP and Scottish Nationalists each returned one.

Chapter six

CAN THE LAW SECURE WOMEN'S RIGHTS?

INTRODUCTION

Legislation has been a key instrument for securing women's rights. The steady improvement in the rights of married women, for example, over the last 130 years, can be charted partly in terms of a series of Acts of Parliament. When women organise themselves for political action to improve their economic and social position, demands for legislation have been a natural focus of campaigning; and pressure for new laws has usually united a wide spectrum of women's organisations and enlisted the support of male Members of Parliament or of political parties. So promoting legislation to extend the rights of women has always been a central concern for feminism. On the other hand, women have often been disappointed by the results of new laws, and there are numerous factors which combine to limit the effectiveness of law as a means of radical change in behaviour and attitudes. So there is a need to look more closely at the role of law and what it can or cannot achieve.

Our aim here is to focus in particular on laws designed to prevent discrimination, to examine the purpose of passing laws like the Sex Discrimination Act and to discuss the problems of making such legislation work. In addition to a general discussion on the role of law let us look in more detail at the specific form the key laws designed to secure women's equality have taken – we concentrate on the Equal Pay Act and the Sex Discrimination Act – and to assess their achievements over ten years and their obvious omissions. The means of enforcement available and the role of the EOC in making use of the laws and campaigning about inadequate implementation also require analysis.

The effectiveness of law is influenced not only by general social and economic factors and by specific provisions of the laws concerned but also by the political and legal context within which the law has to operate. It is therefore interesting to observe how British legislation on women's rights has been affected by membership of the EEC and by decisions taken by the European Courts. It is also relevant to consider briefly why passing laws may be less effective in Britain than in some other countries with different constitutional, legal and political traditions.

Finally, in this chapter we explore two interesting and controversial questions which have been debated in the context of legislating for women's rights. The first is whether it is desirable to go beyond forbidding discrimination against women to incorporate the principle of positive discrimination in favour of women in order to combat deep-seated inequalities. The second question is whether it is compatible with claims for total equality with men for women also to ask for certain kinds of special protection under the law. Both these issues raise theoretical problems about interpreting equality, rights and justice; the second also involves asking about the real aims of feminism and looking at women's position in society.

CAN LAWS STOP DISCRIMINATION?

One reason for passing laws to forbid discrimination is to try to influence attitudes. Passing a law gives moral authority and the added weight of official government policy to the principle that discrimination is wrong, so promoting long-term social acceptance of the right to equal treatment. Those who believe strongly that discrimination is justified may continue to oppose or ridicule the law, but legislation tends to have the effect of influencing the tone of official and public comments on the issue and so probably of shifting middle-ground opinion. Legislation is also likely to influence the attitudes of the group suffering discrimination by making clear that equal treatment is a right, not a privilege or an exception.

The most immediate reason for passing a law is to influence behaviour, since it is easier to promote outward compliance than to change deep-seated personal beliefs or attitudes. Thus a law on discrimination is designed to influence the behaviour of relevant institutions – companies, trade unions, banks, building societies or schools for example – and to alter the rules by which they operate. But behaviour and attitudes are not of course wholly separate; where discriminatory behaviour is normal it reinforces acceptance of discrimination, and so ending explicit discrimination is also likely to bring about gradual acceptance of equal treatment as the norm.

A third reason often cited for legislation is to give the protection of the law to persons who may not themselves be prejudiced but have to work in a strongly prejudiced social context, and so find it difficult to avoid discriminating. Once the law is passed they can refuse to discriminate on the grounds that they have to obey the law. This argument was first evolved in relation to the civil rights struggle by blacks in the USA and applied particularly to the Deep South, but has been transferred to the British context to strengthen arguments for legislation against first racial and then sexual discrimination. It may apply with rather less force to sexual discrimination in this country since in recent years prejudice has not in most cases been so overt and so extreme as to force individuals to discriminate. But since quite a lot of discrimination at work stems from traditional attitudes to what is men's and women's work, employers might be able to appeal to the Sex Discrimination Act to justify putting women into 'men's jobs'.

Finally, of course, the purpose of legislation is not only to change attitudes, influence behaviour and give moral backing to those who wish to practise equal treatment, but to provide means of enforcing a change in social and economic practices. British laws against discrimination have on the whole sought to persuade rather than invoking the sanctions of law, on the grounds that this approach was more appropriate in an area involving general social attitudes and relationships between people. The Race Relations Board set up under the 1965 Race Relations Act had no direct enforcement powers or powers to investigate individual complaints adequately; the emphasis on conciliation was so dominant in the Board's procedures that in three years no case of discrimination reached the courts, though the Board had sole responsibility to act on behalf of individual complainants. A further Act in 1968 widened the scope of measures to combat discrimination, but maintained the belief that persuasion was the best policy. By the mid 1970s, however, there was acceptance of the need to provide for means of enforcement, which were included in both the 1975 Sex Discrimination Act and the 1976 Race Relations Act. But, as we will see below, whether these powers should be used remained controversial in relation to the Sex Discrimination Act.

It is interesting to note that in Britain the theoretical justification for legislation against discrimination was elaborated in relation to race, and the White Paper proposing the Sex Discrimination Act simply repeated the reasons given for the Race Relations Act. In addition, both the laws against racial and sexual discrimination drew heavily on the theories and legal experience of the United States. The law has in practice, however, been used less effectively in Britain than in the

USA, partly because of differences in their legal and political systems, to be considered briefly later.

It may be misleading to press the comparison between the discrimination suffered by blacks in our society and the discrimination suffered by women too far. Women are 52% of society, not a minority, which in one sense makes their inequality even more unjust. In both cases discrimination is worse for those at the bottom of the class system, but proportionately more women enjoy the advantages of being born into the middle or upper classes. But the greatest difference is that women do have a special role in the family in our society, and are physically different from men: this is the source of much discrimination at work. As a result, legislation to prevent discrimination is more complex in the case of women, has to include special provisions like maternity leave and raises difficult questions about exempting women from certain kinds of work and the need for protective legislation for women.

What are the limits of law? One set of considerations concern the inherent limits of law in changing the nature of society. The first limitation is the impossibility of transforming deep-seated attitudes by simply passing a law. One of the standard objections to legislating against discrimination has been that it is necessary to change people's hearts and minds to achieve real change. This objection is too sweeping to constitute a valid argument against legal measures which, we have argued above, can effect some alterations in both public attitudes and institutional behaviour. But it is nevertheless true that ingrained attitudes based on historic social practices do change only slowly, and therefore laws may promote lip-service to the principle of equal treatment and token gestures towards implementing it, without resulting in any fundamental alterations in the economic and social structures of society.

Lack of real change may, however, be ascribed less to the inflexibility of social attitudes than to the intractable nature of economic forces and of other social factors. Laws can alter overt and simple forms of discrimination, but not the way the economy functions. It has often been argued for example that in the United States federal government legislation and Supreme Court decisions could end segregation in public places in the South, but failed to touch the realities of *de facto* discrimination in the North: the segregation of most blacks in the slum ghettos, the poor education received by most black children, the high unemployment rate among black people and their concentration in the lowest-paid jobs when they could get work. Legislation against racial discrimination in this country has failed to alter a similar pattern among the black population, and as we saw in Chapter 4 women also still tend to be clustered at the bottom if their position is measured in terms of income, job status or political power. The position of both blacks and women is also worsened by economic depression.

Have there been observable social and economic constraints on the effective operation of the Equal Pay and Sex Discrimination Acts? The answer is clearly 'yes'. The importance of attitudes among both employers and male workers is indicated by the steps taken by many employers to minimise the effects of the Equal Pay Act on their wage structure. Employers' federations examined and gave advice on implementation of the Act, and measures suggested included reclassifying jobs and perhaps slightly changing the content so that men and women could not be directly compared, or to cut down on jobs being done by both men and women. One management memorandum suggested that men could still be paid more than women by giving them long-service payments (i.e. no maternity leave), merit payments for qualifications or 'competence', attendance bonuses and payments for willingness to work overtime (NCCL 1975: 8–9). Research carried out by the London School of Economics (LSE) between 1974 and 1977 on the effects of the Equal Pay and Sex Discrimination Acts found that while there was a clear failure to comply with the law in only a few cases, there were numerous examples of possible non-compliance. But even more important was the effect of perfectly legal measures taken to ensure that the Equal Pay Act had as little effect on women's wages as possible (Snell 1979: 43–7). Some employers also admitted that they were prepared to ignore the Sex Discrimination Act. One personnel manager told the LSE researchers that: 'Legislation doesn't mean a company will act differently. We won't change our personnel decisions, just how we go about them. Just as we keep a "good" mix on race by finding reasons to reject most Asians, we will find reasons to reject women for some jobs.' (Snell 1979: 49.)

Later research by the EOC also suggested limited compliance. A 1979 survey of 768 establishments found that 5 per cent were prepared to admit openly to breaking the Equal Pay Act, and although a third had job-evaluation schemes, only 4 per cent of these had been revised or introduced to promote equal pay. The Sex Discrimination Act appeared to have a very limited impact. Only 18 per cent of the establishments surveyed had changed their practices to meet the Act's requirements, and in many cases this meant changing their advertising for jobs. Only a small minority could and would produce a written policy on equal opportunities, and only 3 per cent practised some form of positive discrimination. But there were some signs of marginal improvement: in 6 per cent of the establishments women were doing jobs they had not formerly done; and 14 per cent of managers said promotion opportunities for women had increased, about half of them attributing this improvement to changing management attitudes as a result of legislation (EOC 1981c: 8–11).

A number of different motives for minimising the effects of the equality laws can be discerned. The most obvious is economic: employers do not normally wish to pay higher wages to their workforce. But employers were also influenced by anxiety about the reaction of the men working for them if women were to receive equal pay, and the LSE study found evidence that male workers did sometimes react strongly (Snell 1979: 46). Employers also argued that men would object to women in supervisory posts. In addition, some employers were motivated by their own sense of what was traditional and fitting in the employment of men and women, or by a belief that women were less able to be reliable workers. The CBI had opposed a law to ban sex discrimination in 1972 on these kinds of grounds, as we saw in Chapter 2. Some managers told the LSE study that Sex Discrimination was not needed because men and women were in the jobs they did best; others admitted discrimination but saw no need to change their personnel practices (Snell 1979: 48–9). Employers also tend to resent Government legislation and interference in general.

The role of the trade unions is clearly important too, since unions were in a position to strengthen or weaken women's right to equal pay in negotiating details of job-evaluation schemes or collective agreements. Unions could also help women take a case to industrial tribunals. But many unions still tended to be more concerned for their male than their female members in the 1970s, despite growing membership among women. So trade unions did not usually exert effective pressure on employers to implement the spirit or even the letter of the Equal Pay and Sex Discrimination Acts.

Economic constraints have to some extent been recognised in legal decisions about the operation of the equality laws. Questions concerning volume of work and the level of profits have been debated in a number of equal pay cases as a factor which may justify unequal pay (EOC Annual Reports 1983: 5). But the major economic pressures derive of course from mass unemployment. The recession has undermined women's bargaining position and increased job segregation, which has always been a key cause of inequality. Since the equality laws were passed economic conditions have become increasingly unfavourable to women achieving equality at work.

Despite the importance of broader social and economic factors in creating a climate favourable or unfavourable to the implementation of laws against discrimination, it is also necessary to look at the actual scope of the laws and the means of enforcement available. The effectiveness of laws depends in part on legal considerations relating to the wording of the Acts and the procedures for hearing complaints of discrimination. On these grounds it is widely accepted that the existing laws could be improved.

LOOPHOLES IN THE EQUAL PAY AND SEX DISCRIMINATION ACTS

The loopholes in the Equal Pay and Sex Discrimination Acts include both the numerous exceptions not covered by anti-discrimination legislation, and the gaps left by the actual content and drafting of the Acts.

Certain institutions are excluded from the operation of the Acts: the armed services are not covered by either the Equal Pay or Sex Discrimination Acts; private households and firms with less than six employees, private clubs and churches are excluded from the Sex Discrimination Act. Certain issues are also excluded; notably retirement age and pensions. Perhaps most important of all, previous parliamentary legislation (or regulations under that legislation) is not covered by the Sex Discrimination Act. Hence the exclusion of immigration rules, taxation and social security where discrimination in various forms has persisted. These gaps can of course be filled by other measures designed to promote equality – as happened to some extent under the Labour Government. But supplementary laws and rules are easier to repeal than the Sex Discrimination Act itself, and as we have seen in Chapter 4 the Conservative Government has weakened or reversed some of the measures designed to strengthen women's rights.

The Equal Pay Act has also been criticised for its wording, which fails in practice to cover many women workers. The Act requires equal pay for 'like work' with that of a man employed by the same firm or group of firms; since women are often segregated in 'women's work' they often cannot claim equal pay under the terms of the Act. The Act did allow another venue for women to claim equal pay: if their work had been assessed of 'equal value' under a job-evaluation scheme. Much then depended on the scheme; some schemes were deliberately altered to favour men in preparation for the coming into force of the Equal Pay Act, for example by giving higher value to lifting heavy weights than to manual dexterity (Snell 1979: 45). In addition the Act covered collective provisions – employer's pay structures, collective agreements negotiated with the unions and Wage Council orders – so that explicit pay discrimination between men and women in such agreements could be challenged. Nevertheless, the LSE study found that in 15 of the 26 establishments studied groups of women were not able to claim equal pay under any provision of the Act; these were women in such traditional female roles as cleaners and canteen assistants, clerks and secretaries. In most cases the groups concerned were quite small, but in one organisation 4,000 women typists were not covered by the Act (Snell 1979: 38).

The Sex Discrimination Act has less obvious gaps in its wording and covers a wide range of issues. It also includes one very important principle: it prohibits 'indirect discrimination', that is, practices which in effect operate against women. The concept of indirect discrimination grew out of the experience of the American Supreme Court in interpreting the Civil Rights Act; the Court decided that even if no intention to discriminate were present certain apparently neutral rules in practice could operate to the detriment of a particular group, and incorporated this principle into its decisions in 1971. The British Home Secretary, Roy Jenkins, decided to include indirect discrimination in the Sex Discrimination Act after a visit to the USA. Indirect discrimination is certainly relevant to the problems faced by women at work; for example certain age bars for training, recruitment or promotion can penalise women who have taken time off to have children. But the Sex Discrimination Act nevertheless clearly lacks bite; employers did have to take account of the Equal Pay Act even if only to evade it, whereas we have seen that many did nothing at all in response to the Sex Discrimination Act.

A NCCL survey of the operation of the two Acts after their first year of being in force, did find a few specific gaps in the Sex Discrimination Act revealed by tribunal cases. For example it failed to prohibit the practice of some companies and universities of refusing to allow husband and wife to work in the same department, a practice which operated against the wife. The wording of the Act also allowed an employer to dismiss a woman who announced her intention of getting married, since the Act only forbade discrimination against women on grounds of marriage if they were already married. Tribunal cases also showed that some forms of discrimination were not properly covered by either Act. A clerical worker, Mrs Meeks, claimed that it was indirect discrimination to pay part-time workers at a lower hourly rate than full-time workers, since the overwhelming majority of part-timers were women who also had family responsibilities. But the Sex Discrimination Act did not cover pay, whilst under the Equal Pay Act Mrs Meeks could not compare herself with a relevant man and the Act does not in any case include the concept of indirect discrimination (Coussins 1976: 64–70).

ENFORCEMENT OF THE ACTS

Even laws containing loopholes may have impact if rigorously enforced, but it has been agreed by all commentators that there are in practice often considerable difficulties in taking a case under the equality laws to industrial tribunals or courts. Enforcement should not of course be measured solely by the number of legal cases or by the number won by the complainants; women may complain successfully to their employers without having to go to a tribunal, and trade unions or the EOC may negotiate a settlement under the equality laws before a case is heard. The EOC does in fact spend quite a lot of time in arranging such settlements. Nevertheless, it seems probable that employers will be more likely to settle out of court if they envisage a legal case is likely to go against them. If women face difficulties in knowing whether they have a case under the Acts and then have to overcome major obstacles in applying to tribunals or courts the enforcement provisions are clearly unsatisfactory.

Women have found it easier to know if they were suffering discrimination under the Equal Pay Act than under the Sex Discrimination Act, presumably because pay rates are easier to discover. The LSE study found that no women in the organisations they surveyed had brought cases of discrimination to tribunals, or even raised them within the organisation, mainly because women applying for jobs or for promotion often had no means of knowing if discrimination did occur. Even if they suspected it, proof was very difficult. Therefore, in the early years there were far more cases under the Equal Pay Act than under the Sex Discrimination Act: 1,256 cases were heard under the Equal Pay Act between 1976 and 1980 and 345 were successful, compared with 394 cases under the Sex Discrimination Act of which only 96 were upheld. Under both Acts only about a third of the applications initially made reached a tribunal or court – the rest were settled or withdrawn for various reasons.

On the other hand, cases under the Equal Pay Act fell off much more sharply after the first two years, and were reduced to a trickle in the early 1980s. Women either despaired of using the Act effectively after initial enthusiasm or became increasingly aware of their need for a job at any price as unemployment rose and more women found themselves having to keep a family. The number of Sex Discrimination Act cases has remained at an average of about 200 applications a year, perhaps because of the range of issues involved.

The responsibility for taking cases under both Acts to industrial tribunals (or to the civil courts in non-industrial cases under the Sex Discrimination Act) lay with the individual woman. It also stacked the cards against her, since she did not have adequate powers to demand relevant information and was not entitled to legal aid in presenting her case before a tribunal, though she might get some legal advice in advance. She also risked creating bad relations with her employer. Some women were able to get union support, especially for equal pay cases, though only about a fifth got this kind of support in the first two years. Others were given advice by the EOC or NCCL, and a few were legally represented by one of them. But many women had no expert help in presenting their case against their employer to a tribunal.

Women were further handicapped by the procedures laid down under the Acts and the way they were implemented. All applications lodged by complainants were sent to the Advisory, Conciliation and Arbitration Service (ACAS), which had the task of trying to settle the case before it went to a tribunal. It has been questioned whether ACAS is the most appropriate body to deal with cases involving discrimination. The role of ACAS is to conciliate and seek a compromise between employer and employee, and to avoid cases reaching a tribunal; whereas the purpose of many women may be – as the ACAS 1978 Report noted – to uphold the principle of non-discrimination. Research by Jeanne Gregory, who tried to contact applicants whose cases were dropped in 1978, found that in her sample half of those who had been contacted by ACAS had not found the officers helpful, and some felt that they had been put under pressure to accept an unsatisfactory settlement. A minority of women also felt the officers were positively unsympathetic to them, and it is clearly relevant here that extremely few officers are women. The four men in the sample who had complained under the Sex Discrimination Act and been contacted by ACAS found the officers helpful (Gregory 1982: 79–84). The numbers in this survey were small – 82 altogether of whom only 56 had been seen by an ACAS officer – but its findings were partly confirmed by complaints received early on by the NCCL about the behaviour of some ACAS officers (Coussins 1976: 17–18).

If a woman reached an industrial tribunal she faced the problem that the initial burden of proof that her pay was unequal, or that she had suffered discrimination because of her sex, lay with her. So under the

Equal Pay and Sex Discrimination Acts – contrary to the practice of other employment legislation in the 1970s which put the onus of proof on the employer – the employer gained the benefit of the doubt. Some women who appeared to have a very strong case lost before the tribunal.

It is arguable that in some cases tribunals failed to apply the law properly. Tribunals are composed of a legally trained chairman aided by two members of a panel of lay members available for tribunal hearings; the main responsibility lies with the chairman. During 1978 the NCCL observed sixteen tribunals in action and also monitored the written decisions of tribunals, and concluded that some showed a lack of understanding of the admittedly complex provisions of the Acts. There were some clearly anomalous tribunal decisions: for example a tribunal held that the Leicester Council for Voluntary Service was justified in paying a woman playleader £400 p.a. *less* than her male co-worker because she had *more* responsibility for supervising the overall project than he did, and this constituted a 'practical difference' under the Act (Coussins 1976: 26–7). The NCCL found some chairmen who went out of their way to be helpful to women who lacked legal representation, or to point out other possible legal remedies in their written decisions if the tribunal had dismissed a case. But it also found evidence of clear prejudice among some tribunal chairmen, and pointed out that in 1976 only 27.9 per cent of the panel of lay members were women, and there was no obligation for a woman to be on a tribunal dealing with sex discrimination cases (Coussins 1976: 43–7).

In addition to all the other hurdles a woman has to face in taking a case to a tribunal, there is the possibility of victimisation by her employer. The possibility of dismissal is a strong deterrent, especially in a period of high unemployment, and the fact that the Sex Discrimination Act prohibits victimisation for pursuing equal rights does not prevent it happening. There is clear evidence that women have been dismissed for asking for equal pay. For example two women clerks were dismissed by South Pembrokeshire District Council after they had made an application for equal pay with district rating officers (Coussins 1976: 67). In another case a woman buyer started Equal Pay proceedings in 1976 because a male buyer who was twenty years younger and with no previous experience was earning over £800 p.a. more than she was. The company made her redundant in April under the cover of some reorganisation and dismissed her in November. She won the equal pay claim, though the company appealed, and was eventually awarded £3,671 in compensation for unfair dismissal and victimisation in November 1978 (EOC n.d.: 99).

Women can, of course, take their cases to higher courts. In practice employers were more likely to appeal against the finding of an industrial tribunal that went against them, but some women also pursued their cases to the Employment Appeals Tribunal which, unlike the lower tribunals, could set legal precedents. Beyond the Appeals Tribunal either party could take the matter to the Court of Appeal or the House of Lords. But for an individual to approach the higher courts takes a long time, is prohibitively expensive and normally impossible without support from a body like the EOC. The first case under the Sex Discrimination Act reached the House of Lords late in 1979, and concerned the important principle whether employers were obliged to divulge relevant documents to complainants, even if these were confidential. Cases of both sexual and racial discrimination were involved and the EOC and the Commission for Racial Equality were represented in an advisory role. Employers' records were needed to prove possible discrimination in promotion procedures. The Lords ruled that confidential documents should be produced if they were essential to the case, but left the decision on the relevance of the documents to the tribunal concerned, which was empowered to inspect them.

The other channel for enforcing employment legislation is to refer collective agreements or employers' pay structures to the Central Arbitration Committee. The responsibility for doing so lies with the Secretary of State for Employment, with trade unions in the case of jointly negotiated collective agreements or with the employer. In the early years after the passage of the equality laws the Committee played a positive role in scrutinising provisions in collective agreements and had concerned itself with forms of indirect discrimination. But the powers of the Committee were curbed by a 1979 High Court ruling denying the Committee's right to amend covertly discriminatory pay structures, and this meant in effect – as the EOC noted – a narrowing of the scope of the Equal Pay Act affecting collective agreements (EOC Annual Reports 1980: 45; 1981: 5).

Because of perceived loopholes in the Equal Pay and Sex Discrimination Acts and weaknesses in enforcement, concerned organisations like the Fawcett Society, the Equal Pay and Opportunities Campaign and Women in Media all proposed changes. The EOC itself formally proposed a list of amendments to the Government in 1980: in addition to the abolition of some exemptions, it proposed that the Equal Pay Act be extended to cover indirect discrimination, to enable equal pay for work of equal value, to allow a woman to compare herself with a 'hypothetical man' and to exclude part-time working as grounds for paying a lower hourly rate. The EOC urged that the burden of proof in cases before tribunals should be shifted from the individual making the complaint to the employer or institution concerned, and it also suggested extending the powers of the Central Arbitration Committee to scrutinise collective agreements for pay structures for direct and indirect discrimination (EOC Annual Reports 1981: 39). The NCCL produced an even more comprehensive set of amendments in 1983: it wanted to amalgamate the two Acts, to make discrimination in relation to death or retirement illegal, and to strengthen sections of the Sex Discrimination Act that now allow for some positive action on behalf of women. Proposals to strengthen enforcement included making it possible (as it has been in the USA) to bring actions not only on behalf of individuals but on behalf of a 'class' of persons likely to be affected by discrimination, and either to train ACAS officers in how to apply the equality laws or preferably creating a new group of 'equality officers' attached to the EOC (Scorer and Sedley 1983).

The Government submitted a group of Amendments to the Sex Discrimination Act that were passed by Parliament in November 1986, and that were designed to extend its scope rather than the enforcement provisions. Small businesses and partnerships, previously excluded, now fall under the Act. So do private households, but a genuine occupational qualification has been introduced which allows sex discrimination in certain circumstances, for example where close contact with an individual is involved, as in nursing undertaken in the home. The new Amendments also stipulated that collective agreements between employers which entailed direct or indirect discrimination based on sex or marriage would become void and would have to be renegotiated.

One provision was a response to a European Court ruling in 1986, when a nurse, Miss Helen Marshall, won her case against her local health authority, complaining that she had been forced to retire earlier than she wished simply because she was a woman. The Court in Luxemburg ruled that compulsory retirement of women at an earlier age than men constituted discrimination on grounds of sex and was contrary to EEC law. So the 1986 Amendments require all employers to set equal retirement ages for their staff in future.

A more controversial clause concerns the issue of protective legislation, and will mean that women will no longer be exempted under the Factories Act from working night shifts. The EOC has supported removing special restrictions on women doing manual work in industry on the grounds that it limits their opportunities, but the

TUC has wished to retain this restriction to protect women's interests, and ensured that the 1975 Act did not repeal protective legislation.

THE ROLE OF THE EQUAL OPPORTUNITIES COMMISSION

Proposals to reform the laws tend to include provisions to strengthen the powers and widen the role of the EOC. But commentators have queried whether, especially in the early years, it made good use of the powers it already has. As the body officially responsible for overseeing and helping to ensure implementation of the Acts, the EOC's performance is clearly relevant to an assessment of how far existing legislation has worked.

Under the Sex Discrimination Act the Commission has responsibility for making available information about the Acts and their implementation and advising the Government on how they are working; its broader brief is to work towards the ending of discrimination. The Act envisages that one of the key instruments for enforcing compliance with the laws would be the conduct of formal investigations, under which the EOC would have the right to demand documents and question witnesses, and could then issue a non-discrimination notice, which could be upheld by the courts. In addition, in proven cases of persistent discrimination, the Commission had the right to seek a court order. The EOC was given discretion to assist individuals to take cases to tribunals and courts where a question of principle was involved, or where other special circumstances arose, but it was not intended that the Commission should devote a large proportion of its resources to pursuing individual cases.

There were bound to be disagreements about the strategy the Commission should adopt and whether it should spend much of the time operating discreetly behind the scenes or should opt for a more publicity-seeking and campaigning stance. But the way in which the Commission was set up ensured that it would use its powers cautiously. The members of the Commission were appointed by the Home Office, following normal procedures for setting up quangos; that is, by ensuring representation of the powerful interest groups associated with Government and to draw on a panel of acceptable establishment figures. Interests represented on the Commission were the CBI, TUC, and the fields of education and law, and there were individuals representing Scotland and Wales. All nominees from women's rights organisations and recognised feminists were excluded, though there was one representative of family planning. The composition of the EOC could be seen as an example of how Civil

Service procedures tend to blunt and transform the purposes of politicians, since Roy Jenkins did appear to be seeking an effective policy against sexual discrimination. Alternatively, it can be viewed as an example of the growing corporatism of British politics in the 1970s, since both the CBI and the TUC had three representatives each on a Commission of at most fifteen members. Either way it was a Commission unlikely to make maximum use of its powers. The representation of the CBI was particularly inhibiting since one of the main groups the Commission had to deal with were employers. One of the CBI representatives wrote to Confederation members that CBI influence was responsible for the EOC deciding to issue advisory guidelines to employers, rather than codes of practice which could (under a clause of the 1976 Race Relations Act) be admitted as evidence in tribunal cases (Byrne and Lovenduski 1978: 137, 143).

The Commission was also hampered by the need to ensure representation of the two main parties, since the Conservative Party favoured a more low-key and conciliatory approach to women's rights. This problem was magnified by the fact that the Chairman (*sic*) Betty Lockwood was a former full-time Labour Party worker at Transport House and her deputy, Lady Howe, was a Conservative, and that both worked full-time for the Commission. The EOC also had to bear in mind that if a Conservative Government came to power it might decide to curb the EOC's role, and was more likely to do so if the Commission had made itself very controversial. Byrne and Lovenduski (1978: 46) suggest in their analysis that the problems posed for this kind of body by the alternation of political parties with opposed views on many issues, 'adversary politics', may have encouraged 'foot dragging' by the Commission.

The EOC was strongly criticised by many feminists for lack of achievement in its first two years, and in particular its failure to use its enforcement powers. For example the EOC pursued only two formal investigations between 1976 and 1978: one into the Tameside Education Authority, publicly accused of sending twice as many boys as girls to grammar schools; and one into the Electrolux Company where there were widespread complaints about a discriminatory grading system. The Tameside inquiry may have been prompted by the Labour Government, engaged in a confrontation with the Conservative local authority over its refusal to go comprehensive, and the Electrolux inquiry was initiated by Mr Justice Phillips of the Employment Appeals Tribunal, who publicly suggested the EOC should investigate the company. Neither inquiry was satisfactory; the Commission failed to unearth evidence at Tameside and the

Electrolux inquiry dragged on for two years and ended with the EOC issuing a non-discrimination notice covering matters the company had already acted upon. The EOC did take up quite a few cases before industrial tribunals and a few before the courts, but Jeanne Gregory argued that the EOC interpreted the terms of the Act too narrowly and concentrated on developing case law, whereas the Commission for Racial Equality with a similar brief has extended legal aid much more widely to those with a real case and as a result individuals continued to invoke the Act, whereas fewer women came forward to contest sexual discrimination (Gregory 1982: 86). There were also individual complaints that the EOC backed down from giving legal aid and switched support to more winnable cases.

The comparative inactivity of the Commission in its first two years was due not only to the composition of the Commission and its attitudes, but to specific administrative problems, and conflicts between the staff and Commissioners. Because the Commission was set up in a hurry it took time to recruit qualified staff; Civil Servants seconded to the Commission were often used for inappropriate jobs, and the Commission was early on deluged with individual enquiries which diverted energies from its real task of evolving a more general strategy. Early lack of clear administrative direction from the top was compounded by ideological conflicts between staff and Commissioners. Many able people committed to the aims of equality for women were recruited – about 75 per cent of them women – but many felt the EOC should be pursuing a clearer and more activist policy. This frustration led to in-fighting and bitterness, a very high initial staff turnover and to a major confrontation between staff and Commissioners at a weekend conference in June 1978. One result of this weekend was the emergence of a group within the Commission sympathetic to the aims of the staff (Coote 1978a: 734–7).

After its initial problems the EOC has taken a stronger line on use of enforcement powers. It launched four more formal investigations into employment conditions in 1979, but these also proved to be long drawn out: provisional reports on SOGAT and the Leeds Building Society were submitted to the organisations in 1982, but final reports were not completed until 1984. An inquiry into discrimination in the appointment and promotion of women teachers in one school was finished in 1983, with the finding that the law on sex discrimination had not been broken but procedures had not been properly followed. The fourth inquiry into a college of further education was delayed by a court injunction, and resumed again in 1983. So the Commission continued to have difficulties in the use of this instrument for preventing discrimination. But it has reversed its earlier decision not to produce a code of practice for employers: a draft code was published in 1980 and a revised draft circulated in 1982; the EOC submitted a final draft to the Secretary of State in 1984 to be placed before Parliament. The EOC has expanded its legal aid to individuals: between 1981 and 1983 it was involved in well over 100 tribunal or court cases each year, and has backed a number of cases up to the Court of Appeal and the House of Lords.

The Commission has generally adopted a more positive and comprehensive programme since 1978. It has initiated or supported a wide range of research and produced numerous publications, and has been less shy of publicity than it was initially. It has also become more willing to give money to feminist organisations and to work with them on various issues, perhaps influenced by the fact that two Commissioners identified with women's rights were appointed (Meehan 1985: 140, 222). The EOC became involved in the 1980s in promoting positive action to create equal opportunities, and has cooperated with some local authorities, financial institutions, industrial companies and trade unions to widen training and jobs available to women. A campaign to promote women in science and engineering (WISE) was launched by the EOC in 1984 jointly with the Engineering Council.

The EOC has, however, on the whole maintained a low-key consultative approach in trying to influence the policy of public bodies and the Government, though it did advertise in the press on tax and social security issues. It has given evidence to public inquiries and Royal Commissions on various topics, and has formally commented on government legislation in fields like immigration and maternity leave. But much of the time the EOC has operated behind the scenes in consulting with bodies like ACAS and the Manpower Services Commission and with various Civil Service departments. The Commission has quite often found itself obstructed at this level; the Department of Education and Science for example tried early on to remove education from the remit of the EOC. Lack of cooperation by public bodies and the Civil Service may be ascribed to normal bureaucratic resistance to external 'interference' and has occurred under both Labour and the Conservatives. But the notable lack of enthusiasm for women's rights displayed by Mrs Thatcher's Government has clearly put no pressure on Civil Servants to cooperate with the EOC.

Given the Conservative Government's lack of sympathy for policies designed to ensure equality for women, and its general penchant for deregulation of the economy, the EOC has suffered less from cuts since 1979 than might have been expected – and less than the Commission for Racial Equality. This fact could be seen as a vindication of the EOC's previous strategy of maintaining a fairly low and non-controversial profile. On the other hand, it could equally be seen as evidence that the Commission had failed to use its powers vigorously and had in practice conformed to the Conservative model of its proper role (Meehan 1982: 16).

LIMITATIONS ON LAW IN THE BRITISH CONTEXT

One set of reasons for the failure of the equality laws to have the radical results many hoped for lies not in the drafting of the legislation or the possible over-caution of the EOC but in the way law operates in the British legal and political context. Recourse to law has been a crucial element in the campaign for civil rights by black citizens of the USA and later by feminists, both in terms of federal legislation and in terms of court rulings favourable to civil rights. By contrast the use of law is less effective in Britain.

One important difference is the lack of a written Constitution and of a formal Bill of Rights in the UK. In the United States the Supreme Court has a specifically political role in interpreting the Constitution and in adjudicating whether governmental or other practices infringe the rights of individuals under the Constitution, and the tendency to reach broad decisions in principle extends down to lower courts as well. In the American system the courts can restrain the Government and can interpret legislation in the spirit of the Constitution. By contrast British courts now have a more limited role, and tend to interpret government legislation more narrowly.

There are other differences in the practices of courts and in the attitudes of ordinary citizens to use of the courts to redress their wrongs. American courts are less closely bound by judicial precedents than in Britain and admit a wider range of evidence; for example when the Supreme Court ruled in a famous decision in 1954 that segregated education was unconstitutional, it reversed a much earlier decision which had reached the opposite conclusion, and in reaching its decision it allowed sociological evidence about the impact of separate schools and colleges for blacks in the Deep South to be considered. Americans are also a more litigious people than the British – the courts seem to be viewed as a natural source of redress, whereas in the UK the Dickensian view that the law is an arcane and labyrinthine process that benefits only the lawyers, and brings nothing but grief to individuals rash enough to engage in civil suits, still lingers. In the field of industrial law British trade unions have been chary of working through tribunals and have in the past much preferred to pursue their aims through collective agreements and strike action when necessary. British attitudes to law and to courts or tribunals reflect the fact that the ethos of British political life is less democratic, less egalitarian and less individualistic than in the USA. Government and the judiciary have been instruments of class privilege in the eyes of ordinary people, whether they have responded by accepting the situation or by uniting in working-class solidarity to fight it.

The objective differences in the role of the courts and the different attitudes towards them have meant that whereas American pressure groups frequently resort to court action, British pressure groups have done so more rarely. Nevertheless, it can be argued that attitudes are changing in Britain, that many in the legal profession see a case for a Bill of Rights and a wider role for the courts, that legal aid for defence of the underprivileged is more widely available since the development of radical law centres in the late 1960s, and that the fact of laws which forbid racial and sexual discrimination encourage resort to legal redress. Political movements in the 1960s and 1970s also encouraged a strong sense that members of various groups have rights, and this consciousness has of course increased markedly among women themselves. The fact that in the first two years after the Equal Pay Act came into force about 2,500 applications were filed, despite all the inhibiting factors for the individual women involved, suggests quite a widespread willingness to assert their rights.

In addition it might be argued that cumulative experience of the operation of the Equal Pay and Sex Discrimination Acts may encourage more women to take their case to the tribunals or courts, especially if successes for the individuals involved are given publicity. Such cases can also be expected to have some impact on the practices of various institutions. Two well-publicised cases with obvious implications for future practice were brought by a policewoman and by the parents of three schoolgirls. In the first case an attractive policewoman was removed from car patrol duty because her superiors heard rumours that she was having an affair with her male partner; she complained and was then moved from the traffic division back on to the beat. The industrial tribunal upheld her complaint of sex discrimination and victimisation (*Guardian* 22 Dec. 1983). In the second case the EOC supported a complaint about discrimination against girls in the education system: eight girls had to spend an extra year at primary school because they were not allowed to move into a higher class which was too big. The ostensible reason for keeping the eight back was that they were the youngest, but parents of three of the girls alleged sex discrimination, which was admitted by the former headmistress and education authority. The county court heard the case in 1984 and ordered compensation, and the EOC commented that it had received evidence of this kind of practice elsewhere and hoped that this would prove a test case (*Guardian* 13 Nov. 1984).

There is also evidence that although the tendency for tribunals has been to interpret the equality laws narrowly – for example the Employment Appeals Tribunal found in three cases under the Equal Pay Act in 1978 and 1979 that part-time working in itself constituted a 'material difference' that justified lower hourly rates – some legal decisions have been more broadly based. An encouraging precedent was set by an Employment Appeals Tribunal ruling in June 1984 covering part-time work. Sara Holmes, who was employed by the Home Office, asked after her second child was born if she could be transferred to part-time work. The Home Office had refused, and to told her to return full-time or else resign. The Appeals Tribunal found that the Home Office had been guilty of indirect sexual discrimination in refusing to recognise the problems of a woman with children, and so had broken the law. This decision recognised that over 90 per cent of part-timers are women; it also marked a broad interpretation of the Sex Discrimination Act and its purposes (*Guardian* 18 June 1984).

Perhaps the most important reason why the role of law in combating discrimination is becoming more effective in Britain is that the British legal system is now supplemented by appeal to European Courts, and the British Government is bound by its membership of European bodies to respond to certain European Court rulings. Britain does subscribe to the rights written into the Treaty of Rome and the European Convention on Human Rights, and, as Elizabeth Meehan has noted, European Court rulings tend to cover broad questions of principle and to be in some ways similar to the kind of rulings made by the US Supreme Court (Meehan 1985: 170–1). Therefore, somewhat reluctantly Britain is responding to a different legal tradition and being held accountable for infringements of individual rights.

THE IMPACT OF EUROPEAN COURTS

Interpretations of the laws against sexual discrimination have been considerably strengthened by the rulings of the European Court of Justice at Luxemburg, which decides on whether there is a clash between domestic law and the Treaty of Rome. The European Court of Justice was set up as one of the organs of the Common Market and gives rulings when requested to do so on violations of the EEC Treaty; its decisions are binding on member states. So when Britain eventually joined the EEC in 1973 it also became subject to Court rulings. The Treaty of Rome impinges on interpretation of the equality laws because Article 119 requires member states to apply the principle of men and women receiving equal pay for equal work. Interpretation of this Article was strengthened by two EEC Council Directives. The first, issued in 1975, defined the principle of equal pay to mean 'for the same work or for work to which equal value is attributed', and specified that job classifications must use the same criteria for men and women. A further Directive in 1976 on implementing the principle of equal treatment stated that there should be no indirect discrimination by reference to marital or family status and that women should be guaranteed the same working conditions.

A number of sex discrimination cases have been referred to the European Court of Justice by higher courts in the UK. The first case sent by the Court of Appeal to the European Court was concerned with the question whether a woman could claim equal pay with her male predecessor. The industrial tribunal that heard the case of Mrs W. Smith, a stockroom manager, found that she should not have been paid £10 a week less than the previous man who had the job. But the Employment Appeals Tribunal and the Court of Appeal both took the view that under the Equal Pay Act a woman could only compare herself with a man doing a similar job in the same firm at the same time. The Court of Appeal, however, wanted clarification on how European law applied. The European Court found that Article 119 covered cases where a male predecessor earned more than his female successor, and was not limited to men and women doing equal work at the same time. As a result the Court of Appeal then ruled that European law overrode the Equal Pay Act on this point, and found for Mrs Smith. Following on the European Court ruling, a woman won a case before an industrial tribunal in 1982 when she claimed a right to equal pay with a male successor, and the EOC commented that a number of claims for equal pay with the man previously holding a job were being settled satisfactorily before they reached a tribunal (EOC Annual Reports 1983: 5).

The issue of part-time working was referred to the European Court for an interpretation of Article 119. The case was initiated by a woman sewing-machinist who worked thirty hours a week. The company concerned, Kingsgate Clothing Productions Ltd, had equalised the rate for full-time men and women in 1975, but brought in a new lower rate for part-timers. The woman, Mrs Jenkins, claimed an equal hourly rate of pay with full-time men; the industrial tribunal had found against her on the grounds that part-time working was a genuine 'material difference' under the Equal Pay Act. When Mrs Jenkins appealed to the Employment Appeals Tribunal she relied on Community law, not the Equal Pay Act, since the Appeals Tribunal had already dismissed three part-time cases under the Act. The Appeals Tribunal, therefore, asked the European Court to adjudicate and it found that part-time work alone did not provide grounds for lower hourly rates, if it was an indirect way of paying women less, but that employers could cite valid reasons (for example an economic need to encourage full-time work) for paying lower rates to part-timers. National courts had to decide each case on its merits. The EOC (Annual Reports 1983: 5) noted that the European Court's finding had assisted a number of women part-timers to get their cases settled before they reached an industrial tribunal.

Several problems concerning pensions and retirement have been referred to the European Court. The Court has ruled that an addition to salary to cover contributions to a pension scheme which applied to men, but not to women, constituted 'pay' within Article 119, and also found that unequal fringe benefits associated with retirement could be covered by Article 119, and so breached the EEC Council Directive on equal treatment (EOC n.d.: 18–19). But when a man, Mr Burton, complained that it was unjust a woman could qualify for redundancy pay at a younger age than a man, the Court decided that national rulings on different retirement age for social security purposes did not constitute discrimination, nor did redundancy rulings related to that age (EOC n.d.: 22–3). The Court has, however, subsequently in 1986 ruled in favour of Helen Marshall's contention that she suffered discrimination in being forced to retire from her job earlier than a man, as we noted earlier (*The Times* 27, Feb. 1986).

The most important case of all that has come before the European Court of Justice was brought by the EEC Commission itself. The Commission alleged that the British Government was in breach of its obligations under the Treaty of Rome because its national legislation did not allow for individuals to claim equal pay for work of equal value, and that the Equal Pay Act did not meet the requirements of Article 119 and the EEC Council Directive on Equal Pay. The Court ruled in 1982 that the Act did not meet tht Treaty of Rome requirements, and as a result the British Government had to change its domestic laws. The Government did so, though rather grudgingly as noted in Chapter 4. The method chosen was to issue an Order under the European Communities Act, and many commentators thought the form of the

Order would make equal pay difficult to claim and that it was almost incomprehensible.

The decisions taken by industrial tribunals have on the whole confirmed the difficulty women have in proving 'equal value'. The EOC reported two cases in 1984 where the women lost: in one the tribunal ruled there were no reasonable grounds for determining that the work was of equal value and refused to appoint an expert to look into the problem; and in the other the tribunal decided there was no sex bias in a job-evaluation scheme (EOC Annual Reports 1985: 4). When a nursery nurse, Marion Leverton, based her comparison on clerical and administrative staff employed in local government, the tribunal found that she did better through working shorter hours and having more holidays and was not entitled to a pay increase (EOC Annual Reports 1986: 6-7). There was one widely reported victory when Julie Hayward, a cook in a Birkenhead shipyard, won the right in November 1984 to equal pay in a comparison with male painters, joiners and thermal insulation engineers. Her case was supported both by her own trade union, the Boilermakers, and by the EOC. But her victory was short-lived. The employers refused to equalise the less favourable terms in her contract by paying her the same as the men, arguing she would on balance then be better off. So the case went back in 1985 to the tribunal, which this time backed the employers, and held that 'pay' included more than basic pay and so rejected her right to equal wages. Julie Hayward then took her case to the Court of Appeal as an important test case for the application of the equal value amendment to the Equal Pay Act. The Court ruled in March 1987 that her work could be considered equivalent to that of male workers, but that if fringe benefits such as free lunches and sick pay were taken into account her total pay was at least as good as that of her male colleagues, so she was not entitled to equal wages. This meant in practice that she was paid £25 less every week in return for potential sick pay if she lost many weeks' work every year. The EOC noted that this ruling would make subsequent claims even more difficult (*Guardian* 6 Mar. 1987). Women may do better if their trade unions tackle the regrading issue through collective bargaining, or threaten to use the equal value amendment, but do not have to go to the tribunals. TASS, the engineering staffs union, did win pay rises for women on this basis, in one case securing a pay rise of £2,000 a year for a despatch office supervisor (*Guardian* 3 Aug. 1985).

The main impact of European law on equal rights for women has been as a result of Article 119 of the Treaty of Rome. But certain cases of discrimination can be argued in terms of the European Convention of Human Rights, and individuals can appeal to the European Court of Human Rights in Strasburg, set up as an organ of the Council of Europe in 1949. Partly because Britain does not have its own Bill of Rights, but has signed the European Convention, quite a wide range of cases have been brought against the British Government under the Convention, including issues of personal privacy and the treatment of prisoners. The Joint Council for the Welfare of Immigrants took Britain to the Court over its 1980 Immigration Rules on the grounds that they constituted both racial and sexual discrimination. The Court ruled in May 1985 that tight immigration rules did not necessarily amount to racial discrimination, but that Britain was guilty of sexual discrimination in refusing to allow women legally settled in Britain (but not British citizens) to be joined by their husbands, when men in the same position could bring in their wives. The Government is bound to comply with the ruling, but can choose to do so by restricting the rights of men to bring in their families rather than by being more generous to foreign women. The initial reaction by the Government suggested it would choose the more restrictive course; later it announced new rules limiting the right of wives to join their husbands (*Guardian* 12 July 1985).

POSITIVE ACTION AND POSITIVE DISCRIMINATION

British adherence to European law may have brought interpretation of anti-discrimination legislation closer to the American legal tradition, but it has not affected British attitudes to positive discrimination which still diverge from American practice. During the process of implementing equal rights for blacks and for women in the United States it has become accepted that groups which have suffered from cumulative discrimination in the past need special help and some preferential treatment in order to have genuine equality of opportunity. Under this approach a number of institutions of higher education reserved quotas for groups suffering from discrimination. A Supreme Court ruling in 1978 in the Bakke Case did challenge the constitutionality of quotas based purely on race, but the Court at the same time upheld the constitutionality of 'affirmative action' schemes designed to eliminate the disadvantages created by previous discrimination. Positive discrimination continues to create controversy in the USA, but is quite widely accepted as a legitimate and necessary tactic. So far in Britain advocacy of a vigorous programme of positive action and positive discrimination is associated with the Radical Left and lacks mainstream support.

It is possible to distinguish between positive action, which seeks to encourage members of the group suffering discrimination and to widen opportunities open to them, and positive discrimination which gives preference to members of the group for education, jobs or promotion over people with equal or better qualifications. The dividing line may be fairly thin between positive action and positive discrimination, but the Sex Discrimination Act sought to draw the line by allowing forms of special training for women but by not allowing employers to discriminate by reserving jobs for women, except under the category of 'genuine occupational qualification'. The Act does allow reserved seats for women on committees in trade unions, employers' organisations or professional associations in order to achieve reasonable representation, and special training to encourage women to hold union posts, but it forbids discrimination in the actual selection of candidates for union office (Home Office 1975: 34–6).

The central argument for both positive action and positive discrimination is that deep-seated attitudes and the social or economic obstacles facing disadvantaged groups cannot be overcome simply by legislating for formal equality of opportunity. Therefore, to create real equality of opportunity it is necessary to make it easier for members of that group initially to gain education and to make their way in occupations previously closed to them. There are possible supplementary arguments in favour of positive discrimination: one is the need for 'role models' to raise the expectations of young members of the group – for example since Mrs Thatcher became Prime Minister girls perceive that women can hold powerful positions in our society; the other is that there are certain occupations where the presence of women (or blacks) positively benefit the group they represent – medicine and law are two obvious examples.

There are two main objections to legalising positive discrimination (which may not apply to positive action). The first is based on the basic philosophy of law, that everyone should be treated equally by the law; explicit discrimination (even if it is positive discrimination in favour of a disadvantaged group) infringes this precept. As the NCCL points out there is one exception to this approach in British law – the disabled are covered by an Act which requires employers to have a small quota of disabled people on their staff. The second objection rests on a general appeal to fairness or individual rights: why should a qualified white man lose a place at a university or a job because of a policy of giving preferential treatment to women or black people? It is also sometimes argued that positive discrimination may patronise individuals selected under this policy and undermine them by making it appear that they have been chosen primarily because of sex or race and not on their merits.

Detailed argumentation depends on the precise form of positive discrimination being considered, but what is basically at stake is a conflict between two kinds of liberal theory, one stressing individual rights and equality under the law or the relevant rules for educational or occupational advancement, the other stressing the need to supplement formal equality by taking account of real differences in opportunity due to social class, racial and sexual prejudice. Conservatives will support the first form of liberalism in these disputes and socialists the second, but it is essentially a debate within liberalism.

Provisions for positive action could be seen as a neat compromise, recognising the strength of social obstacles faced by many women without raising the problems of principle involved in positive discrimination. But it is debatable whether positive action to promote special training is effective unless there are also measures to ensure those trained can go on to get jobs. The immediate problem, however, is that positive action is unlikely to occur on a wide scale without pressure to enforce it. The NCCL proposed in 1983 that the Government could encourage employers to undertake positive action to promote equal opportunity for women and ethnic minorities, by only offering government contracts to firms that had proved their commitment to equal opportunity. This measure has been used in the United States since the mid 1960s.

Governmental action to promote positive action programmes depends on a sympathetic government. At present some local authorities have taken action to use their powers and to refuse contracts to firms which do not appear to be granting genuine equal opportunities to women or racial minorities. The GLC for example decided in April 1985 to ban Kit Kat chocolate bars from premises for which it was responsible because the manufacturers would not fill in an equal opportunities questionnaire (*Guardian* 22 April 1985). But the reaction of some Conservative back-benchers has been to urge the Government to legislate to prevent local authorities from using their economic powers to uphold the principle of equal opportunities.

PROTECTIVE LEGISLATION

The question of positive action or positive discrimination affects all underprivileged groups; but only women are covered by certain kinds of protective legislation at work. As a result they are debarred from certain kinds of work seen as involving special risks to their health, for example working underground as miners; they are also excluded from working on night shifts in factories (but not in other kinds of work). Whether or not women should continue to have this kind of special protection when they are claiming equality, and whether it hinders or benefits them is an issue which has divided supporters of women's rights.

There are a number of arguments for repealing this kind of protective legislation. Laws to protect women and children engaged in factory work derive from the Victorian era, and are associated with an ideology that views women as the 'weaker sex' and in need of paternalist care. When women are claiming equality with men at all levels, there is a prima-facie case that special exemptions for women are inappropriate. In addition, it can be argued that these exemptions tend to exclude women from some better-paid manual jobs which they are in fact capable of doing – American women have campaigned successfully for the right to become coal-miners for example. The main issue in Britain is doing shift work at night; the EOC argued in a detailed analysis of the protective laws that women's inability to work at night means they earn less than men who can, because night shifts are better paid. It also means that women are sometimes excluded from training and jobs which require experience of night work and are not eligible to become foremen or managers in these cases. The Factories Act did allow employers to apply for special exemption for women to work nights, but employers were often reluctant to do so (EOC 1979a). If women were to be drafted into night work in factories, however, they would need proper child-care facilities and the EOC recommended the need to provide safe transport.

The main objection to removing the barrier to women doing night shifts is that in practice women, because of their household commitments, are much less able to undertake work at night than men. A related objection is that once employers were able to require women to do night work many women would be vulnerable to being pressured into accepting night shifts, even if they faced considerable domestic difficulties or dangerous journeys. The NCCL Rights for Women Unit launched a bitter attack on EOC proposals to repeal protective legislation, without even requiring prior provision of necessary child-care services (Coussins 1979). The NCCL argued that according to the EOC's own survey evidence most women did not want to work nights, and that it was now illegal for women to receive a lower rate of basic pay on the grounds that their hours were less flexible. The NCCL conceded that there were certain cases in which women could be penalised by protective legislation restricting their opportunities, but the thrust of their argument was that greater protection should be extended to men rather than less protection accorded to women by a process of 'equalising up' rather than 'equalising down'.

The disagreement between the EOC and the NCCL was not entirely centred on divergent interpretations of how to promote women's rights on this issue, it also reflected a clash of interests between employers and unionists. Repeal of protective legislation was espoused by the CBI and generally opposed by the TUC; the NCCL took the union side in this conflict and argued for better conditions for all workers. But the debate about protective legislation does raise issues of principle for feminism, including the question of what kind of equality women are seeking and whether there are some circumstances where women do need special protection not accorded to men. Since the 1986 Amendments to the Sex Discrimination Act will mean repealing special protection for women in industry, it will be possible to judge the effects on women in practice.

CONCLUSION

Bringing about changes in women's economic position through use of the law is a slow and frustrating process. Although many feminists joined the campaign to get a Sex Discrimination Act on the statute books, feminist commentators now often stress the ineffectiveness of the equality laws. This disillusionment is understandable, especially when apparent progress – for example in getting the concept of work of 'equal value' incorporated into the application of the Equal Pay Act – is then nullified by industrial tribunal decisions. Nevertheless, legislation has brought about real if still very limited gains for women in employment, and the role of the European Courts has made a significant contribution to women's rights, despite the reluctance of the British Government to implement Court decisions generously.

Even inadequate legislation is helpful in influencing general attitudes to women's rights, influencing women's own expectations and encouraging them to fight for their rights. But it is important to strengthen the legislation so that the scales are not tipped against an individual woman trying to prove her case. It is also essential to provide the political backing needed for lengthy legal proceedings. Women who have won notable victories have usually had organisational backing from the EOC or NCCL, or in the case of immigration the Joint Council for the Welfare of Immigrants, which can provide expert legal advice and necessary funds, and ensure publicity. A government predisposed to support women's rights could do a great deal by strengthening means of enforcing the equality laws and by setting an example as an employer.

The success of the laws cannot, of course, be measured solely by cases before courts and tribunals. One of the most important functions of this legislation is to set a framework for employers and trade unions to operate in. The EOC has intervened to help settle many cases before they get as far as a tribunal, and the unions can also seek agreement using legal action as a possible sanction. The most encouraging aspect of the equal value provision now applicable in principle to equal pay is that three unions in particular have taken up the cause of their women members: TASS (as noted above), APEX which covers clerical staff and in which women make up over half of the union membership, and the General Municipal and Boilermakers Union, (GMBATU) about a third of whose members are women, which has appointed equal opportunity officers. The unions can use the tribunals to try to set a precedent, but can also press for change through collective bargaining.

Individual attempts to use the law without adequate organisational backing and in an unfavourable political and economic context can at best only result in limited successes. But the law can be a valuable instrument of change if well framed and enforced, if it is backed by political pressure and supplemented by positive action and general economic and social policies strengthening women's position.

Chapter seven

FEMINIST THEORY AND SOCIAL CHANGE

Feminists have always believed that social change is needed to achieve full rights for women, and feminist movements have often combined demands for specific and immediate reforms with more revolutionary aspirations. Because any development of feminist theory requires women to ask fundamental questions about the origins of their oppression, including cultural and psychological definitions of human nature and the role of the family, feminists often look for far-reaching solutions. Moreover, the very fact of participating in a social movement and sharing a new consciousness is in itself frequently a thought-provoking and radicalising experience. So it is not surprising that advocates of the new feminism originating in the 1960s have put forward controversial ideas for social change.

Our purpose in this chapter is to look at some of the main strands in feminist thought and the models of social change they recommend, and to clarify how far they relate to established traditions of political thought. A thorough examination of all recent feminist theory is beyond the scope of this book, but it is relevant to sketch in the range of answers given to the question: in what kind of society could women really have equal rights with men?

In order to give the discussion greater precision, feminist answers to this question are discussed in rather more detail in terms of four crucial categories for present feminist analysis: *the family, work, politics* and *war*. There are of course other issues of considerable importance, like the causes of violence against women and the critique by some feminists of 'male' rationality and science. But the four categories chosen here raise many of the basic questions about women's nature, the institutional conditions of equality and the possible contribution women can make to creating a better society for everyone. Ideal prescriptions for change can also be related to present realities.

LIBERAL FEMINISM

Liberalism is the body of ideas that feminists in Britain or in \
society might most naturally turn to when developing a theory to
justify women's rights, since it is the dominant ideology of our society.
Moreover, liberal values are inherently compatible with feminist
claims to equal rights with men, since liberalism stresses the rights of
all individuals to freedom, autonomy and a voice in how they are
governed. Indeed, historically, liberalism is the first social theory that
offered the possibility of equality to women, since it developed in
opposition to theories stressing a political, social and sexual hierarchy
based on tradition, 'nature' and the order ordained by God in the
Scriptures. But because liberalism evolved in a context in which the
private sphere of the family was excluded from political demands for
equality, in which traditional social attitudes remained strong, and in
which the Church upheld women's subordinate role in the family,
liberal feminism took time to develop.

There are British feminist writings dating from the seventeenth
century, the period when liberalism first emerged as a political force,
but the first major feminist statement was Mary Wollstonecraft's
Vindication of the Rights of Woman, written in 1792 (Wollstonecraft
1967), in which she extended rationalist ideas to embrace women as
well as men. She argued that, women were potentially as capable of
rational and moral self-development as men, that they were stunted by
being reared to fit an artificial image of weakness and femininity, and
degraded by having to study to please men. Her prescription for the
emancipation of women was education: girls and boys should be
educated together for citizenship by a national system of education
based on day schools. Wollstonecraft is primarily concerned with
middle- and upper-class women and she assumes that the purpose of
education is to make them better wives and mothers and members of
society. There are intimations of more revolutionary social change in
her book, but no explicit proposals. Education has always been
advocated by liberals as a means of replacing ignorance and prejudice
by knowledge and enlightenment, and liberal feminists have looked to
education to widen the narrow mental horizons imposed on women by
domesticity. But later feminists saw that it was only a beginning.
Freedom and equality for women required legal reform, the possibility
of economic independence and the right to influence political
decisions through the vote. These arguments were developed in the
middle of the nineteenth century by John Stuart Mill – the most
influential and representative British theorist of liberalism – and by

Harriet Taylor, his close friend and later his wife, who influenced his thought on many issues, including feminism. They argued that the despotism men exercise over women in marriage not only led in some cases to great cruelty, but had a degrading effect on the men who exercised power and on the women who had to cultivate the art of pleasing and propitiating their masters. Like Wollstonecraft they also pointed to the fact that ambitious women tried to exercise power through their husbands, but lacking education and a wider experience were tempted to use their influence for selfish and capricious ends. Equal rights for women were necessary not only to remedy the injustice done to them, great as that was, but also to promote the moral and intellectual progress of humanity (Rossi 1970).

Liberal ideas and values have been the basis for all the central political and legal reforms achieved in the 100 years since Mill and Taylor formulated a then radical plea for women's rights. The movement for women's suffrage from the 1860s to the First World War drew on the logic inherent in liberal thought to extend the vote to all adult persons. Demands for higher education and access to the professions appealed to the liberal commitment to encourage individual self-development and promote social enlightenment. Demands for reform of divorce and property laws rested primarily on a claim for married women to be treated as individuals with their own rights, not simply as appendages of men. There is still scope to uphold feminist claims by invoking liberal beliefs and a good deal of support for women's rights still rests on liberal assumptions and commitments. At a theoretical level liberalism provides a strong framework for reformulating a feminist manifesto for women's rights, and some of the numerous writings by women and men on the injustices still suffered by women have been primarily inspired by the liberal tradition.

It is at first sight odd, therefore, that only one widely known and influential theorist of the contemporary Women's Movement is usually classified as a liberal feminist: the American writer Betty Friedan. In her book *The Feminine Mystique* she attacked the cultural and ideological pressures that encouraged women to define themselves purely in feminine and domestic terms, and urged them to realise their full potential at work and in public life. Although Women's Liberation in this context meant primarily a change in consciousness and using opportunities that already existed, a liberal feminism did imply seeking legal reforms to ensure that women had genuinely equal opportunities, a strategy pursued by Friedan through her organisation NOW. In Britain recent legislation for women's rights has arisen out of liberal commitments. But neither the new feminist movement, nor its main theoreticians, have been satisfied that liberalism could answer women's needs.

There are a number of reasons why liberalism seems inadequate today as a framework for developing women's rights. Liberalism is now a status quo ideology and appears to have less potential and appeal as a basis for demanding radical change than it did in the past. More specifically, liberal prescriptions like extending education and giving women the vote are seen to have brought about improvements, but to have failed to emancipate women. The legislative measures adopted since 1970 have underlined the message that legal equality is necessary, but not sufficient, to create real equality. Feminists have therefore asked why the structure of our society appears inherently to perpetuate the inequality of women.

SOCIALISM AND FEMINISM

Socialists would argue that the greatest weakness of liberal feminism is that it focuses on formal legal rights and equality of opportunity, and does not tackle the fundamental problems of poverty and economic subordination which prevent most women from enjoying full opportunities. Socialist feminists have often in practice been particularly concerned to unionise women workers so as to secure better wages and conditions, to improve the social services available to women including nursery provision, and to strengthen women's rights to welfare benefits. At a theoretical level there is, as we have noted in earlier chapters, some overlap between the kind of approach embodied in the parliamentary socialism of the Labour Party and modern welfare liberalism, which does recognise the need for welfare benefits and state regulation of the economy to protect workers, and in relation to sexual discrimination sees a case for positive discrimination in favour of women.

There are many varieties of socialist thought, but feminist theory has primarily engaged itself with the Marxist tradition, partly because Marxism offers an ambitious attempt at comprehensive social explanation, and partly because it also promises revolutionary social change, so it seems to provide a possible theoretical framework for explaining the inequality of women, and for ending it. Marxism argues that the proclaimed legal and political equality granted by bourgeois liberal society is undermined by the fundamental inequalities in real power created by the economic system. The economic powerlessness of the workers, with no resources but their labour, leaves them at the mercy of individual employers and of booms and slumps. This lack of economic power means that, in practice, the state and the law operate against the interests of the workers, whilst dominant social attitudes and the institutions which shape opinion assert the justice and necessity of the capitalist system. The position of women seems in some ways analogous: women appear to form a permanent underclass in terms of low wages, low status and lack of political influence, and a Marxist critique of liberalism seems to offer an approach to uncovering the roots of women's inequality behind a façade of equal opportunities.

Marxist categories lend themselves most directly to examining why women tend to be at the bottom in the job market. Feminists have explored the concept of a 'reserve army of labour' to explain women's economic role under capitalism. Marx argued that the capitalist system needed a potential work-force of workers who could be drawn into new branches of production, easily switched between different jobs and easily laid off when no longer wanted. In addition to providing a pool of flexible labour, the reserve army plays a useful role for employers by tending to depress wage rates, or increase worker productivity, by providing potential alternative labour. In some ways women seem to be an ideal reserve army; married women can be drawn into work when required and allowed to vanish back into the home when their labour is not needed, as happened in and after both world wars. Married women do not impose a burden on the state (so long as their husbands are at work) and tend to be invisible in the unemployment statistics, so they do not create political embarrassment. Their wages are usually low because of assumptions about women's work and the belief that the husband is the main wage-earner (Beechey 1982). Whether women workers are especially dispensable in times of recession, as feminists have often assumed, has been debated (Bruegel 1979). Sexual segregation of jobs may, as suggested in Chapter 4, often prevent men replacing women. Moreover, the concept of women's work, as opposed to men's work which carried a 'family wage', has in the past probably prevented women workers from driving down wage rates of unionised male workers. But in the changing circumstances being created by the second industrial revolution, due to introduction of new technology, men and women may be drawn into more direct competition, although it seems at least as likely that new forms of sexual segregation of work will develop. Women's possible role as a reserve army may vary in relation to changing economic conditions.

Marxist ideas can also be extended to examine the importance of women's unpaid domestic labour in reproducing the labour force – women have and look after children – and in maintaining the male workforce. The man's wage in effect buys the labour of his wife. This economic argument can be widened into an assessment of the way in which paradoxically capitalism has benefited from the pre-capitalist institution of the patriarchal family (Benston 1982). The sale of consumer goods may be expanded by advertising that targets women as housewives anxious to be good wives and mothers. Domesticity has apparently tended to encourage among women an apolitical conservatism in their social attitudes, so wives have quite often opposed the more militant trade-unionism of their husbands. Moreover, home life may make the boredom and frustrations of work more tolerable to many male workers – creating a sphere where they are boss, their physical and sexual and emotional needs catered for and comfort provided. This latter role is often assigned to the family in contemporary functionalist sociology. Whereas early capitalism threatened to destroy totally the working-class family, later legislation and economic developments reconstructed it, removing children and many wives from the factories and producing higher wages for the husband. Today, when market competition has been reinstated as the basis for most economic and social relations by Mrs Thatcher's conservatism, the family is assigned the task of inculcating moral values and social responsibility and a sense of duty. The family is also seen as the ideal unit for caring for the old and the sick, so lessening the burden on the Welfare State.

But although Marxism has suggested interesting ways of analysing women's position under capitalism, it has not met feminist requirements. True, in principle Marxism espouses the equality of women, and Marx himself once wrote that the level of civilisation could be measured by the position of women within it; but the emancipation of women is assumed to be simply a by-product of creating socialism. Moreover, until socialism is achieved orthodox Marxist thought suggests that women's problems are subsumed under the struggle between the major social classes. The more dogmatic Marxist groups have indeed reacted in a hostile way to the new feminist movement on these grounds. Marxist theory has paid only limited attention to the roots of women's special oppression; the only major Marxist text on this topic is Engels' pamphlet on *The Origin of the Family, Private Property and the State* (Engels n.d.), though Marx criticised the bourgeois family in the *Communist Manifesto*.

Engels and some later Marxists have explored the role of the family in oppressing women (Charvet 1982). The monogamous family of bourgeois society (the only type of family of direct interest to Western feminists) has been presented as the basis of property relations: strict chastity was imposed on the wife so that the father could ensure his property was passed on to his real heirs. The man was under no such restriction, as the flourishing trade in prostitution in the Victorian era testified. The bourgeois form of marriage is based upon an apparently free contract founded on free choice. But the appearance of freedom and equality for the nineteenth-century woman was as illusory as it was for the worker entering into a contract with his employer. Women had no real choice except marriage, and once they entered into it they were legally subordinate and became in effect their husbands' property. The legal terminology which defines a widow as the 'relict' of her late husband reflects the concept of women as chattels. This oppression of women has been made tolerable by the ideology of romantic love, which encourages an idealisation of the woman and persuades her that she serves her husband out of devotion.

Marxists have therefore tended to see the emancipation of women – when they have envisaged it at all concretely – as a result of transforming the nature of the bourgeois family. Women would become free through becoming part of the general work-force, so gaining economic equality with men and at the same time they would acquire the broader political consciousness that domesticity had denied them. Thus far the prescription is much the same as most liberal feminism – though socialist theory presumed the workers as a whole would gain new freedom and power once capitalism had been overthrown. But whereas liberals have continued to idealise the 'bourgeois family', Marxists have assumed the family will lose its function of transmitting property rights and will change its nature. A free and equal relationship between the man and woman could still mean a marriage contract, but implied freedom of divorce. An end to the husband treating the wife as 'an instrument of production' suggested transferring most or all the work involved in the household – child care, cooking and cleaning – from the individual family to the community. Whilst Marx and Engels assumed the ideal was a permanent partnership between a man and woman, some later Marxists envisaged a more radical abolition of the family. Alexandra Kollontai, one of the few women prominent in the Bolshevik Party in the early years after the Russian Revolution, advocated free love in the sense of freedom to change sexual partners frequently in response to personal love and desire; and envisaged children would be cared for in collectively run homes. But the advent of Stalinism meant a strengthening of the traditional family unit, strict divorce laws and an emphasis on women's childbearing role.

Many feminists in the Women's Liberation Movement were sceptical about the relevance of Marxism to their concerns. One reason was that in their view Marxist theory was really almost exclusively concerned with the liberation of man, and gave at best marginal attention to the real problems of women. Indeed, since the 1920s Marxism had shown even less interest in the woman question. The other main reason was that the position of women in official socialist societies, although upheld by ringing declarations of equality, appeared on investigation to be in many ways worse than under Western capitalism. Socialist societies have stressed the right of women to work, have opened up professions to them and provide child care for young children. But the result, for a number of reasons, has been very far from real equality. Traditional cultural attitudes to women in Russia were more reactionary than in most of Western Europe, and these attitudes received political reinforcement during the Stalinist period. As a result women have been allowed to undertake heavy manual labour (less common now than in the past when there was a manpower shortage) and even during the war to fight in the armed forces, but their pay and status has remained relatively low. Feminised professions in the USSR, for example medicine, are correspondingly low in status. Although women have been represented at the lower levels of political power, there have been even fewer women at the top of politics in the Soviet Union than in the West. But where the average woman in the USSR does significantly worse than her Western counterpart is that the double burden of a job and housework is a great deal more onerous for her. This is partly because the Soviet Union has been a much less efficient consumer society, so shopping may mean queuing for hours to get basic food and goods. In addition, Russian men are even less likely to give a hand with the housework than men in Britain or America, and their entrenched patriarchal attitudes have not been challenged. A small independent feminist movement arose briefly in the USSR in the late 1970s, only to come under immediate surveillance by the KGB. One of the main complaints of this feminist samizdat was the low standard of care during childbirth and during abortions, still frequently used as a substitute for contraception, which is not well publicised. Moreover, the available methods are unsatisfactory (Almanach 1979). Cultural conditions in some socialist countries in Eastern Europe are closer to those in the West. But Hilda Scott, who lived in Czechoslovakia as a working mother, wrote a book on the theme *Does Socialism Liberate Women?* and came up with the clear answer 'no' (Scott 1974).

Juliet Mitchell took on board the inadequacies of existing socialist theory, and the failure of existing socialist societies to emancipate women, and sketched in the outlines of a more comprehensive approach (Mitchell 1981). Her aim was to find Marxist answers to feminist questions. She argued that the position of women had to be understood in terms of four distinct but interconnected social roles: in production, i.e. the general workforce; in the reproduction of children; as sexual objects; and in the socialisation of children. The three latter roles are all combined within the family. Mitchell concluded that the liberation of women required that they gain freedom in all four contexts simultaneously. Greater freedom in one area had tended historically to lead to greater oppression in others: for example in China emphasis on liberating women in production had led to the promotion of women in society, but had been accompanied by rigorous sexual repression. There was no single panacea like the right to work or sexual freedom. She also suggested that women's liberation would only be possible in the economically developed societies of the West. Since she wrote her original book on *Woman's Estate* Mitchell has pursued her interest in the ideological definition of woman's nature largely through an exploration of the implications of psychoanalysis for feminism (Mitchell 1975). She defends the validity of Freud's theories and their relevance for feminism against the attacks of many feminists. In seeking the roots of patriarchal culture in psychoanalysis Mitchell, although she maintains a commitment to Marxism, is moving away from mainstream Marxist debates into an area being explored by many radical feminist theorists.

RADICAL FEMINISM

Much of the feminist writing of the 1970s and 1980s cannot be classified in terms of existing traditions of political thought. Feminists raised questions about the nature of the female condition, about women's attitudes to themselves and the social images imposed upon them, about men's fear and hatred of women, and about the causes of women's powerlessness and oppression. These concerns have led feminist writers to explore the nature of social conditioning in contemporary society and to explore men's and women's attitudes to women reflected in literature. The search for the origins and changing forms of women's oppression has led to anthropology and social history and often to psychological theories. The influential books in the early stages of the Women's Movement tended to be wide ranging in their comments and reflections, and to draw on a variety of academic

disciplines. Eva Figes' *Patriarchal Attitudes* (Figes
Germaine Greer's *Female Eunuch* (Greer 1981) both fa.
category; so to some extent do the early radical feminist
writings by Kate Millett and Shulamith Firestone. But both ....atter
also attempted an ambitious, systematic theoretical explanation of
women's oppression.

Two of the key ideas of the Women's Movement – the concept of
patriarchy transcending different historical periods, and the belief that
'the personal is the political' – were both developed by Kate Millett in
Sexual Politics (Millet 1985). She defined 'patriarchal government' as
the institution 'whereby that half of the population which is female is
controlled by that half which is male', and deduced two main
principles of patriarchy: men dominate women, and older men
dominate the younger. Millett claimed that patriarchy was a deeply
entrenched 'social constant' that ran through all economic and social
structures and political regimes and found expression in all religions,
though the forms of patriarchy differed in detail and individual
exceptions to patriarchal rule could be found. Because patriarchy
governed the relations between men and women, individual personal
and sexual relationships reflected the social structure of power
relationships and the associated psychological attitudes. In this sense
personal relationships and attitudes were necessarily 'political'.
Millett also touched on themes that were developed later by other
writers in her attempts to delineate the bases of patriarchy, for example
the tendency in social thought to identify women with the realm of
nature dictated by her biology and to identify human culture with
masculine energy, creativity and intelligence; and the association of
women with impurity in patriarchal myth and popular attitudes.

One theme explored by Millett, that women despite differences of
social class tend as a group to be an inferior social caste to all men, is
taken up as a central theoretical statement by Firestone (1979) in her
book *The Dialectic of Sex*. She asserts that the sexual class division
rooted in the biological differences between men and women is the
original and most basic class division of all, and she seeks to link
Marxist analysis to a feminist interpretation of Freudianism to 'arrive
at a solution' to the oppression of women. She accepts the distinction
between women identified with nature as a result of the 'natural
division of labour' involved in the reproduction of the species, and
men identified with culture. As a result her prescriptions for women's
liberation are the most far-reaching attempt to transcend women's
biological nature; not simply by demanding the right to contraception
and abortion, as the Women's Movement as a whole has done, but

anticipating the technological possibility of artificial methods of reproduction. Firestone believed at the time she was writing in the late 1960s that cultural taboos were holding back research into artificial reproduction, but developments since then in embryo research and genetic engineering have brought the possibility closer. She believes that 'pregnancy is barbaric' and looks forward to the possibility that women may be freed from the curse of Eve – to bring forth children in pain and travail (1979: 188).

Firestone went further than most feminists in accepting that in one sense biology was destiny for women, though she rejected the stereotype that women found their true satisfaction in being wives and mothers even more strongly than most other feminists. The early theorists of the new wave of feminism implicitly accepted that traditional masculine pursuits were superior to traditional womanly pursuits. One source of this attitude is a heritage of political theory that has excluded the household (the sphere of women and slaves in classical Greece) from the realm of truly human endeavour – that is, of creation (art and crafts), thought (philosophy and science) and politics. Within this tradition childbearing, child-rearing and all forms of domestic work are seen as essentially subhuman and menial activities. Feminists were also reacting against the idealisation of woman as mother and housewife, but as nothing else, in the prevailing social ideology in which they had grown up. They were aware too that in the past frequent pregnancy had often been a burden on women's health and energy, and that the mother's responsibility for looking after her children until they were adult had tended to make women wholly dependent on their husbands. Finally, many feminists wanted on principle to abolish the nuclear family of father, mother and children isolated from the rest of society in their homes. Greer in particular saw the nuclear family as a prison in which women are restricted and miserable and so tend to tyrannise over their children and scheme to restrict their husbands. She also saw the family perpetuating the psychological repression of women and the process whereby growing girls are trained to be 'daddy's little girl' for life.

Despite their rejection of the traditional feminine roles and of the kind of character and attitudes associated with 'femininity' in social stereotypes, and to some degree in practice, the theorists of the Women's Liberation Movement did not accept a purely masculine definition of ideal human nature, as tacitly many earlier feminists had done. The new feminism had after all emerged partly in response to the exaggerated assertion of an ultra-masculine culture on the political Left. Kate Millett's *Sexual Politics* exposed in detail the brutal masculine attitudes to women and sex displayed by the men in the novels of admired writers like Henry Miller and Norman Mailer. There was a general sense that a feminist revolution must mean more than women imitating men. Greer suggested that prevailing masculine criticism of woman's nature could be explained by men's desperate struggle to suppress parts of their own personality. She added: 'if women understand by emancipation the adoption of the masculine role then we are lost indeed, because there will be no counterweight to the blind male aggressive drive that is leading us to destruction' (1981: 136). So the goal was to liberate both sexes from their previous limiting roles and character stereotypes, for women to become more independent and assertive and for men to become more gentle and caring. Some feminist psychologists writing in the early 1970s envisaged an explicitly androgynous human nature and tried to characterise it (Heilbrun 1973; Kaplan and Bean 1976).

In the years since the first wave of writings that elaborated the new feminism there has been a switch of emphasis both in many theoretical works and within sections of the Women's Movement itself. Firstly there has been a re-evaluation of women's traditional role, and a celebration of women's fertility, their motherhood and the creative values and abilities deriving from women's own subculture. Related to this trend, feminists ceased to criticise the stunted or castrated nature of women's psychological development within patriarchal society, and to stress that women had developed strengths within their subordinate culture. These talents included a responsiveness to emotion, and an intuitive understanding, which should not be abandoned for a masculine ideal of objective rationality, but developed into a new autonomous female personality. Androgyny was rejected as an aim. These views could be seen as a logical development of two components of the Women's Movement: the stress on sisterhood and the power of women acting independently and together; and the emphasis on consciousness-raising, whereby women explored not only their present predicament but their own potential arising out of their experience and awareness. Claiming the positive elements in women's historical experience and values is a natural strategy for a movement with revolutionary aspirations. The socialist movement built on the comradeship and solidarity of working-class experience and trade union struggles, and projected these values into the ideal of socialism. Socialist research and writings seek to recapture a history, tradition and cultural heritage for the working class. The Women's Movement has, after an initial tendency to denigrate women's particular experience as well as their past struggles and achievements in a wider sphere, had the same impulse to recover women's past in order to re-create their present. This impulse has led in diverse directions: to sustained critiques of masculine culture, in particular the effects of an alienated pursuit of science and technology and the prevalence of aggression and war; to examination in depth of positive and negative cultural implications of the exclusive role of mothers in rearing young children; to the search for a totally separate female culture; and to attempts to reconstruct and revive pre-patriarchal culture based on goddesses of fertility and pre-patriarchal attitudes to life and religion (Eisenstein 1984: 45-145). In its more extreme manifestations this later wave of radical feminist thought involves a total break with existing cultural attitudes, for example a rejection of 'male rationality', and rejection of all political movements and traditions that can be associated with a male-dominated society (Daly 1978). This phase of radical feminism has raised many important and interesting theoretical questions, but in its extreme forms not only splits off feminism from both liberal and socialist parties and attitudes, but divides feminists themselves. There have been useful debates between those espousing the ideas of the early radical feminists and socialist feminists on whether or not patriarchy can be understood as a transhistorical social form based on a biological division, and whether women in any meaningful sense form a class analagous to socio-economic classes (Rowbotham 1982, Alexander and Taylor 1982). These debates have had direct implications for political strategy, and the possibility of a united women's movement. The extreme form of radical feminism renounces both rational debate and politics for a separatist culture based on a revolution in consciousness.

It is beyond the scope of this chapter to attempt even a brief summary of the theories arising out of this second stage of radical feminism. But it is relevant to note here that a reassertion of values within women's traditional experience as mothers has not been confined to new feminist writers. This change in mood has extended to some of the pioneers of the Women's Liberation Movement, and has been most visible in the recent books by Germaine Greer and Betty Friedan. Greer's book *Sex and Destiny* (Greer 1984) has puzzled many readers, since its celebration of childbearing and motherhood, its attack on modern methods of contraception, and its uncritical idealisation of traditional societies and extended families for their methods of dealing with sexual relations, childbirth and child-rearing, seems anti-feminist in its themes and implications. But the underlying rationale is indicated by Greer in an introduction to a 1981 edition of the *Female Eunuch*, in which she comments that the Woman's

Movement has won pyrrhic victories: the right to abortion when governments were anxious to control population, so that childbearing itself has become 'subversive'; the right to modern contraceptives, which have proved to be harmful to health in the West and are now being exported to the Third World; and token public and legal concessions at a time when in reality women on average have grown poorer. She also claims that women have discovered 'that the isolation of women from other women is even more bewildering and crippling than the exclusion of individual women from public affairs'. So there is much to learn from the segregated life-style of women in Asia and Africa, a life-style that is being broken up by modernisation (Greer 1981: 12–14). These concerns clarify the point that in principle Greer is still seeking the liberation of women, but in the context of repudiating the values and arrogance of Western 'developed' society, and of seeking to recapture the strengths of segregated female societies.

Friedan's recent book *The Second Stage* (Friedan 1983) looks at the dilemmas facing the daughters of many of the feminists of the 1960s. She notes that whereas her own generation had seen a job as a means of independence and self-fulfilment, and a necessary escape from domesticity, young women who had taken a career for granted had begun to yearn for motherhood, but did not know if they could combine children with work. The overall thrust of Friedan's argument is that feminists have in the past allowed the far Right to monopolise awareness of the importance of the home to women as a source of power and satisfaction; the 'second stage' of feminism needs to find ways of allowing women to enjoy the creative aspects of motherhood and the home, while avoiding the isolating and crippling effects domesticity often induced in the frustrated housewives of the 1950s. These concerns lead us into an examination of the prospects for women in the family, and in the spheres of work and politics in the future.

THE FAMILY

Questions concerning the family have necessarily been central to debates about women's emancipation. Liberal feminists have never queried the values of the Western-style family – provided the wife has legal equality – but have disagreed whether most women can be expected to fulfil their main role within the home or whether all women require paid employment outside the home to ensure them independence, self-respect and use of all their talents. John Stuart Mill favoured the first option, whereas Harriet Taylor stressed that women needed actual and not simply potential careers. Within the feminist movement during this century there has been some oscillation between urging women to make their way in the outside world – a priority up to the First World War and again in the 1960s – and a desire to strengthen women's independence and dignity within the home.

So far the liberal solutions have not proved satisfactory. If women stay at home economic dependence inevitably tends to create personal dependence upon the man who is the wage-earner. Attempts to remedy the problem that a woman who stays at home normally has no money of her own, and that money is essential for real freedom and equality in our society, have proved wholly inadequate. Children's allowances have only been paid direct to mothers as a result of continuing feminist pressure (this principle is indeed once more under threat) and are always too low to do more than provide a minimum for the children concerned. Given increasing demands on the Welfare State and political and economic difficulties in finding adequate resources, it is almost inconceivable in the foreseeable future that women in Britain will receive from the state the equivalent of a proper wage for looking after children or the elderly. It is not, moreover, entirely clear that this would be desirable, as it would put pressure on women to stay at home; and if housewives received more than a basic allowance there would be political demands to provide official supervision to ensure they were earning their money and meeting government requirements. On the other hand, if women do go out to work they usually get, as we have seen in earlier chapters, a very low wage, and so are still far from being in a position of genuine financial independence. Furthermore, they then have to undertake the dual responsibility of housework and child care inside the home as well as a job.

For those socialist and radical feminist writers who have seen the break-up of the nuclear family as the prerequisite of women's liberation, the central problem has been how to organise child care outside the family. The Israeli kibbutz has been cited as a possible model, with the emphasis on communal rearing and education of children. Firestone tackled the problem squarely, and suggested the creation of households of about ten adults who would contract to take care of a child for as long as was required. Originally the households would include the natural parents, but Firestone looked forward to a time when the natural ties were severed and a baby acquired an extended 'family' based purely on choice and not on kinship. She also explored the possibility of reducing the period of childhood

dependency by giving children adult rights and freedoms, arguing t
the concept of childhood is itself a largely artificial construct o
modern industrialised society, and imprisons children. This is an
approach which was explored during the 1970s by other radical writers
who noted that pre-industrial societies tend to involve children much
earlier in the work of the community and to educate them in the
process of work (Holt 1975).

Radical alternatives to the family come up against two obvious and
important objections. Any attempt to separate parents from primary
responsibility for looking after their own children runs counter to the
very strong desire of many women, including quite a few feminists, to
have and care for children. Many men also desire to become fathers.
The motives for wanting children may sometimes be questionable, and
parents do not automatically love their own babies. But the
desperation of many infertile couples suggests that there is a genuine
need to be fulfilled, and the fact that most parents (in particular most
mothers) feel a strong bond with their children is a relatively good
guarantee that children will be loved and well cared for. This point
brings us to the second objection to trying to dismantle the family: that
the alternatives one can envisage in the context of contemporary
Western society look worse. Experiments in community living suggest
that they are usually short-lived (unless based on a common set of
strong beliefs and strict discipline) and communities generate their
own emotional tensions. Whilst voluntary communities may provide
interesting examples of alternative life-styles, no government could
legislate for communal care of children as a substitute for the family.
The only feasible solution on a national scale would be to institute
children's homes run directly or indirectly by the state. But to treat all
children like orphans and to give Government such total control over
bringing up children are both repugnant propositions.

There are, moreover, positive arguments in favour of the family. In
modern society it is a sphere of privacy, affection and intimacy; and in
the home women and men can find a degree of dignity and self-
fulfilment which may be denied to them at work and by society as a
whole. It can, for instance, be argued that the survival of strong family
bonds among the working class has been, however functional the
family may be for capitalism, a very positive gain for both the men and
women involved (Cliff 1984). The ideal of love and constancy between
husband and wife is a genuinely attractive ideal, and not simply a myth
to subjugate women. Moreover, the virtues embodied in motherhood
of duty, unselfishness and tenderness are vital for any society, however
much women who accept the values of the motherly role have been

risk sacrificing their own genuine interests. But it is
to move from accepting the real values inherent in an
sentimentalising a far from ideal status quo.

al feminist case for abolishing the family unit is
..., the feminist arguments for changing conditions within
the family and the way in which the family relates to the wider society
are extremely cogent. Previous chapters have enumerated the
emotional problems of mothers isolated in their homes with young
children, and the economic, practical and psychological disadvantages
of total dependency on a man. There is an even more fundamental
consideration, that the orthodox division of roles within the family
may be an instrument for perpetuating women's social inferiority. In
the past this may have been true because young children perceived the
generally inferior position of women being mirrored within the family,
where the father was the figure with real power and authority. But if
the analysis is pushed back to the stage of infancy, then the role of the
mother becomes crucial. Two feminist writers have drawn on a form of
psychoanalytic theory to locate men's fear and hatred of women, and
women's tendency to accept male dominance, in the helplessness of
infants before an all-powerful and hence threatening mother figure
(Dinnerstein 1977; Chodorow 1978). The detail of their analysis
varied, but both conclude that the deep-rooted attitudes of men and
women can only be changed if men take a more active part in looking
after babies and young children. Even if this theory is not valid, it is
certainly plausible that a more equal role in the home for husbands and
wives will influence boys' and girls' perceptions of masculinity and
femininity.

It is not very fruitful to discuss whether the family is desirable in the
abstract without at the same time looking at what is happening to it in
reality. We examined the relevant trends in Chapter 3, so here it is only
necessary to summarise them. Women have gained sexual freedom
and control over their own reproduction, through availability of
contraception and access (though not always easy) to abortion. While
sexual freedom can be double-edged, putting them under more
pressure to make themselves sexually available to men, and perhaps
requiring them to use contraceptives which may damage their health,
women have gained greater freedom to decide whether or not to marry.
They have also, if they do marry, gained greater freedom of divorce.
The divorce rate has risen steadily since the 1950s, and women are a
higher proportion of those seeking divorce. But marriage still remains
popular; many of those who divorce go on to remarry. However, as a
result of higher rates of separation and divorce the number of single

parents has also been rising steadily, and about 90 per cent of them are single mothers.

The other trend we have noted is for increasing numbers of married women to go out to work and, since the onset of high unemployment, for quite a few to become the sole wage-earner. So the family in which the mother stays at home to look after the children whilst the husband provides for them all is now the exception rather than the rule. But women with children under school age are more likely to stay at home still, some presumably because they want to and others because of the lack of child-care facilities. Women desperate for a paid job may have to find unofficial child minders.

Is it possible in the light of these trends to suggest social changes which would be desirable and realistic? The approaches worth exploring further are to make more provision for child care and communal services that would ease the burdens for married women and single parents; to take further the sharing of child-rearing and housework between wives and husbands; and encouraging changes in patterns of work which enable both men and women to work part-time, work from home, or to move in and out of jobs.

The original demand of the women's movement for twenty-four-hour free nurseries has been associated with the belief that women ought to have full-time careers, and not interrupt them for their children. But the case for them is much wider. Provision of nurseries on a large scale would give women genuine freedom of choice whether to take up full- or part-time work when their children were very young; but it would in addition give support to women who most need it, for example single mothers or mothers in danger of battering their children. Another step that would help working mothers would be to make arrangements for children to stay longer at school to work or play, supervised by additional part-time staff.

Friedan suggests that families could be less isolated and share housework by a change in housing design, so that flats and houses would be built round communal areas, where tasks like cooking and laundry could be shared and people could meet for recreation. She recognises that cooperative organisation of housework could cause personal conflicts; but if each family retained a reasonable degree of privacy and there were clear contractual requirements when entering this kind of tenants' association or housing cooperative it could work. Liberal and socialist approaches come together in this kind of proposal, though there are important questions to be asked about how it would work: would, for example, the families involved pay for their extra amenities through the cost of their home, or would local government contribute to creating communal services in council housing and deprived areas? A central question for feminists would be whether all the communal tasks, whether unpaid or possibly paid, were done by women.

Persuading men to play a larger part in looking after their children is a process that has already begun. In a small number of cases couples have deliberately exchanged roles, with the man staying at home to look after the children; but this is still exceptional. More commonly the husband helps out a bit in the evenings and weekends. But there has been a significant shift in attitudes compared with thirty years ago: it is no longer uncommon to see a man pushing a push-chair for example. One specific way to promote a stronger move towards equality in caring for children is for the state to recognise the father's responsibilities and allow paternity leave when a baby is born, and for both parents to be granted time off by employers to look after sick children. Sweden launched a sex-role equality programme in 1968, and recent figures indicate that a quarter of fathers take some time off to look after their baby during its first year. The International Labour Organisation adopted the principle of paternal leave in 1981 (Scott 1984: 149–51).

Equality within the family and a fair sharing of home responsibilities depends, however, on a more radical restructuring of the world of work. One requirement is a more flexible career structure which would enable people to take several years off work without risking permanent loss of a similar job and damaging the possibility of future promotion. At present this is most important for women, but men are much more likely to drop out for a while to look after children if their work prospects were not to suffer as a result. A few large economic institutions have begun to make special provision for women employees who have babies, but the Government could establish an important precedent within the public sector. There are, however, more fundamental questions involved about how we conceive of work in the future, and whether we change our expectations of a full-time job until retirement.

WORK

An interesting attempt to characterise an economy in which women could achieve full equality and in which women's values would be realised is made by Hilda Scott in her book *Working Your Way to the Bottom* (1984). She argues for a much more flexible approach to paid work, in which both men and women would be encouraged to spend more time in higher education, and to retire earlier, and in which there would be a growth in part-time working and job sharing. As a necessary corollary Scott wishes to place increased social emphasis and value on unpaid work, whether in the home or in the wider community, and to rely more on volunteers to maintain local community services. Her aim is to create a new conception of work, to avoid mass unemployment as a result of new technology, and to foster the values of an economy based on human needs rather than one dominated by criteria of profit and productivity and subordinate to technological 'progress'. She draws on the work of a number of writers who have seen a reordering of economic priorities as a necessary element in developing a society based on feminine values.

The case for a more flexible workforce would be accepted by many with differing political goals, given the problems posed by new technology and the threat of permanent rates of high unemployment. Prescriptions for more part-time work and for working out of the home fit in with the existing trends that we considered in Chapter 4. But as we saw, these trends far from being a panacea at present mean poverty, insecurity and lack of rights for most of those involved. Part-time work necessarily means a fairly low income (except perhaps in the case of scarce skills), but this could be acceptable in a family where two people are working part-time, if part-time jobs are well protected in terms of minimum wages and conditions and are linked into pension schemes. Whether many people would be willing to trade-off leisure and more time at home against money (if they had a real choice) is certainly in part a matter of values; at present women are probably more likely to make such a choice, but men need to do so too if the result is not to perpetuate women's inequality in the economy. But whether lower level personal incomes are tolerable also depends considerably on broader economic and social factors, for example whether decent low-cost housing is available, the nature of public transport and the availability of communal forms of recreation.

More provision for periods of vocational training or retraining throughout life is clearly essential in a changing economy, and Britain is behind many other countries in making such provision. The main feminist issue here is to ensure women's access to training for a wide range of jobs. But if the aim is in addition to create more leisure, then adult education in the broadest sense is needed. A variety of institutions might provide part-time or full-time courses, the Open University, for example, has been especially valuable for women, but an expansion of education implies an increase in government investment in universities and colleges.

Greater reliance on volunteers to run social services makes sense in both economic and social terms. It can be argued that the growing burden on the Welfare State, especially as a higher proportion of the population becomes elderly, must be met by increasing reliance on voluntary help. Scott cites evidence from Sweden – a country noted for its high expenditure on welfare and its correspondingly high taxation levels – that the solution envisaged there is more reliance on volunteers. Secondly, if people are working on average shorter hours, retiring earlier and living longer than in the past, many may wish to do something useful. There is already a flourishing tradition of voluntary work in this country on which to draw, and the feminist movement has created its own special services for women like refuges for battered women and rape counselling. But voluntary work is not going to be politically acceptable if it is offered as a sop to the long-term unemployed, to married women as an alternative to a job or as a substitute for adequate government provision. Moreover, voluntary services rely on a framework of local government support, as the crisis being created for many organisations by the abolition of the metropolitan councils, and so of an important source of funds, has dramatised.

Government economic policy affecting employment and welfare and legislation on rights at work are all therefore crucially important in determining the environment within which part-time working and voluntary action take place. Priorities in allocating government funds also become vital at a time of economic and social change. Decisions about the application of new technology, the kinds of energy supplies we rely upon, the sort of agriculture we promote, the levels of affluence we aim for and the degree of economic equality we require will be made consciously or by default in the next twenty to thirty years and shape the nature of post-industrial society. If women's interests are to be protected and if the directions we take are to reflect womanly values, then women need to start exerting real influence on the decisions made.

POLITICS

Four main questions are worth examining here: can women best promote their goals inside or outside formal politics; do women in power necessarily support women's interests; how can women's representation in government be increased; and is it possible to define 'womanly' policies – for example in relation to war and peace?

The argument for working within the political system is that ultimately the decisions are made within the Civil Service and by government ministers and are ratified or occasionally altered by Parliament. Government policies are shaped by attitudes within political parties and by party manifestos, though these usually undergo modification once a party is in power. The problem of trying to work within the power structure to achieve change is that those who do manage to get to the top are under great pressure to conform to prevailing standards and attitudes. This has certainly been true in the past of many women.

Radical and innovative ideas have always come from movements operating outside the centres of political power. These movements can generate great energy and confidence, challenge existing attitudes and beliefs, and experiment with ways of tackling social problems and with forms of self-organisation. If movements are at all successful they bring about a shift in social awareness which then filters into mainstream political parties and institutions and promotes some reform. Highly organised pressure groups can also bring significant pressure to bear on specific legislative issues. The women's movement has over the last twenty-five years achieved both a significant shift in attitudes and particular legal gains. But movements do have important limitations. They lack real power, influence and resources; energy and enthusiasm flag after a while, especially when people find themselves having to fight the same battles again and again and see their victories easily reversed. Moreover, by developing new ideas in enclosed internal debates, movements run the risk of losing touch with majority attitudes and social reality, and of becoming sectarian and dogmatic. The Women's Movement has certainly faced the first problem and has also shown tendencies towards sectarianism, though on the whole feminism remains remarkably resilient and politically relevant.

The best way to achieve significant political reforms is to build a strong movement to influence the general climate of opinion and at the same time to strengthen representation for the cause within the political system, which can be achieved most directly through getting supporters into Parliament. Campaigns on some issues gain parliamentary support across all political parties, and this has been true of some women's rights issues like abortion. But where wider economic and social issues are at stake it is usually necessary to win support within one of the main political parties more likely to implement the programme required. Feminists are still battling in the Labour Party to achieve better representation, though by 1986 they had won strong policy commitments to women's rights.

Feminists cannot, however, automatically assume that women

elected to Parliament or achieving influence within a political party will support women's interests. Women who enter political life identify with a range of political parties, and in the past many have not thought of themselves as feminists. Moreover, even where they have wished to espouse women's rights they have been at a disadvantage through being in a small minority in an environment unsympathetic to women's issues, which have been defined as marginal. In addition, talented and strong-minded women politicians have sometimes reacted against being identified primarily with questions traditionally associated with women.

Two factors are likely to influence the readiness of women parliamentarians to support women's rights and interests. One is the strength of feminist pressure groups and attitudes outside Parliament. During the 1970s women MPs began to demonstrate a greater feminist consciousness and solidarity than they had done earlier (Randall 1982: 105). The other is the number of women who are elected. If there were a significant increase in women's representation then women MPs would cease to be an isolated minority and would be psychologically as well as politically better placed to act effectively to promote women's rights. Joni Lovenduski (1986a), after a rather gloomy survey of the role of women in European legislatures, suggests that there may be a 'critical mass', a certain level of representation which will tend to have this effect.

Is it then possible to increase the very low proportion of women in the British Parliament? One approach is to try to encourage women generally to stand as candidates and to help them develop skills in public speaking and the necessary self-confidence. This is the strategy adopted by the 300 Group formed as an all-party pressure group. Another is to work within political parties to secure a policy favourable to selection of women. By 1986 the SDP, Liberal Party and Labour Party had all made inclusion of one or more women on candidates' short lists mandatory, but progress in increasing the proportion of women standing has so far continued to be slow. A third possible approach, which might have more immediate results, is to campaign for a change in the British electoral system. The case for such a change in terms of increasing women's representation has been made by Elizabeth Vallance (1984). She argues that in single-member constituencies where only one candidate out of those standing is elected to Parliament, the pressure on constituency parties who hope to win the seat is to choose 'the standard product, largely middle-class, middle-aged, and overwhelmingly male' (308). If proportional representation were adopted, parties might be under pressure to include women to ensure a balanced list, though it has also been suggested that national lists drawn up by parties are more likely to favour women than multi-member constituencies where local parties still dominate selection (Castles 1981: 21-6). But all forms of proportional representation increase the chances of smaller parties, and women are already better represented as candidates for the Scottish Nationalist Party and the Green Party. Proportional representation would also make it realistic to consider fielding candidates specifically standing on a women's rights platform. Comparative figures for other West European legislatures strongly suggest that proportional representation, in particular a list system, is a factor in the significantly better (though still low) proportion of women in other legislatures. Increased numbers of women in Parliament would not in itself immediately ensure greatly enhanced power for women in political life: that requires women to get to the top in a range of institutions that influence policy. But it would be symbolically important and would assist the passage of legislation to strengthen women's rights at work.

Women interested in fundamental social change may favour increasing the number of women in positions of power as a first step, but they are likely to want to change the structure of power itself as well as altering the policies pursued by Government. This raises the question whether it is possible to identify a political theory or approach to politics based on feminine rather than masculine values.

There are considerable difficulties in identifying a set of specifically womanly values; it raises the question whether women's biological role as mothers necessarily influences women's attitudes, and whether permanent values can be satisfactorily deduced from a cultural inheritance based on women's subordination in society. But it can be claimed that there are certain qualities and attitudes to life which at present are primarily associated with women: concern to preserve life, a desire to look after people and be responsive to their feelings, and giving greater priority to human needs than pursuit of power or of scientific knowledge for its own sake, regardless of results.

Even if it is possible to identify a cluster of womanly values, it is clearly a mistake to go on to assume that all women will espouse these and all men will not. In terms of character traits it is generally agreed that in varying degrees all women and men share both recognised feminine and masculine traits. In terms of specific moral and social beliefs, many women accept ideologies hostile to womanly values, and many men support ideologies that favour womanly priorities. In the case of women who enter the official political arena, it has in the past been more likely that they would support women's rights in a limited sense than that they would identify themselves with a political programme embodying womanly values, largely because most political parties have not centrally incorporated these values.

On the other hand, it is relevant to note that women have often been active and prominent in movements outside the official political arena, movements for basic human rights like the abolition of slavery, movements concerned with social welfare and peace movements. Women have indeed exerted social pressure in these spheres in periods before they were legally entitled to vote and stand for office; but they have continued to play a large part in such movements and often seem to prefer this style of politics. This fact has relevance for debates about women's degree of interest in or participation in politics, and about their attitudes to political issues (Evans 1984). It is possible to suggest that even in periods when feminism has not been a significant political force, many women have wanted to redefine the prevailing conception of what 'politics' is really about.

WAR

Since 1980 feminists in both Europe and the United States have developed political arguments linking feminism to ecological concern to end increasing pollution of the environment as a result of modern industrial technology and procedures and widespread use of chemicals in agriculture, and to prevent the destruction of the world by nuclear weapons. The aim is not only to ensure women full rights, but to transform political and social priorities in order to preserve the future by bringing about a change in consciousness. This programme implies decentralising the power now vested in central governments, and vast corporations, and increasing democratic control. This fusion of feminism with environmentalist and peace movements has achieved its greatest political impact so far in the West German Green Party. The Greenham women have become a symbol of the link between radical feminism and opposition to war and the technologies of destruction. But these concerns have also found expression in literature and in writings on politics. The East German novelist Christa Wolf (1984) engages in an exploration of the links between war and male domination in her novel and related essays *Cassandra*. Hilda Scott takes these links for granted in the final chapter of the book we have already discussed, pointing to enormous expenditures on armaments in the midst of poverty and famine, and Marilyn French (1986) in *Beyond Power* argues that man's lust for domination now threatens to destroy the world; only a woman-centred morality and woman's form of power can prevent this.

Although this contemporary strand of feminist thought and action gives priority to saving society as a whole, it does simultaneously posit that only in a peaceful society, in which womanly values are widely held and respected, will women achieve full equality and dignity, and so escape from their long history of cultural and social subordination. It is impossible here to explore this proposition in detail. But it is intuitively plausible if one looks at societies and ideologies that exalt war and militarism and notes the subordinate role they assign to women and the contempt in which by definition they hold womanly values, which are identified with weakness and cowardice. Fascism, the ideology and movement that drew on the ideal of men joined in comradeship in the trenches and proving their manhood in war, relegated women to the kitchen and bedroom. Juliet Mitchell (1981: 103) suggested plausibly in *Woman's Estate* that the historic root of women's oppression was not a division of labour in which women were excluded from heavy physical work – pointing out that there are many places in the world where women do almost all the heavy work in agriculture – but women's physical disadvantage when it came to fighting. Some modern wars have helped to liberate women, but that is either because they have created great social and economic dislocation, requiring women to fill men's jobs, as in the two world wars; or it has been because war has been waged to create a social and political revolution and so has liberated women from previous servitude, as in the case of the Chinese Communists. But the ethos of war itself and the attitudes associated with societies geared to war, emphasise manly virtues epitomised by fighting and dying on the battlefield, and promote aggression and toughness.

In modern Western societies the military sphere is still the one most hostile to women. They have no role in the military hierarchy that runs the armed services and defence ministries, and are scarcely present in the numerous scientific laboratories and design departments that fashion new weapons. Military strategy, the realm in which intellectual 'toughness' substitutes for actual fighting, is male dominated. It is still inconceivable that a woman would become Minister of Defence; though in Sweden two women have been Ministers of Disarmament, illustrating an association between women and the goal of peace.

Women have in fact come closer to participating in the actual armed services than in the mainly civilian power hierarchy that is associated with them, and have attained positions of command within the services, though almost all armies still exclude women from actual combat units. Whether women have a right and a duty to fight on equal terms with men is one of the most difficult questions that has faced the feminist movement. When the question of conscription arose in the United States under President Carter the women's movement split. What is involved is a conflict between the equal rights tradition of feminism that demanded the same rights and responsibilities as men, and the tradition that sees feminism's role as transforming the society in which both men and women operate. Both strands have always been present in the women's movement going back to the early suffragists, but this division has become sharper and clearer since the 1970s. Betty Friedan (1982) illustrates an interesting ambivalence in a chapter of her latest book, in which she describes a visit to the American military academy at West Point, where women have been admitted on the same terms as men. She is proud of the ability of women she meets to survive in this male chauvinist environment and to retain some degree of femininity; but she also has misgivings whether integration into the armed forces was really what the Women's Movement wanted.

Many complex issues are involved in a general discussion of whether women should ever be willing to fight in wars, unless feminism is equated with total pacifism. But it can be powerfully argued that feminists should resist many tendencies in contemporary society to glorify violence and to subordinate social goals to military priorities and criteria. Feminists anxious to shake off an image of women's timidity and weakness and powerlessness should not look to the armed forces to give women scope for bravery, self-assertion and power over men or machines. The possibility of peace is undermined by the belief held by too many men that soldiering is a test of true manliness, and by the wishful fantasies projected on to crude images of violent self-assertion displayed for example by the Rambo films. These attitudes and fantasies are frequently reflected in the posturing of men in power and linked to desire for national self-assertion. Possession of nuclear weapons is closely related to images of potency and prestige, which distort the political and strategic arguments. Moreover, when the whole direction of science and industry is dominated by military requirements, true to a considerable extent of both the USA and USSR and both halves of Europe, then general social needs are neglected and institutions perverted from their real purposes: universities for example are conscripted into doing widespread military research.

The women who struggled to achieve the vote sometimes looked forward to a time when women's political influence would bring about an end to war. This dream now looks naïve, because it overestimated the power the vote alone would bring and assumed too readily that women would rebel against the values of a male-dominated society. Feminists now have a more acute awareness of the political and social obstacles to be overcome and change in consciousness required if peace is to be made possible. After the experience of two world wars and living under the shadow of a third, feminists are also possessed of a much greater sense of urgency. Among the rights they seek for themselves and their daughters is the most basic human right of all – the right to life. The feminist literature of the last twenty-five years reflects a change of emphasis from primary concern for women's rights and freedom to a much greater concern about the whole direction of society, and whether there will be an earth for women to inherit.

CONCLUSION

When looking at the changing position of women in Britain over the last forty years we can reach very different conclusions. Many women who have lived through this period are aware of the greater opportunities now open and changes in attitude. Feminists, however, tend to stress the continuing inequalities suffered by women, especially at work, and to suggest that little has been achieved by legal reform.

This books argues that there have been significant advances for women since 1945. Women's specific legal rights have been greatly strengthened thanks to feminist pressure, laws passed by the Labour Government in the 1970s and to decisions by the EEC European Court. Married women with children have a recognised right to continue going out to work if they wish to do so. Women's access to higher education and to professional and managerial jobs has improved and more women are moving into positions of economic and political power, though there are still ludicrously small numbers in Parliament and central Government. Most political parties and trade unions are in the late 1980s showing much greater awareness of women's rights and needs than they were ten years ago. Feminists have succeeded in putting violence against women on the public agenda and challenged male hierarchies and prejudice in areas like medicine. Attitudes among women and towards women have changed considerably since the 1950s, and the injustices suffered by women have become more visible.

These gains are, however, still precarious and there is a long way to go before women achieve full equality and secure policies which meet their particular needs. Indeed, for large numbers of women trying to support themselves and their families on very low wages or inadequate benefits the position appears to be getting worse not better. Women still face great problems too in trying to combine motherhood and a job. Rapid progress is impeded by the strength of continuing prejudice and social inertia, and by the difficulties women encounter in fighting for equal rights, for example when they try to make use of the equality laws. But, in addition, new political and economic forces threaten to reverse what has been won.

The 1980s have seen a resurgence of moral and cultural conservatism combined with right-wing populist politics exemplified by Mrs Thatcher and Mr Reagan. Feminists feared the new Conservative Government's agenda included dismantling the Welfare State and forcing women back into the home to look after the sick and the elderly as well as the young. But cuts in welfare have been limited by active resistance, electoral considerations and cross-party opposition, whilst economic factors are leading more married women to go out to work. So far the Thatcher Government's commitment to deregulate the economy, leading to reduced protection for part-time and low-paid workers and cuts in maternity rights, has had the most widespread impact on women; though restrictions on the rights of immigrant women have been more overtly discriminatory.

Mass unemployment has been a product of general recession, specific government policies and a long-term switch from an industrial to a post-industrial economy. Many women have lost their jobs, but the growth of part-time and low-status jobs which has also occurred has usually provided new jobs for women. So the main problem for women workers is that they lack rights and security at work, and the great majority are still clustered at the bottom of the economic hierarchy. Automation and the new information technology could perpetuate the economic inequality of women unless they assert their ability to do the jobs controlling the technology and, even more important, have a say in the use society makes of it.

A government committed to women's rights could promote numerous measures which would improve women's position. Minimum wages, rights for part-time and homeworkers, provision of crèches, implementing the EEC Directive on paternity leave, and strengthening the Sex Discrimination Act and Equal Pay Act would all buttress women's rights at work. In the longer term, girls and women need more access to training for skilled jobs and a more flexible pattern of work and promotion that allows women or men to take time off to look after children. Positive action is now being taken by campaigning groups and most political parties to ensure that more women enter political life at all levels. But Britain still lags behind most of Europe, and strong positive discrimination in favour of women on selection committees for parliamentary and local candidates, or institutional reform, is needed. For example, provisions for a reformed second chamber to replace the House of Lords could be designed to ensure women were likely to be well represented.

Equal rights for women, who make up over half the population, are a prerequisite for achieving social justice. But protecting women's rights is organically linked to promoting the rights of the poor and disadvantaged and to ending discrimination based on the arbitrary grounds of race. This is so not only because the poor are most often women, and black women suffer from a dual discrimination, but primarily because women's rights will only be secured in a context of respect for the rights of all and of policies designed to ensure a just society.

REFERENCES

Alexander, Sally (1974) 'The nightcleaners' campaign', in *Conditions of Illusion* (eds Sandra Allen, Lee Sanders and Jan Wallis) Feminist Books.

Alexander, Sally and Taylor, Barbara (1982) 'In defence of patriarchy', in *The Woman Question* (ed. Mary Evans) (first published in *New Statesman*, Dec. 1979).

Almanach (1979) *For Women about Women*, No. 1. Translated and published as *Woman and Russia: First Feminist Samizdat*, Sheba Feminist Publishers 1980.

Arnold, Eric (1985) 'The appliance of science: technology and housework' *New Scientist*, No. 1452, 16 April.

Atkins, Susan and Hoggett, Brenda (1984) *Women and the Law*, Blackwell.

Banks, Olive (1981) *Faces of Feminism*, Martin Robertson.

Barratt, Michele and Roberts, Helen (1978) 'Doctors and their patients: The social control of women in general practice', in *Women, Sexuality and Social Control* (eds Carol Smart and Barry Smart), Routledge and Kegan Paul.

Beechey, Veronica (1982) 'Some notes on female labour in capitalist production', in *The Woman Question* (ed. Mary Evans), Fontana (first published in *Capital and Class*, 1977).

Benston, Margaret (1982) 'The political economy of Women's Liberation', *in The Woman Question* (ed. Mary Evans) (first published in *Monthly Review*, 1969).

Blackstone, Tessa (1984) 'Inequality in British Universities' *AUT Woman*, No. 1 Spring 1984.

Bruegel, Irene (1979) 'Women as a reserve army of labour: a note on recent British experience', *Feminist Review*, No. 3, also reprinted in *The Woman Question* (ed. Mary Evans), Fontana, 1982.

Bullock, Alan (1967) *The Life and Times of Ernest Bevin*, Vol. 2, Heinemann.

Butler, David and Sloman, Anne (1980) *British Political Facts 1900–1979*, 5th edn, Macmillan.

Butler, David and Stokes, Donald (1971) *Political Change in Britain: Forces Shaping Electoral Choice*, Penguin.

Byrne, Paul and Lovenduski, Joan (1978) 'The Equal Opportunities Commission', *Women's Studies International Quarterly*, No. 1.

Calder, Angus (1982) *The People's War: Britain 1939–1945*, Granada.

Carr, Steve (1984) *Changing Patterns of Work*, Workers Educational Association, Studies for Trade Unionists, Vol. 10, No. 4, Dec.

Castle, Barbara (1980) *The Castle Diaries 1974–76*, Weidenfeld and Nicolson.

Castles, Francis G. (1981) 'Female legislation representation and the electoral system', *Politics*, Vol. 1, No. 2, Nov.

Central Advisory Council for Education (England) (1959) *Fifteen to Eighteen* (Crowther Report), HMSO.

Central Advisory Council for Education (England) (1963) *Half Our Future* (Newsom Report) HMSO.

Central Statistical Office (1970) *Social Trends*, No. 1 (ed. Muriel Nissel), HMSO.

Central Statistical Office (1983) *Social Trends*, No. 13 (ed. Deo Ramprakash), HMSO.

Charvet, John (1982) *Feminism*, Dent.

Chodorow, Nancy (1978) *The Reproduction of Mothering: Psychoanalysis and the Sociology of Gender*, University of California Press.

Cliff, Tony (1984) *Class Struggle and Women's Liberation: 1640 to the Present Day*, Bookmarks.

Coote, Anna (1978a) 'Equality and the curse of the quango', *New Statesman*, 1 Dec.

Coote, Anna (1978b) 'Hellbent on destroying the Domestic Violence Act', *New Statesman*, 16 June.

Coote, Anna (1978c) 'The Tories strange affair with women', *New Statesman*, 13 Oct.

Coote, Anna and Campbell, Beatrix (1982) *Sweet Freedom: The Struggle for Women's Liberation*, Picador (Pan Books).

Coote, Anna and Gill, Tess (1974) *Women's Rights: A Practical Guide*, Penguin.

Coote, Anna and Kellner, Peter (1980) *Hear This Brother: Women Workers and Union Power*, New Statesman Report No. 1.

Coussins, Jean (1976) *The Equality Report*, National Council for Civil Liberties.

Coussins, Jean (1979) *The Shift Work Swindle*, National Council for Civil Liberties.

Crewe, Ivor (1983) 'The disturbing truth behind Labour's rout', *Guardian*, 13 June.

Crewe, Ivor (1979) 'Who swung Tory?' *The Economist*, 12 May.

Crossman, Richard (1977) *The Diaries of a Cabinet Minister: Volume Three, Secretary of State for Social Services 1968–70*, Hamish Hamilton and Jonathan Cape.

Currell, Melville (1974) *Political Woman*, Croom Helm.

Daly, Mary (1978) *Gyn/Ecology: The Metaethics of Radical Feminism*, Beacon Press.

Daniels, W. W. (1981) 'Employers' experiences of maternity rights legislation', *Department of Employment Gazette*, July.

Department of Employment (1973) 'The fall in the labour force between 1966 and 1971', *Department of Employment Gazette*, Nov.

Department of Employment (1974) *Women and Work: A Statistical Survey*, Manpower Paper No. 9, HMSO.

Department of Employment (1975) *Women and Work: A Review*, Manpower Paper, No. 11, HMSO.

Department of Health and Social Security (1974) *Report of the Committee on One-Parent Families* (the Finer Report), Cmnd. 5629, 2 vols, HMSO.

Dinnerstein, Dorothy (1977) *The Mermaid and the Minotaur: Sexual Arrangements and Human Malaise*, Harper and Row.

Eisenstein, Hester (1984) *Contemporary Feminist Thought*, Unwin Paperbacks (Allen and Unwin).

Ellis Valerie (1981) *The Role of Trade Unions in the Promotion of Equal Opportunities*, Equal Opportunities Commission and Social Science Research Council.

Engels, Friedrich (n.d.) *The Origin of the Family, Private Property and the State*, Foreign Languages Publishing House, Moscow (first published 1884).

Equal Opportunities Commission; (1977) *Income Tax and Sex Discrimination*; (1978) *Women in the Legal Services*; (1978/79) *Research Bulletin*, Vol. 1, No. 1 (Winter); (1979a) *Health and Safety Legislation: Should We Distinguish Between Men and Women?*; (1979b) *With All My Worldly Goods I Thee Endow ... Except My Tax Allowance*; (1981a) *Behind Closed Doors*; (1981b) *Investigation into the Numbers of Women Appointed to Public Bodies*; (1981c) 'Women and underachievement at work', *Research Bulletin*', No. 5 (Spring); (1982) *Women in Universities*; (1986) *Women and Men in Britain: A Statistical Profile*; (n.d.) *Towards Equality: A Casebook of Decisions on Sex Discrimination and Equal Pay, 1976–1981*. (n.d.) *'It's not your Business, it's how the Society*

Works': The Experience of Married Applicants for Joint Mortgages.

Equal Opportunities Commission Annual Reports; (1979) *Third Annual Report, 1978*; (1980) *Fourth Annual Report, 1979*; (1981) *Fifth Annual Report, 1980*; (1982) *Sixth Annual Report, 1981*; (1983) *Seventh Annual Report, 1982*; (1984) *Eighth Annual Report, 1983*; (1985) *Ninth Annual Report, 1984*; (1986) *Tenth Annual Report, 1985.*

Evans, Judith (1984) 'The good society? Implications of a greater participation by women in public life', *Political Studies*, Vol. 32, No. 4, Dec.

Ferguson, Marjorie (1983) 'Learning to be a woman's woman', *New Society', 21 April.*

Figes, Eva (1978) *Patriarchal Attitudes,* Virago (first published 1970 by Faber and Faber).

Firestone, Shulamith (1979) *The Dialectic of Sex: The Case for Feminist Revolution,* Women's Press (first published in Britain in 1970 by Cape).

Fogarty, Michael, Allen, A. J., Allen, Isobel and Walters, Patricia (1971) *Women in Top Jobs,* Allen and Unwin, PEP Report.

Fogarty, Michael, Allen Isobel and Walters, Patricia (1981) *Women in Top Jobs 1968-1979,* Heinemann Educational Books, Policy Studies Institute Report.

Fogarty, Michael, Rapoport, Rhona and Rapoport, Robert (1971) *Sex, Career and Family,* Allen and Unwin, PEP Report.

Fransella, Fay and Frost, Kay (1977) *On Being A Woman,* Tavistock.

French, Marilyn (1986) *Beyond Power; On Women, Men and Morals,* Jonathan Cape.

Friedan, Betty (1982) *The Feminine Mystique,* Penguin (first published in Britain in 1963 by Gollancz).

Friedan, Betty (1983) *The Second Stage,* Sphere Books.

Gaffin, Jean (1977) 'Women and cooperation' in *Women in the Labour Movement* (ed. Lucy Middleton) Croom Helm.

Gavron, Hannah (1966) *The Captive Wife: Conflicts of Housebound Mothers,* Routledge and Kegan Paul.

Gregory, Jeanne (1982) 'Equal pay and sex discrimination: why women are giving up the fight', *Feminist Review*, No. 10, Feb.

Greenhall, Stella (1966) *Women and Higher Education,* National Union of Students, Education and Welfare Department.

Greer, Germaine (1981) *The Female Eunuch,* Granada (first published in Britain in 1970 by McGibbon and Kee).

Greer, Germaine (1984) *Sex and Destiny: The Politics of Human Fertility,* Picador (Pan Books).

Hakim, Catherine (1981) 'Job segregation: trends in the 1970s', *Department of Employment Gazette*, Dec.

Hakim, Catherine and Dennis, Roger (1982) *Homeworking in Wages Council Industries*, Department of Employment, Research Paper No. 37.

Hall, Ruth E. (1985) *Ask Any Woman: A London Inquiry into Rape and Sexual Assault*, Falling Wall Press.

Heilbrun, Carolyn G. (1973) *Toward a Recognition of Androgyny*, Alfred A. Knopf.

Heron, Liz (1983) 'Sisterhood re-examined', *New Statesman*, 1 April 1981.

Hills, Jill (1981) 'Candidates, the impact of gender', *Parliamentary Affairs*, Vol. 34, No. 2, Spring.

Holland, Janet (1981) *Work and Women: A Review of Explanations for the Maintenance and Reproduction of Sexual Divisions*, Bedford Way Papers, No. 6, University of London, Institute of Education.

Holt, John (1975) *Escape From Childhood: The Needs and Rights of Children*, Penguin.

Home Office (1975) *Sex Discrimination: A Guide to the Sex Discrimination Act*.

House of Commons (1968) *Parliamentary Debates (Hansard), Session 1967-68*, Fifth Series, Vol. 759, 28 Feb., HMSO.

House of Commons (1972) *Parliamentary Debates (Hansard), Session 1971-72*, Fifth Series, Vol. 829, 28 Jan., HMSO.

House of Commons (1973a) *Parliamentary Debates (Hansard), Session 1972-73*, Fifth Series, Vol. 849, 2 Feb., HMSO.

House of Commons (1973b) *Parliamentary Debates (Hansard), Session 1972-73*, Fifth Series, Vol. 850, 14 Feb., HMSO.

House of Commons (1973c) *Special Report from the Select Committee on the Anti-Discrimination (No. 2) Bill, Session 1972-73*, 26 June, HMSO.

House of Commons (1973d) *Parliamentary Debates (Hansard), Session 1972-3*, Fifth Series, Vol. 856, 8 May, HMSO.

House of Lords (1972-73) *The Select Committee on the Anti-Discrimination (No. 2) Bill, Sessions 1972-72 and 1972-73*, 2 vols, HMSO.

Hurstfield, Jennifer (1980) 'The part-time trap', NCCL, *Rights*, Vol. 4, No. 5, May-June, 1980.

Kaplan, Alexandra G. and Bean, Joan P. (eds) (1976) *Beyond Sex-Role Stereotypes: Readings Towards a Psychology of Androgyny*, Little, Brown.

Kellner, Peter (1983) 'Anatomy of a landslide', *New Statesman*, 17 June.

Klein, Viola (1957) *Working Wives*, Institute of Personnel Management.

Labour Party Study Group on Discrimination (1972) *Discrimination Against Women*, Opposition Green Paper.

Leman, Joy (1980) ' "The advice of a real friend". Codes of intimacy and oppression in Women's magazines 1937-1955', *Women's Studies International Quarterly*, Vol. 3.

Lewis, Jane (1983) 'Eleanor Rathbone and the family', *New Society*, 27 Jan.

Lister, Ruth (1973) *As Man and Wife? A Study of the Cohabitation Rule*, Poverty Research Series, No. 2.

Lovenduski, Joni (1986a) 'The distaff syndrome', *Guardian*, 14 Jan.

Lovenduski, Joni (1986b) *Women and European Politics: Contemporary Feminism and Public Policy*, Wheatsheaf Books, Harvester Press.

McDonald, Oonagh (1977) 'Women in the Labour Party today', in *Women in the Labour Movement* (ed. Lucy Middleton) Croom Helm.

McCarthy, Margaret (1977) 'Women in trade unions' in *Women in the Labour Movement* (ed. Lucy Middleton) Croom Helm.

McGoldrick, Ann (1985) *Equal Treatment in Occupational Pension Schemes*, Equal Opportunities Commission.

Meehan, Elizabeth (1982) 'Implementing equal opportunity policies: some British–American comparisons', *Politics*, Vol. 2, No. 1, April.

Meehan, Elizabeth M. (1985) *Women's Rights at Work: Campaigns and Policy in Britain and the United States*, Macmillan.

Millett, Kate (1985) *Sexual Politics*, Virago (first published in Britain in 1971 by Rupert Hart-Davis).

Mitchell, Juliet (1975) *Psychoanalysis and Feminism*, Penguin.

Mitchell, Juliet (1964) 'Women's education', *New Left Review*, No. 28, Nov.–Dec.

Mitchell, Juliet (1981) *Women's Estate*, Penguin (first published 1971).

Morton, Liz (1984) *Women and Work in the West Midlands*, West Midlands Low Pay Unit (reviewed in 1984).

Myrdal, Alva and Klein, Viola (1968) *Women's Two Roles: Home and Work*, 2nd rev. edn, Routledge and Kegan Paul.

National Council for Civil Liberties (1975) *Equal Pay and How to Get It*.

National Council for Civil Liberties (1980) *Annual Report*; (1981) *Annual Report*.

National Union of Teachers (1980) *Promotion and the Woman Teacher*, A National Union of Teachers Research Project, published jointly with the Equal Opportunities Commission.

Nicholson, Nigel and Metcalfe, Beverley Alban (1985) *The Career Development of British Managers*, British Institute of Management.

Pulzer, Peter G. J. (1975) *Political Representation and Elections in Britain*, 3rd edn, Allen and Unwin.

Randall, Vicky (1982) *Women and Politics*, Macmillan.

Rasmussen, Jorgen S. (1983) 'Women's role in contemporary British Politics: impediments to parliamentary candidates', *Parliamentary Affairs*, Vol. 36, No. 3, Summer.

Riley, Denise (1979) 'War in the nursery', *Feminist Review*, No. 2.

Rogers, Barbara (1983) *52% Getting Women's Power into Politics*, Women's Press.

Rossi, Alice S. (ed.) (1970) *Essays on Sex Equality by John Stuart Mill and Harriet Taylor Mill*, University of Chicago Press.

Rowbotham, Sheila (1978) 'The beginnings of Women's Liberation in Britain', in *The Body Politic: Women's Liberation in Britain* (ed. Michelene Wandor) Stage 1.

Rowbotham, Sheila (1982) 'The trouble with "patriarchy" ', in *The Woman Question* (ed. Mary Evans) Fontana (first published *New Statesman*, Dec. 1979).

Royal Commission on Trade Unions and Employers' Associations 1965-68 (1968) (Donovan Report) Cmnd. 3628, HMSO.

Rush, Michael (1981) 'The Members of Parliament', in *The Commons Today* (ed. S. A. Walkland and M. Ryle) Fontana.

Savage, Wendy (1986) *A Savage Enquiry: Who Controls Childbirth?*, Virago.

School Curriculum Development Committee (1986) *Gender, Science and Technology: Inservice Handbook*, Longman Resources Unit.

Scorer, Catherine and Sedley, Ann (1983) *Amending the Equality Laws*, National Council of Civil Liberties, Women's Rights Unit.

Scott, Hilda (1974) *Does Socialism Liberate Women? Experiences from Eastern Europe*, Beacon Press.

Scott, Hilda (1984) *Working Your Way to the Bottom: The Feminization of Poverty*, Pandora Press (Routledge and Kegan Paul).

Sharpe, Sue (1976) *Just Like a Girl: How Girls Learn to be Women*, Penguin.

Smart, Carol (1984) *The Ties That Bind: Law, Marriage and the Reproduction of Patriarchal Relations*, Routledge and Kegan Paul.

Snell, Mandy (1979) 'The Equal Pay and Sex Discrimination Acts:

their impact in the workplace', *Feminist Review*, No. 1. Article based on LSE research project 1974–77 on the implementation and effects of the Acts.

Trades Union Congress (1983) *Women in the Labour Market*.

Vallance, Elizabeth (1984) 'Women candidates in the 1983 general election', *Parliamentary Affairs*, Vol. 37, No. 5, Summer.

Vanek, Joann (1980) 'Time spent in housework', in *The Economics of Women and Work* (ed. Alice H. Amsden), Penguin.

Westergaard, J. H. and Resler H. (1975) *Class in a Capitalist Society: A Study of Contemporary Britain*, Basic Books.

White, Cynthia (1970) *Women's Magazines: 1963–1968*, Michael Joseph.

Willmott, Peter and Young, Michael (1957) *Family and Kinship in East London*, Penguin.

Wilson, Elizabeth (1977) *Women and the Welfare State*, Tavistock.

Wilson, Elizabeth (1980) *Only Halfway to Paradise: Women in Postwar Britain 1945–1968*, Tavistock.

Wilson, Harold (1974) *The Labour Government 1964–70*, Penguin.

Wilson, Harold (1977) *The Governance of Britain*, Sphere Books.

Wilson, Harold (1979) *The Final Term: The Labour Government 1974–1976*, Weidenfeld and Nicholson and Michael Joseph.

Wolf, Christa (1984) *Cassandra: A Novel and Four Essays*, Virago.

Wollstonecraft, Mary (1967) *A Vindication of the Rights of Woman*, W. W. Norton (first published 1792).

Zweig, Ferdynand (1961) *The Worker in an Affluent Society*, Heinemann.

PERIODICALS AND PAPERS CITED (without giving authors)

Guardian, Daily Telegraph and *The Times; New Society, New Statesman, Spare Rib*; NCCL, *Rights, Civil Liberty*, CPAG, *Poverty* (organisational journals); *Money Which?, Marxism Today*.

INDEX